D1760016

A History of Council Housing in 100 Estates

RIBA Publishing

John Boughton

© RIBA Publishing, 2023

Published by RIBA Publishing, 66 Portland Place, London, W1B 1AD

ISBN 978 1 91412 463 1

The right of John Boughton to be identified as the Author of this Work has been asserted in accordance with the Copyright, Designs and Patents Act 1988 sections 77 and 78.

All rights reserved. No part of this publication may be reproduced, stored in a retrieval system, or transmitted, in any form or by any means, electronic, mechanical, photocopying, recording or otherwise, without prior permission of the copyright owner.

British Library Cataloguing-in-Publication Data
A catalogue record for this book is available from the British Library.

Commissioning Editor: Clare Holloway
Assistant Editor: Scarlet Furness
Production: Richard Blackburn
Designed and typeset by Sarah-Louise Deazley
Printed and bound by Short Run Press, Exeter
Cover image: Architectural Press Archive / RIBA Collections, colourised by Sarah-Louise Deazley

While every effort has been made to check the accuracy and quality of the information given in this publication, neither the Author nor the Publisher accept any responsibility for the subsequent use of this information, for any errors or omissions that it may contain, or for any misunderstandings arising from it.

www.ribapublishing.com

Contents

About the Author

John Boughton is the author of *Municipal Dreams: the Rise and Fall of Council Housing* and the blog Municipal Dreams, a record of local government reform and council estates across Great Britain. The book has been an Amazon best seller in its category and was selected by Rowan Moore as an Observer Book of the Year. The blog has had as of September 2022, 1.9 million views and 1.2 million visitors.

John is an Honorary Senior Research Fellow in the School of Architecture at the University of Liverpool.

Acknowledgements

A book of this type could not have been written without the help of many organisations and individuals over the years. There are too many to mention in this brief entry but my research and writing has been dependent on the work of academics, local historians and archivists, who have all contributed inestimably to its detail and analysis. For a variety of personal and practical reasons, I was unable to take up the grant to support my research offered by the Society of Architectural Historians of Great Britain but I am very grateful for their generosity and support. I would like to thank the School of Architecture at the University of Liverpool for appointing me an Honorary Senior Research Fellow and have benefitted immensely from the university's research facilities and resources.

Some individuals have been of especial help in providing images and information on particular case studies and I would like to acknowledge the help of Dan Lucas of Nottingham City Homes, David Martyn, Senior Conservation Architect at Bristol City Council, Professor Gerry Mooney of the Open University in Scotland, Rose Pipes in relation to the Stockbridge Colonies, Martin Rogers of the Rosyth Garden City Association, Dr Ian Waites of the University of Lincoln, Peter Warrington of Burnage Garden Village, and David Weir of the Craigavon Historical Society. My apologies to many other worthy people whose names I have omitted.

My thanks to Clare Holloway at RIBA Publishing for her conscientious reading of the manuscript and thoughtful advice and to Richard Blackburn and the design team who have created such an attractive volume.

My final and greatest thanks go to my wife Michele Grant who has once again been the rock on which this endeavour is built.

Introduction

In 1980, there were well over 5 million council homes in Britain, housing around one-third of the population. The right of all to adequate housing had been recognised in the 1948 Universal Declaration of Human Rights and reaffirmed in the 1966 International Covenant on Economic, Social and Cultural Rights. But long before that popular notions of what constituted a 'moral economy' and elite concerns, both philanthropic and repressive, had also, in varying ways, advanced the principle that everyone was entitled to adequate shelter as constituted by the standards of the day.

Historically that entitlement was fulfilled, very partially at least, by feudal authorities and the Church. After the Dissolution of the Monasteries in England in the 1530s, private charity and a nascent local state assumed greater responsibilities. An emergent capitalist order, population growth and mobility, and new forms of social hierarchy increased housing pressures and intensified tensions around a contested right to adequate housing. Almshouses, funded by private benefactors, and the lesser-known 'parish houses' provided by local government came to represent the main attempts to meet the housing needs of those unable to provide for themselves. Workhouses, particularly after the harsh New Poor Law of 1834, were designedly a far more punitive attempt to accommodate the poorest of the parish.

Industrialisation from the late 18th century, and the unprecedented growth of towns that followed brought new urgency and a far greater political salience to the housing question. The 'Condition of England' debate among writers and social commentators of the 1840s expressed alarm at the mass – or, more accurately, newly concentrated and inescapably witnessed – poverty of the era and, in the context of Chartism (the world's first mass working-class protest movement), its social and political dangers. Benjamin Disraeli famously talked of 'Two nations … the rich and the poor'.

Others in the upper classes feared the disease – which could breach Victorian social divisions – and alleged criminality that characterised the worst areas of slum housing. Sanitary and public health reform followed haltingly in the Public Health Acts of 1848 and 1866; permissive legislation requiring activist local authorities to enforce its modest terms. The 1875 Public Health Act, requiring newly built houses to be self-contained with their own sanitation and water supply, would have a greater impact. Around 2.5 million so-called 'bye-law houses' were built by 1910 – the two-storey terraced housing typical of swathes of urban Britain (though Scotland would cleave to its distinct multi-storey tenement tradition). The improvement or, where necessary, demolition of unfit housing, enforced by local Medical Officers of Health and councils, was the other side of this coin. It was small-scale at this time but would assume huge importance in the following century.

In laissez-faire Britain there was little appetite for a more constructive state role, but housing reformers and politicians invested hopes and sometimes hard cash in what was known as 'five per cent philanthropy'. The first of these companies was formed in the 1840s, building 'model dwellings' for the working classes and promising that return to their financial supporters. The hope was that such model dwellings might also create a 'model' working class.

That was unlikely, not least because of the inability of such private efforts to meet the pressing scale of housing needs. Increasingly, central government looked to local as its agent. The latter's role – particularly after the creation of an effective machinery of borough, county and district local government from 1889 – would distinguish British social housing from that of much of Europe. The 1890 Housing of the Working Classes Act empowered councils to build housing. A few of the more ambitious did – some 24,000 homes by 1914.

A more democratic politics and strengthened upper-class fears about the 'fitness' of the British working class in the light of increased international competition, alongside genuine humanitarianism, encouraged renewed interest in housing reform. Ebenezer Howard's Garden City ideals provided the preferred physical form for many, at least in moderated cottage suburb form, but his organisational model could not compete with the logistical and financial power of local government.

The First World War – a total war that demanded a contented domestic workforce and a soldiery rewarded for its sacrifice – provided the great impetus for further reform and laid the foundations of council housing as we know it. In form, this was supplied by the Tudor Walters Report; legislatively by the generous provisions of the 1919 Housing Act. Cottage homes were the ideal; inner-city conditions often required denser tenement housing. Around 1.1 million council homes were built between the wars, but the pace and quality of new housing reflected the spending priorities of central government and its policy preferences. From 1930, however, a shared determination to clear slums and build anew set a precedent that would be fulfilled on enormous scale from the mid-1950s.

The Second World War (and the Blitz that devastated many cities) and the election of the first majority Labour government intensified the housing drive and brought with it new planning ideals and a contested Modernism that had hitherto had little impact in conservative Britain. Suburban estates remained the dominant form, but high-rise solutions that promised greater housing density emerged both as design preference and perceived planning necessity. An average of 126,000 council homes were built annually between 1945 and 1979, many most dramatically in the era of mass council housing, promoted by governments of the left and right, that characterised the 1960s.

Construction defects, particularly in the poorly executed system-building programme, helped foster a backlash against what critical politicians and commentators came to see as the overweening and impersonal scale of much of this newer housing. New and attractive forms of low-rise, high-density public housing did little to reverse this receding tide. Politics – in the form of an increasingly sceptical attitude towards the role of the state, and among an emergent New Right a veneration of the free market, and economics – a desire

A History of Council Housing in 100 Estates

to curtail public spending – recast the narrative. Margaret Thatcher was their avatar. Council housing became a problem, not a solution.

The contemporary housing crisis and a small uptick in council housebuilding in recent years, often with a commitment to high-quality and sustainable design, may yet mark a new chapter in the longer story. For me, this is a moment to both celebrate the achievements of the past and better understand its missteps. Thus armed, we might build better, just as we need to build more, in the future.

Bottom
A housing mix in the Cranbrook Estate, Tower Hamlets'

CHAPTER 1

A 'Prehistory' of Social Housing

The housing of the poor has for the most part been a matter for the poor themselves. In medieval and early modern times, they might have taken over an existing or newly subdivided home. Newbuild homes might have been supplied by a landlord at a suitable cost, but could also, when a modest assemblage of timber, thatch and wattle and daub sufficed, have been self-built. (The availability of land, dependent on manorial control or encroachment onto common land, was more fraught.) For those lacking the extended family network that might otherwise provide support and unable – rather than unwilling – to provide for themselves, there might, if they were lucky, have been a safety net.

A Christian tradition of monastic alms-giving can be dated to the Synod of Aix in 816. From food and money doled out at monastery gates, monastic charity expanded until by the early medieval period some 300 institutions in England offered residential care to the sick and elderly of their local community. Sometimes such efforts were supplemented by the Christian charity (or guilty consciences) of the country's secular elites. Almshouses, catering especially for the aged poor, became more common.

The break with the Catholic Church (1534 in England and Wales; 1560 in Scotland), the dissolution of the monasteries and the suppression of religious charities that followed changed this picture. Perhaps half the Church-based institutions previously providing care and accommodation for the sick and elderly closed. Private charity increased; the early modern state became more active. What some have called a 'mixed economy of welfare' developed.[1]

The Poor Law, decreed by the central state but administered by the parish, set the terrain on which this mixed economy played out. It was predicated, in essence, on the fear and resentment of the 'sturdy beggars' that plagued the imaginings of the Elizabethan elite, but tempered by pragmatism and a genuine concern for the 'impotent poor'. A 1547 law requiring parishes to provide accommodation for the sick and infirm, and the 1576 Poor Law stipulating that a poor person who refused to work be committed to a workhouse mark the competing poles of policy

and sentiment. Parishes, administered by the local gentry and well-to-do, were given responsibility for poor relief in 1597. Many provided 'parish houses' as accommodation for the poorest of the community.

Outdoor relief, particularly after Gilbert's Act in 1782 (which permitted the elderly and young to be placed in so-called poorhouses and the unemployed to be provided work or given an allowance in their own homes) became more common by the late 18th century. The New Poor Law of 1834 infamously decreed that all those unable to support themselves be placed in the harsh and intentionally deterrent conditions of the 'reformed' workhouses.

The 1834 Act reflected population growth and pressures in an era of unprecedented industrialisation and urbanisation. Britain's population had increased by two-thirds in a century to reach 10.8 million by 1800; in 1900, it stood at 41.4 million. The problem of the urban poor – or frequently, in elite eyes, the problems they caused – assumed new prominence.

'Model dwellings', funded by the Victorian upper classes and often in the form of austere tenement blocks, were one response but provided little relief from their surrounding squalor. As some in the working class grew more prosperous in the later 19th century, self-help cooperative and co-partnership ventures emerged but these too could do little to address the larger problem of slumdom. A laissez-faire state reluctantly embarked on a programme of sanitary and public health reform. Over time, as more positive attitudes towards state intervention prevailed and sheer necessity dictated, this would mitigate the worst of urban conditions. An infrastructure of fresh water supply and sewerage initially took centre stage, but the provision of decent housing was increasingly understood as an essential corollary. National legislation and local bye-laws set improved standards for new housing and, on an initially small scale, cleared some of the worst of existing habitations. By the turn of the century, however, the failure of the free market to build decent housing for the poorer working class and the inability of non-state actors to make good this deficiency compelled politicians to accept a role for national and local government in the construction of housing.

Almshouses and parish housing

By tradition, the first purpose-built almshouses were established by King Athelstan in York in 936; the oldest in authenticated continuous existence form the Hospital of St Cross in Winchester, founded in 1132. These early 'hospitals' were funded by benefactors, but were generally linked to the Church, and are better understood as hospices in contemporary language. They were created to care for those who, through illness, injury or old age, were unable to care for themselves. By the mid-15th century, they had assumed their predominant later role in accommodating the impoverished elderly, often living rent-free and supported by small allowances.

Around half of perhaps 800 almshouses in existence at the time of the dissolution closed, but private charity bequeathed by local landowners and increasingly by newly emergent mercantile capitalists stepped in. By the mid-1600s, this created around 1,000 such institutions, catering for up to 2% of the country's elderly population. Some became more specialised in serving the indigent of particular trades and guilds. Victorian wealth and philanthropy saw new growth and some new iterations, such as the almshouses established by the Durham Aged Mineworkers' Homes Association from 1898, now managing around 1,700 homes in the northeast. Currently, the Almshouses Association estimates 1,600 independent charities exist, providing homes for around 35,000 residents across the UK.

In a few cases, almshouses might be supported at least in part by the local parish. But parish efforts vary according to the will and wealth of the parish, and circumscribed by national policy, and most went into parish housing. The 1601 Poor Law Act gave parish officials or local Justices of the Peace the right to erect 'convenient houses of habitation for poor impotent people'. Legislation in 1722 encouraged parishes to build workhouses, but often such 'poorhouses' came to provide less institutionalised accommodation for poorer families. John Broad describes 'decentralized decision-making by parish elites' using charitable income and the local rates 'in a variety of flexible and creative ways that did not necessarily entail workhouse building'.[2] While upper-class politicians and commentators increasingly prescribed punitive measures against the poor, popular lore asserted a traditional right of new families to a home of their own.

Parishes might provide this accommodation by building houses or adapting existing property or by paying the rent of families unable to do so themselves. In 1775, the agriculturalist Nathaniel Kent argued that 'if it were not for this excellent law, which obliges parish offices to find habitations for their poor, I am sorry to remark that in many parishes they would literally be driven into the open fields'.[3] In practice, provision varied widely but, at its most generous in Mursley, Buckinghamshire, up to 40% of the village's housing – 39 of 98 homes – was in parish hands. Broad estimates that there were at least 35,000 homes owned by parishes and used to house the poor in 1834. A great many were sold off after the Poor Law Amendment Act of that year, which banned so-called 'out-relief'.

Almshouses: 76–78 Oxford Street, Woodstock, and Caroline Court, Oxford Road, Woodstock

To select one almshouse scheme from a hugely diverse range in age and form is an impossible task, but Woodstock in Oxfordshire offers an unusual example of that 'mixed economy of welfare' referenced earlier. The original alms foundation, established in 1488, was a chantry house of a type abolished in the Reformation, endowed that its inmates might pray for the soul of its wealthy benefactor. It was acquired and managed by the Corporation of the then Borough of Woodstock in 1551 and moved to a new site on 76–78 Oxford Street in the 1590s. The present buildings date to 1724. By the 1790s, it was an unendowed poorhouse, parish housing which survived tenuously into the 1870s.

New almshouses were funded by Caroline, Duchess of Marlborough, in 1797 on Oxford Street (close, but not too close, to Blenheim Palace) for six 'widows or maidens, of the age of 55 or upwards, natives of England and Wales, of sober life and good character'. The residents were provided an allowance of £1 monthly and a small additional sum for cap and gown. No doubt they pondered the words of William Mavor that 'power, riches, and grandeur are little to be envied, except where they are exerted to promote the less fortunate meritorious, and to relieve the distressed'.[4] *Noblesse* did indeed *oblige*.

The building, of limestone ashlar and Welsh slate construction and in typical row form, survives but, unusually, was taken over by the borough council in 1968. Named Caroline Court, it is now sheltered housing and forms part of an attractive larger council estate.

Right
The Duchess of Marlborough's Almshouses, Woodstock

Parish housing

Parish houses took all shapes and forms. Some of them were repurposed buildings, owned by the parish, and adapted to temporarily serve the needs of the poor. One such was the 15th-century manorial courthouse in Long Crendon in Buckinghamshire, which was used to house parish paupers in the 18th century. A similar example is Kenton School, originally a 16th-century church house, in the village of that name in Devon, recorded as early as 1559 as 'for many years used as a habitation of the poor'.[5] Of the same vintage is the former church house in Hurley in Berkshire, similarly employed. Two small cottages were purpose-built in School House Lane, Abbots Bromley in Staffordshire, in 1764 and, this found insufficient, an existing building rented, a former House of Correction. Early local historian Marcia Rice records the building of the local Uttoxeter Workhouse in 1841 when 'the poor old people from our village were "transferred". What a weary seven miles of separation, what suffering this must have meant to them and to those they loved!'.[6] In Bridestowe (Devon), the local vicar secured the erection in 1800 of a purpose-built row of cottages, with two rooms (one up, one down) of 16 square feet only.

Most parish houses, while recorded in the archives, are no longer distinguishable. Many more, of flimsy construction, were rebuilt or simply demolished in the sell-off of parish housing that occurred after the 1834 New Poor Law. It's been largely a lost history, but this early form of 'social housing' deserves recognition.

Left
Long Crendon Courthouse, which served as parish housing in the 18th century

Right
The Reverend Luxmore's parish housing in Bridestowe, Devon, depicted in 1808

Sanitary and building reform and regulation

In 1832, cholera killed some 3,166 people in Glasgow and 5,275 in London. A second outbreak in 1848 killed around 53,000 in England and Wales alone. As the country rapidly urbanised – by the turn of the 19th century, 80% of the population of England and Wales lived in settlements of 2,500 or more; one in three of Scotland's population occupied its four major cities – many more died from more common ailments such as typhus, tuberculosis, scarlet fever, even diarrhoea. The first report of the Royal Commission on the Health of Large Towns and Populous Districts in 1845 found the average age of death of workers and their families in the northern industrial towns stood at between 18 and 28 years of age; over half the children born to these families died before they were five. Such horrifying figures could be multiplied: a product of urban squalor and the 19th-century fact-finding that revealed statistically its deadly consequences.

Effective legislation ensued more slowly. Progressive towns such as Liverpool, whose 1846 Sanitary Act has been described as 'the first piece of comprehensive health legislation passed in England', might promote their own local bye-laws.[7] But early national legislation was permissive, requiring that same zeal and good conscience on the part of still-rudimentary local authorities. The 1848 Public Health Act gave them powers to deal with drainage, water supply and the removal of nuisances. A Royal Commission in 1857 set up 'to inquire as to the best mode of distributing the sewage of towns' and another in 1867 on water supply signalled a growing understanding of how disease was transmitted.

The breakthrough moment came with the 1875 Public Health Act. The legislation, consolidating no fewer than 22 previous Acts and strengthening the reach and enforcement of sanitary regulation, required the setting up of Local Boards of Health and the appointment of Health Inspectors and Sanitary Inspectors. It also stipulated standards for new housing and streets. All homes were expected to possess a privy and form of water supply – however primitive by later standards – and a modicum of light and fresh air, the latter guaranteed by windows of a certain size and streets set at a minimum width of 36 feet (11 metres). Back-to-back housing was formally banned in 1909.

Enforcement of sanitary bye-laws with regard to existing housing was far more dilatory, requiring both the determination of a reforming Medical Officer of Health and the will and spending power of a sympathetic council. Footdee represents a unique and very early example of slum clearance and rebuilding that would gather pace in the years to follow.

Footdee, Aberdeen

The model village, built for the fishing community of Footdee in Aberdeen, is a highly unusual early example of a planned municipal scheme of working-class housing. In the late 18th century, the fishermen on the north side of the Dee harbour, complaining of the dilapidated and unfit condition of their current homes, petitioned Aberdeen Town Council to build new housing for which they would pay appropriate rent. In 1808, the council acceded, planning two squares to replace existing slums. The development was financed, without central government support or approval, from the town's Common Good Fund – a trust (still in existence) dating to the granting of Aberdeen's Great Charter in 1319. The design was entrusted to John Smith, the Superintendent of the Town's Public Works.

Unlike Smith's grander classicist designs in Aberdeen and his later project, Balmoral Castle, this was very basic housing indeed – 28 single-storey, thatched, two-roomed terraced cottages lacking water supply or privies and built of coarse granite blocks. (Many weren't finally improved until the Housing Improvement Act of 1968.) North and South Square formed the original settlement; further streets were added in subsequent decades. After the Town Council began selling off the homes (mostly to sitting tenants) in the 1880s, most received an additional storey and other additions; no. 3 North Square remains an unusual exception. Most cottages possess 'tarry sheds', originally constructed of driftwood, to store work equipment. Mostly listed in 1967 and a conservation area from 1968, the village is now admired for its picturesque qualities, but to some it should be noted as perhaps the country's first council housing.

Left
Pilot Square, Footdee, photographed in 1974

Right
An unaltered cottage (with slate replacing the original thatch) and others with added storeys

Five per cent philanthropy and self-help

'Five per cent philanthropy' combined charity, politics and self-interest. The charity lay in a genuine concern for the conditions of the urban poor felt by its founders and some of its investors. The politics (broadly defined) and perhaps part of the self-interest lay in the concomitant desire to *improve* the working class – to improve their health, of course, but to improve their behaviour too in ways that incorporated them safely into the existing social order. Financial self-interest lay in that promised rate of return secured from rental income.

The first active company, the Society for Improving the Condition of the Labouring Classes (SICLC), was formed in 1844. The Pilrig Model Dwellings Company was founded by the Reverend William Garden Blaikie in Edinburgh in 1849. Their names indicate their intent and approach. The SICLC's first scheme in Streatham Street, Bloomsbury – a sturdy, five-storey, balcony-access tenement block designed by Henry Roberts that provided a template for many to follow – still bears the title 'Model Houses for Families' on its imposing facade.

The big hitters of the movement came later, in the 1860s: the Peabody Trust, the Improved Industrial Dwellings Company and the Artizans, Labourers and General Dwellings Company. By the 1890s they owned and managed some 5,100, 5,350 and 6,500 homes respectively, the latter unusual in comprising principally low-rise suburban housing. Octavia Hill's smaller but well-publicised schemes from the time also abjured the 'barracks-like' – the typical criticism applied – form of most inner-city model dwellings.

What all such enterprises shared was strict management. Tenants, carefully vetted, were to pay their rents regularly and behave respectably, and were evicted summarily if they failed to comply. The regime sat comfortably with the artisans and lower middle classes who were the model dwellings' most frequent tenants, but the relatively high rents excluded the poorest and irregularly employed; the officious oversight alienated others. A contemporary exception to this heavy-handed paternalism was the Edinburgh Co-operative Building Company Ltd, formed in 1861 by striking workers from the building trades.

Around 30 model dwellings companies had been formed by the later century. These were mostly in London, with the Newcastle upon Tyne Improved Industrial Dwellings Company and, a latecomer formed in 1892, the Chester Cottage Improvement Company (backed by the Duke of Westminster) as exceptions. Whatever the mix of good intent and social control represented, and despite the low-cost loans offered by the Public Works Loans Board under the 1866 Labouring Classes' Dwelling Act, it was not a financial model that could address the scale and range of the need.

Stockbridge Colonies, Glenogle Road, Edinburgh

The Stockbridge Colonies are among 10 such schemes in Edinburgh and the first built by the Edinburgh Co-operative Building Company, in the year of its foundation, 1861. (The term 'colony' is said to originate in either the developments' then outlying location or their community of like-minded inhabitants.) The company was set up by building trade workers after a three-month lockout and, unlike later co-partnership ventures of similar ethos, was a joint-stock company based on a capital of £10,000 raised by selling £1 shares. Its aim was to provide decent and affordable working-class housing, for sale or rent, at a time of acute housing crisis in the Scottish capital.

Affordability and the necessary density were achieved by building flats, one atop the other, in sandstone terraces, with the distinctive feature of an external staircase giving access to the upper flat. This saved money and freed up internal space.

At Stockbridge, there are 11 long terraces and three shorter rows. All the tenements have a parlour, kitchen, WC and coal storage area; the single-storey, so-called 'low door' flats have one bedroom; the two-storey 'high door' flats, two. Equipped with kitchen range, sink and tub, water supply and sewerage, and gas-lit, these were high-quality homes for the working class and catered principally, in the words of one company manager, for 'the better class of working man'.[8]

The scheme was commercially successful too, building over 1,000 homes in the Company's first two decades. The Colonies are now among Edinburgh's most sought-after housing.

Top left and right
An illustration from 1872 showing the tenements' separate ground-floor and upper-storey entrances

Bottom left
A Stockbridge Colonies street scene in around 1890

Bottom right
A contemporary aerial view

A History of Council Housing in 100 Estates

Islington Estate, Greenman Street, Islington, London

The Islington Estate was the first of the Peabody Trust's 20 'classic estates' designed by architect Henry Astley Darbishire between 1864 and 1885 and intended for those, in George Peabody's words, of 'an ascertained condition of life such as brings the individual within the description of the poor of London combined with moral character and good conduct as a member of society'.[9] But it was revolutionary in form, rejecting existing street patterns in favour of an arrangement of four detached blocks placed symmetrically around a large open square. In this, it represented, as Irina Davidovici notes, 'a continental urbanity: Hof rather than terrace, îlot rather than sprawl'.[10] It also represented a deliberate shift from the disorderly and close-knit yards and alleys of the slum quarters it replaced. The gates of the estate were closed promptly by its superintendent at 11pm.

The four, five-storey, Italianate-style blocks each comprised 60 one- to three-room tenements with central stairway and corridor access and an unglazed top floor providing laundry and drying facilities. These were 'associated dwellings' sharing WCs and sinks placed at each end of the blocks. This was sanitary and well-ventilated housing, and contemporary accounts detail its lower mortality rates, but it was criticised then and subsequently for its bleak appearance. Modernised and enlarged, it nevertheless continues to provide much-needed affordable accommodation in central London.

Left
Peabody Square, as portrayed in the American *Appleton's Journal* in 1865; the central clock tower is a product of artistic imagination

Right
A contemporary view of the estate and more recent landscaping

Noel Park, Haringey, London

Noel Park was the third of the Artizans, Labourers and General Dwellings Company's estates, officially opened by the company's patron Lord Shaftesbury in 1883. It was built in open countryside to the north of London but close to Green Lanes Station; the belated granting of workmen's fares from the station by the Great Eastern Railway in 1886 provided a major boost to its growth.

The estate, largely complete with some 2,000 homes in 1907, was designed by Rowland Plumbe (recommended to the role by the RIBA) in a series of wide, tree-lined avenues. The homes, semi-detached pairs in long terraces, were built of red and yellow stock brick, with additional detailing, terracotta cills and a mix of slate and tiled roofs: 'the whole being built with the best materials and designed to have bright and cheerful appearance', according to a celebratory account in *The Builder*.[11]

Of the five classes of houses, the most superior were placed centrally, close to church and school, but all possessed scullery, parlour and kitchen, at least two bedrooms and a WC accessed from the yard. While the first-class homes benefited from an additional upstairs toilet, contemporary commentators stressed that a '6 shilling house has the same features and the same finish as a 12 shilling house'.[12] Shops and schools were provided, but no public houses as befitted a respectable artisanal working class.

In 1966, the entire estate of 2,175 homes was purchased by Haringey Council, but it wasn't until the 1970s that facilities now considered standard such as baths, indoor toilets and hot water systems were installed.

Left
The layout and housing of Noel Park as envisaged in the Artizans, Labourers and General Dwellings Company's original prospectus

Right
Superior housing on Gladstone Avenue

Opposite
These elaborate facades further along Gladstone Avenue conceal more modest cottage flats

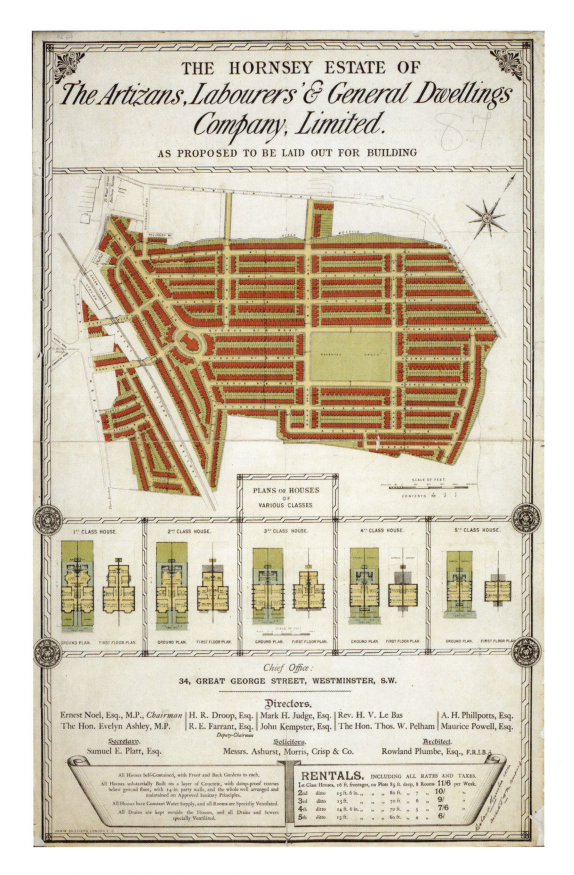

CHAPTER 2

1890–1914: Early Council Housing

The first council housing in recognisably modern form (built by a local authority under national legislation and supported by state finance) was built by Liverpool City Council in 1869: two rather bleak tenement blocks misleadingly named St Martin's Cottages, since demolished. The Labouring Classes Dwellings Act passed three years earlier was directed principally at five per cent philanthropy, but it had empowered local authorities to purchase land and build housing with the benefit of loans at preferential rates from the government's Public Works Loan Commissioners, which was of greater long-term significance. Liverpool was the only council to exploit the legislation. Huddersfield Town Council built five streets of two-storey terraced housing (also long gone) under the terms of the 1875 Artisans' Dwellings Act. But, in the ratepayer-dominated and primitive form of local government at the time, these early pioneers were solitary actors.

The legislative breakthrough came with the 1890 Housing of the Working Classes Act. It strengthened local authority building powers and required that houses lost in clearance schemes be replaced. Crucially, however, the legislation coincided with the creation of a system of more efficient and representative county, borough and district councils. By 1914, around 24,000 council homes had been built across the country.

The continued pace of industrialisation and urbanisation and the housing squalor they wrought was one obvious reason for this relative upsurge. Perhaps more significant was a shift in upper-class thinking, caused partly by witnessing the sheer scale and impact of this new world and partly by the myriad sources – the alarmist, often moralist, pamphlets of religious and humanitarian reformers and the all-too-grounded data of a new breed of social investigators – which charted its consequences. For some in governing circles, those consequences, in the form of a working class unfit to compete industrially or militarily in an increasingly threatening world, imperilled the country's very future; eugenicist concerns about what was called 'National Efficiency' were found across the political spectrum. Pressure from below added its own impetus by the turn of the century, by which time (male) working-class voters formed a majority of the parliamentary electorate, and as the labour movement grew in size and organisation.

In all this, the limitations of the free market, however lauded by those it favoured, were increasingly manifest. That was obviously so in the case of housing, where speculative builders secured their profit margins by building superior houses for those who could best afford them. (Liverpool's first council homes were built because private developers had refused to take on the scheme despite being offered the land and plans to do so.) In broader terms, that wealth of social investigation increasingly encouraged people to understand poverty as a product of individual misfortune rather than personal failing. Whether in Tory Democracy, a paternalist politics updated in electorally competitive form, or in a collectivist New Liberalism (and in pure form among middle-class Fabians and working-class socialists), politicians came in different ways to accept an enhanced and necessary role for the state.

If the case for housing intervention seemed clearer, the form it should take was contested. In the inner cities, multi-storey tenements – similar in style to the model dwellings of five per cent philanthropy – remained the generally preferred solution, assumed to offer sanitary housing more cheaply and at greater density. But many housing reformers, taking their cue from Ebenezer Howard, who first outlined his Garden City ideal in 1898, insisted on cottage homes with gardens front and back. This was a vision taken up on a less grandiose scale in the cottage suburbs designed by municipal architects and the co-partnership ventures which sprang up in the early years of the 20th century. The contest between those who favoured the two-storey house and those who believed flatted accommodation could be not merely practical but desirable would be played out for many years.

A similar argument relating to housing design was fought between the advocates of the picturesque vernacular espoused by the Arts and Crafts movement and critics who, pointing plausibly to the excluding expense of the style, proposed simpler, plainer designs employing standardised components. Raymond Unwin, emerging as the leading architect-planner of the day, endorsed the latter, and this view would prevail after the First World War.

The problem persisted that council rents were generally significantly higher than those charged by slum landlords, and the new housing rarely rehoused the poorest residents displaced by slum clearance. Reformers rationalised this failing by what was called a 'filtering up' theory – that those in the very worst housing might move to the slightly superior housing being vacated by the new council tenants. But this was an issue requiring future resolution.

Municipal tenements and cottage flats

The large municipal tenement blocks which emerged in London and a few other major cities from the 1890s had well-established precedents in the model dwellings erected in earlier decades by five per cent philanthropy. Middle-class mansion blocks, which grew apace in the capital from the 1870s, provided less of a template for obvious reasons, including the lack of lifts in all but a few multi-storey working-class schemes until after the Second World War. That absence of lifts explained the five-storey 'walk-up' limit applied to the new council blocks – a maximum deemed practicable for women with children or men hauling coal.

Despite the essential similarities they shared with the model dwelling schemes that preceded them, municipal developments, particularly those built by the better resourced and more ambitious councils, were generally distinguished by their architectural finesse and scale of construction. The Victoria Square Dwellings, designed by Henry Spalding for Manchester City Council, accommodated over 800 residents in a five-storey, red-brick quadrangle notable for its Queen Anne detailing of terracotta, oriel windows and gables. (Completed in 1894 and now providing supported accommodation for elderly residents, it can claim to be the oldest social housing still in use.)

Spalding was a private practitioner, but among a new breed of committed public sector architects political idealism joined with aesthetic sensibility in a drive to create estates of lasting quality. 'Estates', of course, points to that second distinction – a designation applying not just to size but, at best, to infrastructure. Schools, being built in huge numbers since the 1870 Education Act made elementary education compulsory, were one local authority contribution. Two were built on the London County Council's Boundary Estate, opened in 1900 and the country's first proper council estate, but the council also provided 18 shops, 77 workshops, a central laundry with bathrooms and two clubrooms.

Elsewhere, more modest three- or four-storey tenement blocks might be built, but it was cottage flats – ground-floor and first-floor flats provided in a two-storey dwelling – that best approximated the cottage home ideal in cases where economy and greater density were required. Adjacent to Victoria Square, Manchester built the aptly named Sanitary Street (later renamed Anita Street) comprising facing two-storey tenement terraces with two ground-floor and two first-floor flats sharing a common entrance. The Borough of Richmond, then in Surrey and a surprising early pioneer of council housing, built cottage flats in its 1900 Manor Grove scheme, which enjoyed the additional benefit of separate rear access to a back garden.

London (which built 10,000 council homes before 1914) and Liverpool (some 2,747) were the principal pre-war pioneers of council housing. Contrasting case studies allow us to study this record in greater detail.

Millbank Estate, Westminster, London

Measures to tackle the capital's housing crisis were a major priority for the New Liberal and Labour politicians who formed the progressive majority in the new London County Council (LCC) created in 1889; the ambition not only to clear the worst of the slums but also to build attractive replacement housing that would grace the city. The predominantly young men who formed the permanent staff of the Housing of the Working Classes branch established in the LCC Architect's Department in 1893 shared this aspiration – architects inspired by the radical Arts and Crafts movement of the day that aspired to dignify working-class life and labour, and the aesthetic ideals and social conscience of its leading practitioners such as William Morris, Philip Webb, Norman Shaw and W.R. Lethaby.

The Boundary Estate was the LCC's first great tenement estate; Millbank in Westminster – 17 five-storey, blocks housing around 4,400 people – was its second, completed in 1902. The estate was built on 11 acres of land formerly occupied by the Millbank Penitentiary, which the Royal Commission on the Housing of the Working Classes had recommended be reserved for housing back in 1884. The brownfield site offered the LCC a rare opportunity to rehouse residents from a number of contemporary slum clearance schemes without further loss of housing. The new Tate Gallery, neighbouring Millbank, inspired the naming of its blocks after British artists.

The first completed was Hogarth House, designed by Spalding (the architect of Manchester's Victoria Dwellings) and Cross as part of their winning competition entry to design the estate as a whole. In the event, the LCC found those plans too expensive, and the remainder of the estate was designed in-house by the Housing of the Working Classes branch led here by R. Minton Taylor.

Left
An early drawing of the estate's layout

Right
The original layout plan of Millais and Leighton buildings showing the separate WCs and sculleries provided to some of the tenements

It's a more symmetrical scheme than the Boundary Estate and generally plainer, but it manages to be both imposing and decorous, avoiding that barracks-like feel criticised elsewhere. Its Arts and Crafts inspiration is seen in the high gable ends, tall chimneys and dormer windows of the estate, and particularly in the grand entrance porchways of some of the blocks. Smaller features such as the contrasting use of red and brown brick, occasional rendering and stone dressing add a decorative touch; windows of varying sizes and shapes add variety. Most of the blocks are plain rectangles but some of

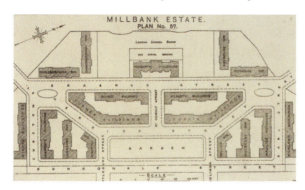

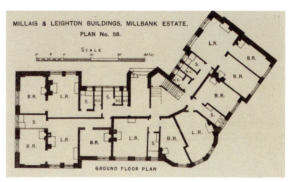

the larger ones are hinged, as it were, around tall pinnacle turrets which served the practical function of providing staircase access.

In terms of the all-important lived experience of the new tenants, room sizes tended to be a little smaller than those of the Boundary Estate and, while the estate escaped the shared facilities of some of the latter's blocks, some WCs were accessed from the hall or landing rather than privately within the tenement. The estate was visited by Edward VII and Queen Alexandra the year after its completion:

> *As evidence of the interest which their Majesties took in everything they saw, it may be mentioned that they subsequently suggested that a larger number of cupboards should be provided, as these would be a great convenience and would add to the tidiness of the rooms.*[1]

Top
Millbank Estate, 1984

Left
Contemporary view of Hogarth House from St Oswulf Street

Hornby Street, Vauxhall, Liverpool

In the 19th century (and beyond), Liverpool suffered the twin problems of housing squalor unequalled in England and a peculiarly impoverished working class heavily dependent on the casual employment offered by the docks. The firmly Conservative council of Liverpool – by the later century, a bastion of the Tory Democracy which purported to both defend throne and empire and elevate the condition of the indigenous working class – had been an early leader in sanitary reform. By 1893, it was reckoned the council had demolished 4,126 insanitary houses and built 1,061 new homes; the problem was that half the displaced population, around 5,000 people in all, were not rehoused. In 1897, the council took the radical decision that henceforth its slum clearance and rebuilding schemes would be dedicated solely to the rehousing of slum dwellers. This was achieved partly by building to quite basic and therefore cheaper standards and, more directly, by guaranteeing rents that were roughly equivalent to those of slum housing.

The Hornby Street scheme, built between 1904 and 1907, was Liverpool's largest to date, involving the demolition of some 511 insanitary homes, housing a population of 2,500. The new scheme comprised 23 blocks of 445 tenements, calculated to accommodate roughly the number displaced by clearance. These were predominantly three-storey buildings with two- and three-bed flats on each level. Facing blocks were placed 21 metres apart to provide the fresher air lacking in the narrow streets and courts they replaced. The overall scheme included a playground, seven shops and a 'keeper's house' from which a council official could exercise some oversight of local conditions and behaviour.

Construction was austere – of 'local grey brick with red brick dressings, buff terra cotta being sparingly used and only in the entrances'.[2] William Thompson,

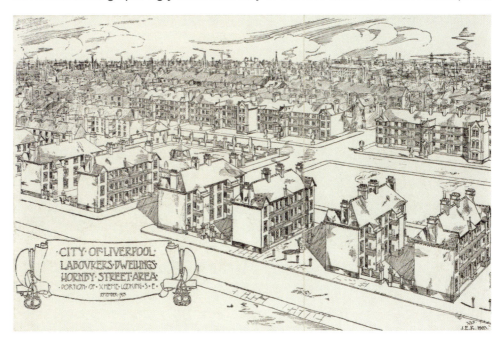

Right
'Labourers' dwellings, Hornby Street area'; an architect's drawing from 1903

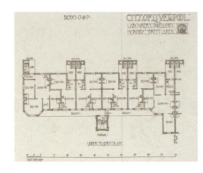

a powerful but very practical advocate of early council housing, also detailed the flooring: 'constructed with small steel joists with coke breeze concrete, the flooring boards being nailed direct on to same'. In an earlier scheme, the city's Medical Officer of Health had described how 'anything which would be likely to attract tenants of a better class has been avoided'.[3]

Such basic accommodation nevertheless represented a marked improvement in living conditions. Each of the new homes contained a separate scullery and WC and 'shoots' which facilitated the disposal of ash and household refuse collected daily. Penny meters supplied gas. A four-room (three-bed) flat rented at between 4s 6d and 5s 3d (23p to 26p) weekly, affordable even in Liverpool where many of the working class subsisted on average wages below 75p a week. Council data revealed that fully 74% of the estate's new tenants came from cleared slum housing, and a rollcall of heads of household listed labourers, carters and hawkers as well as 18 females classified as charwomen.

The Hornby Street housing has since been demolished. Eldon Grove, a later showpiece council scheme opened in 1912 – three-storey tenement blocks with bay windows, half-timbered gables and balconies, even a bandstand – survives, Grade-II listed, but awaiting sympathetic conversion.

Top
This early, undated, plan shows the internal configuration of the blocks

Left
An early, undated, photograph of the Hornby Street tenements

A History of Council Housing in 100 Estates

Balcony access

The balcony-access form is a means by which upper-storey flats are accessed by a shared walkway or gallery leading from a single staircase. It dates to at least the Middle Ages, but it was boosted by the new ideas and plans of 19th-century housing reformers. Its critical advantage, at a time when it was widely believed infectious disease was spread by 'bad air' or 'miasma', was that it offered better ventilation and fresher air than the prevalent staircase-access form. Here, the 'Model Homes for Families' designed by Henry Roberts for the Society for Improving the Condition of the Labouring Classes in Streatham Street in 1850 were indeed to prove a model for much social housing to come.

The weight of existing forms was particularly strong in Scotland, where even the model four-storey tenement plans of the 1860 Report on Houses for the Working Classes of Edinburgh recommended a back-to-back design with a single stairway giving access to 16 flats. Such blocks were built speculatively before being outlawed but were challenged locally by the semi-philanthropic Rosemount Buildings by architect William Lambie Moffat, completed in 1860. A three-storey, balcony-access design arranged around an open quadrangle, the scheme explicitly demonstrated the enhanced light and 'through and through' ventilation advocated by reformers, and would inspire a later generation of municipal schemes in the Scottish capital.

A less touted advantage of the form was that, in reducing the number of stairways required, it tended to be cheaper. This was part of the reason for it becoming the staple design of the plainer forms of early council tenement housing, particularly in London.

As with most things architectural, the form's popularity waxed and waned. In what seems a conscious borrowing from British examples, it was employed by Hannes Meyer in social housing designed by the Bauhaus School in Germany in the late 1920s. Conversely, by the mid-1930s in London, it was criticised for its design deficiencies as improved forms of staircase-access multi-storey housing were promoted. The deck-access 'streets in the sky' reinvented in the 1950s revived this basic gallery-access form.

High School Yards, Cowgate, Edinburgh

Scotland suffered the worst housing conditions in the UK. In 1861, it was reckoned that 71% of Scottish homes, housing almost two-thirds of its population, comprised no more than two rooms.[4] Local construction costs were higher too as a result of the Scottish practice of feuing (in which developers were required to pay an annual fee to the original landowner) and higher building standards. Developers built at greater density and charged higher rents to recoup costs. Scottish tenants – generally lower waged than their English counterparts – were forced to sublet to meet expenses, compounding existing overcrowding.

In 1893, Edinburgh Town Council inaugurated the Old Town Improvement Scheme under the terms of the 1890 Housing of the Working Classes Act. Proto-town planner Sir Patrick Geddes was an important local influence, pioneering what has been described as 'conservative surgery' – a modernising adaptation of existing structures that retained their essence and respected local traditions.[5] New housing built by the council in central slum clearance areas, designed by Burgh Engineer John Cooper, was effectively an improved and more sanitary version of local tenement forms and emulated this approach.

High School Yards, two linked five-storey sandstone blocks in Scots Baronial style, was completed in 1897. The scheme, which unusually included ground-floor shops, comprised 32 flats, each costing around £200 to build. This, the first council housing built in Edinburgh, remained quite basic: one- or two-room, lacking private sculleries and washhouses, with some flats sharing WCs.

Left
The Cowgate front of the blocks with shops

Opposite top
A rear view showing balcony access

Opposite bottom
Balconies colourfully adapted by existing residents

Crucially, however, Cooper's design provided the balcony-access form promoted to provide much better light and ventilation than the foetid blocks it replaced. Rents ranging from 2s to 2s 7d (10p to 13p) for a one-room tenement and 4s to 5s (20p to 25p) were relatively low, though records suggest that the new homes were occupied by the more skilled and better-paid working class.

As infant mortality rates in the High School Yards area fell from a horrendous 247 per 1,000 to 39 in the space of a decade, however, the local impact of Edinburgh's reforms remained impressive.[6] The council followed up the High School Yards scheme with two similar schemes in Old Town – at Tron Square (completed in 1900) and Portsburgh Square (1901).

Darcy Buildings, London Fields, and Valette Buildings, Valette Street, Hackney, London

The case for providing new homes in cases where state-sponsored road-building schemes had demolished working-class housing had been broadly accepted since the mid-1880s and was the major thrust of Part I of 1890 Housing of the Working Classes Act. The London County Council's widening of Mare Street in Hackney, sanctioned in 1900, was estimated to have displaced 526 residents. The duty of the council to rehouse them (or, more accurately, to provide replacement housing sufficient to rehouse that number) was met in two local schemes.

Both these early schemes were of the five-storey, walk-up, balcony-access type. The first, Darcy Buildings (still standing; now Darcy House), was built between 1903 and 1904 on a former almshouse site adjacent to the open green space of London Fields. It may not have been 'the capital architectural feature of the neighbourhood' predicted by the local press, but it remains an imposing presence on the park's fringes and demonstrates some of the design features aspired to by the Arts and Crafts-inspired architects of the LCC in its mansard roofs and ground-floor quoined windows and brick banding.[7] In other respects, the scheme was purposely economical in form, particularly with respect to room sizes. However, the architects exploited its site by placing sculleries and WCs on the rear, walkway side of the block, presenting a more attractive aspect to the park and allowing views over it from most bedrooms and living rooms.

The Valette Buildings (now Valette House) were completed in 1905 to the rear of Mare Street in central Hackney in an area of formerly densely packed slum housing. The design is superficially similar, though the top-storey's horizontal fenestration and the block's striking arched and pedimented courtyard entrance distinguish the block in its otherwise tight urban setting. Room sizes and construction quality were slightly superior to that of its predecessor.

In all, the two new blocks provided accommodation for 606 residents, more than meeting the rehousing requirements of the clearance scheme. The new tenants, though possibly not from those displaced, were local and engaged in the manual trades typical of the area.

Left
Darcy House, the front facade facing London Fields

Right
Valette House, with stairwell and balconies to rear

Garden villages and co-partnership models

The most obvious inspiration of the Garden Villages founded by co-partnership societies in significant numbers before the First World War is Ebenezer Howard. Howard had first outlined his grand vision of economically self-sufficient and socially mixed new towns combining the benefits of sociable urban life and healthy rural living in 1898. The Garden Cities Association (later the Town and Country Planning Association) was formed one year later.

However, there were other significant contemporary influences. The model villages established by the more philanthropic but economically astute employers principally as employees' housing were one, notably Port Sunlight (founded by William Lever in 1888), Bournville (founded by George Cadbury in 1893) and New Earswick (founded by Joseph Rowntree in 1902).

A broader housing reform movement was in full swing. Fred Knee, a trade unionist and socialist, was the tireless force behind the formation of the Workman's National Housing Council in 1899: 'a delegate body representing 150 labour organisations … having for its object the provision by public authority of good houses for all of its people'.[8] Liberal reformers gathered in the Housing Reform Council (which became the National Housing and Town Planning Council), established in 1900.

The latter, representing a more mainstream politics and commanding greater resources, were more immediately influential. It was also more likely to promote self-help housing solutions available to the better-off working class and middle class. Co-partnership was the coming idea before the First World War; a form of housing tenure combining characteristics of the tenant co-operative and limited dividend company. Members bought shares from which capital, alongside loans, the company purchased land and erected housing. Investors and tenant-investors received dividends, generally capped at 5%, when the company had paid off initial debts.

The first modern iteration of the concept came in the Tenant Co-operators Ltd, founded in 1888, but it was Ealing Tenants Ltd, formed by the trade unionist and Liberal politician Henry Vivian in 1901, with its prescribed geographic focus and community ethos, which became the preferred model. Brentham Garden Suburb in Ealing grew to provide several hundred homes, at first in conventional suburban form but from 1906, 'under the influence of the "garden city" idea', in an extension designed by its chief contemporary exponents Raymond Unwin and Barry Parker.[9]

The overall impact of the co-partnership movement is hard to quantify. Up to 36 companies were formed before the First World War, but not all were viable and they inevitably catered for the more affluent who could afford the initial investment they required. They did, however, provide a vital bridge in form between Howard's expansive vision and the less ambitious municipal suburbs emerging to supersede their role in future years.

Burnage Garden Village, Levenshulme, Manchester

The origins of the Manchester Tenants Ltd provide a precise illustration of the forces at play behind the wider movement. There was, firstly, growing concern over the ill-health of the British working class. Some 8,000 of 11,000 Manchester Boer War volunteers had been declared unfit for service, and while local housing reformer T.C. Horsfall believed that 'coal smoke, drinking and licentiousness [were] among the factors which produce this physical deterioration', he was clear that 'bad housing is the chief factor'.[10] In 1902, together with T.R. Marr, he founded the precisely named Citizens' Association for the Improvement of the Unwholesome Dwellings and Surroundings of the People. These middle-class reformers joined with prominent labour activists to form the new co-partnership organisation in a meeting at the committee rooms of the Cooperative Wholesale Society in 1906, perhaps stimulated by a recent address by Ebenezer Howard on 'Garden Cities' to a group of Manchester clerks. Its opening prospectus outlined its aims:

> *We desire to do something to meet the housing problem by placing within the reach of working people, clerks, etc., the opportunity of taking a house or a cottage with a garden at a moderate rent. We believe that in cleaner air, with an open space near to their doors, the people would develop a sense of home life and an interest in nature.*[11]

Burnage Garden Village comprised 144 houses on an 11-acre site in Levenshulme, four miles south of the city centre. The original layout proposed by local architect J. Horner Hargreaves was modified by a distinguished group of advisers (including, most notably, the

Left
The revised and executed plan of Burnage Garden Village

Right
Plan and elevation of a superior three-bedroom parlour house

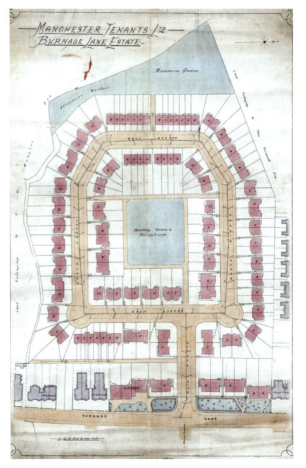

Left
Semi-detached
housing on South
Avenue, shown on
an early postcard

Right
An undated early
postcard showing
the entrance to the
village

Bottom
A detached house
on the corner of
East and South
Avenues

SOUTH AVENUE, GARDEN VILLAGE, BURNAGE.

ENTRANCE, GARDEN VILLAGE, BURNAGE.

ubiquitous Raymond Unwin) to include a central open space with bowling green, tennis courts and clubhouse. The City Council's insistence on bye-law-compliant 42-feet-wide streets was subverted by tree-lined grass verges and broad pavements on each side of narrower metalled roadways. Marr concluded that 'they had not done in Burnage all they would have liked to do, but they had, at any rate, given to the residents of the village rather more of country conditions than most town residents were able to enjoy'.[12]

The housing, at the 12 homes an acre that would become a gold standard, was typical of the cottage-style homes being designed for similar ventures elsewhere – redbrick and roughcast, red-roofed and gabled, mostly semi-detached. Internally, they ranged from two-bed to four-bed, with larger homes enjoying a hall and parlour. Rents corresponding to this provision ranged from 5s (30p) to 11s 6d (57.5p) per week, exclusive of rates. At a time when the local working class generally paid no more than 7 shillings weekly (35p) inclusive of rates, this sum – as well as the initial £10 investment in shares required – clearly precluded most from benefiting from the new estate. Most residents were middle or lower middle class. Unlike Brentham, however, which was sold to a private company in 1936, Burnage Garden Village is still owned and managed by Manchester Tenants Ltd.

SOUTH AVE.

EAST AVENUE

Garden suburbs

In 1910, Patrick Abercrombie, then emerging as Britain's foremost town planner, concluded that 'the keynote of the revival of English Town Planning which has taken place during the past 20 years has been the creation of suburbs of small houses with a strict limitation as to the number per acre'.[13] This was a modest, even pyrrhic, victory for the prodigious efforts of Ebenezer Howard but it recognised the significance of the garden suburbs, which were to become the predominant form of council housing in future years.

The great growth of what might be termed 'corporation suburbia' would come later, but its foundations were laid in the years before the First World War. Most of the earliest council housing – inner city and often associated with urban improvement and slum clearance schemes – was in tenement form, but housing reformers invariably favoured the cottage home ideal. This conflict was played out in a three-day conference on 'Sanitary Reform and Progress' organised by Manchester City Council in 1899. Some members of the council's Sanitary Committee defended its extensive tenement-building programme as practical and cost-effective, but a number considered it 'more in keeping with an Englishman's idea of home that he should have a cottage to himself, and not occupy a portion of block dwelling rooms'.[14] The latter became the Manchester model into the 1960s and found early fulfilment when the council bought 238 acres of land in Blackley on its new northern border in 1904. The new policy had one compelling practical advantage – a purchase price for land of 1p per square yard compared to around £5 in the inner city.

While economics were significant in the choice of councils to build in outlying districts, other factors were necessary to enable it. One was the growth of commuter rail and tram services. Parliament had first authorised workmen's fares in 1860 and their spread was vital to the viability of at least the better-paid workman moving outwards. In Sheffield, the city's Medical Officer of Health contended in 1899 that 'the new and most excellent tramway facilities will do more to relieve the congestion in the central districts than anything else'.[15]

For London in particular, where the London County Council's borders were narrowly drawn, the 1900 Housing of the Working Classes Act, allowing councils to acquire land and build housing beyond their boundaries, was crucial. The LCC acted quickly to build its first 'out-of-county' estate on land acquired in Norbury, Croydon (then in Surrey), in 1900. The Totterdown Fields Estate on land in Tooting purchased the same year was within the county but newly benefiting from an extension of municipal tram services connecting the district to central London.

Legislatively, the 1909 Housing and Town Planning Act was the final piece in the jigsaw allowing the full flowering of the garden suburb. Based on the private 1906 Hampstead Garden Suburb Act, it allowed planners to escape the rigidity of sanitary bye-laws compelling the construction of wide streets and uniform terraces. The Old Oak Estate in Hammersmith, commenced in 1911, would see the municipal cottage suburb in its most complete form.

A History of Council Housing in 100 Estates

Flower Estate, High Wincobank, Sheffield

Sheffield's first venture into municipal housebuilding in the 1890s – the clearance of the notorious Crofts central slum district and the construction of three-storey tenement blocks (eventually completed in 1907 and still standing) – had proved controversial. The housing was more expensive than anticipated and was disliked, even by the chair of the Housing Committee, for its bleak appearance. Its second was intended to be a model scheme.

Top
High Wincobank Estate (Flower Estate) plan

Bottom
Model Cottage Exhibition, Class B gold medallist, architect Frank W. Chapman, 148–150 Foxglove Road, 1907

The council had purchased a greenfield site at High Wincobank – some way northeast of the city centre, but handy for a tramway terminus and the city's east-end steelworks – in 1900. In 1902 it announced a national competition to find the ideal worker's cottage. The winning designs by Chesterfield architect Percy Houfton, erected on Wincobank Avenue and Heather Road, reflected the forward thinking of the day, exemplified in Raymond Unwin and Barry Parker's contemporary Fabian tract *Cottage Plans and Common Sense*: internal bathrooms and WCs, of course; a rejection of the back projections held to impede fresh air and natural light; the replacement of the 'middle-class' parlour with a single larger and more airy living room.

Houfton's double-fronted Class A designs, with upstairs bathroom, represented the acme; his Class B single-fronted housing, which could be built in terraces (with a downstairs bath in the scullery), represented a cheaper compromise. Both, however, with their lowest rent at 7s (35p) weekly, were too expensive for the working class they were intended to serve. The council commissioned a new design, smaller and without bathrooms, from local architect H.L. Patterson, let at 5s (25p) a week.

Despite this pragmatism, the council remained ambitious and it competed successfully to host the 1907 Yorkshire and North Midland Cottage Exhibition organised by the National Housing Reform Committee. The organising committee included, among other such luminaries, the Liberal MP and architect Sir John Tudor Walters (a name of future significance) and the industrialist W.H. Lever, founder of Port Sunlight. Twenty-four acres of the High Wincobank site were set aside for model housing, placed singly or in groups no larger than four at no more than 12 per acre. In the event, it was the site's layout, devised by W. Alexander Harvey, who had earlier devised the plans for Bournville, which received most acclaim. Set around a central axis of

SHEFFIELD COTTAGE EXHIBITION —Nos. 17, 18, 19, & 20.   CLASS B, BRONZE MEDAL. COST £195 PER COTTAGE.

Left
Model Cottage
Exhibition, Class B
bronze medallist,
architect Frank W.
Chapman, 140–146
Foxglove Road,
1907

Bottom left
Model Cottage
Exhibition, Class
B silver medallist,
architects Pepler
and Allen, 17–19
Primrose Avenue,
1907

Bottom right
The same homes
on Primrose Avenue
today

Primrose Avenue (all the estate's roads were given floral titles, hence its overall name), secondary streets were arranged in concentric curves and housing set irregularly and offset at corners to create informal green spaces. This would prove a template for the best of later municipal planning.

The 42 model homes, designed by an array of the progressive architects of the day and incorporating Unwin's key principles, were attractive but more conventionally suburban, and generally criticised as unimaginative by contemporary commentators. They were also, despite the £175 to £225 construction cost limits set by the organising committee, too expensive for the ordinary working-class householder. However, they were bought at cost price by the council as municipal housing. The Conservative charge that the Liberal council was merely 'providing dainty villas for already well-paid artisans' proved to be a major factor in the Liberals' loss of power in 1908.

A History of Council Housing in 100 Estates

Old Oak Estate, Hammersmith, London

The Old Oak Estate has been described as the 'culminating achievement of the [London County] Council's venture into garden suburb planning before the first world war' – a fruition of the design ideals that inspired it and the policy enactments that allowed them expression.[16] That architectural lineage is by now quite obvious in the number of predominantly co-partnership schemes, most notably Hampstead Garden Suburb, which preceded it. But it is seen too in personnel. The LCC's chief architect, W.E. Riley, was a member of the Arts and Crafts-inspired Art Worker's Guild founded in 1884. One of his talented team of project architects was Archibald Stuart Soutar (responsible for 268–274 Du Cane Road and the two blocks on the corner of Du Cane Road and Fitzneal Street) whose brother succeeded Raymond Unwin as chief architect at Hampstead Garden Suburb. The passage of the 1909 Housing and Town Planning Act – when the legislation's promoter John Burns had famously spoken of 'that line of beauty which Hogarth said was in a curve' – was a necessary precondition.

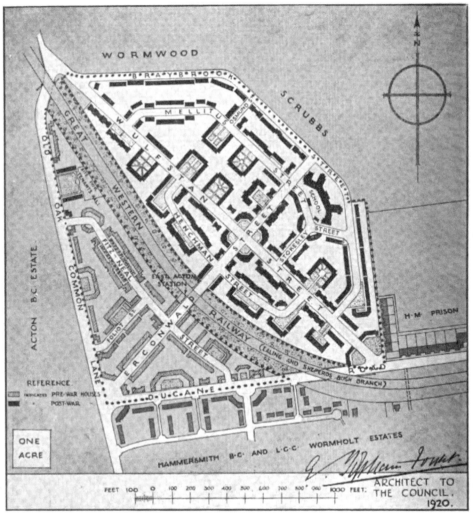

OLD OAK ESTATE

Right
A plan of the estate as completed by 1920

The LCC had bought the 54-acre site in Hammersmith from the Ecclesiastical Commissioners in 1905, a heritage that explains the somehow appropriate archaism of some of the estate's street names: Wulfstan, Erconwald, Mellitus, for example; early bishops of London. Eight acres were sold on to the Great Western Railway to allow the construction of the railway line that bisects the larger estate. Perhaps fortuitously, serious planning did not begin until 1909, and the first working drawings were executed in 1911. The eastern section of the estate was completed just before the First World War.

The first breakthrough in the estate's design is seen in its layout – in its curving streetscapes and carefully designed intersections, a deliberate break with the regular grid of bye-law housing and even the modified grids of the LCC's earlier cottage estates. Particularly notable are the splayed 'butterfly plans' adopted for the corner housing, intended to open vistas and circulate air in a way reminiscent, if not directly inspired, by Unwin's own designs in Hampstead Garden Suburb. Elsewhere, houses are deployed in short terraces, sometimes set back from the street and grouped in styles providing both overall coherence and individual variety.

The council's own account of the estate in 1912 records its housing in typically dry and practical fashion: the proposed erection of 333 cottages and cottage flats of varying sizes, each provided with 'a scullery and the usual offices', though only the larger homes were to enjoy a fitted bath.[17] In fact, most houses were of the smaller type – the result of the decision of the LCC's new Conservative majority to concentrate 'on smaller cottages for those whose needs were "not supplied by other agencies"'.[18]

It's been left to later chroniclers to celebrate its architecture – an updated vernacular of pitched and hipped and tile-hung gables, mullioned window frames and dormer windows, all set in brickwork of rich red and brown amid the profuse greenery of its generous landscaping. While this was a quality occasionally aspired to in the ambition of the immediate post-First World War period, as architectural thinking moved on and finances tightened, it was not one that would be surpassed, as the plainer neo-Georgian style of the estate's westward extension attests.

Left
Du Cane Road

Right
Du Cane Road and Fitzneal Street corner

Opposite
Erconwald Road and Wulfstan Street junction, showing 'butterfly plan' housing

CHAPTER 3

1914–1930: The Impact of War

There had been a small increase in council house construction in the years immediately before the First World War, but it was the war itself that would transform the housing landscape. The enhanced role of the state was seen first in a number of estates built by the government to accommodate defence and munitions workers. However, total war also made more indirect demands. An eight-month rent strike in Glasgow in 1915, sparked by housing shortage and rising prices, forced the imposition of rent controls. The controls themselves were a further blow to a private rental sector already reeling from the standstill in domestic housebuilding and repair caused by the war.

As the labour movement grew stronger, government fears of working-class militancy increased, and assumed more alarmist focus when revolutions erupted first in Russia, then in Germany. The war effort and postwar stability required a contented workforce, soldiery and citizenry. The rhetoric of a 'land fit for heroes' and the housing programme which emerged was knowingly and deliberately, as Mark Swenarton argues, 'an insurance against revolution: its purpose to ensure the survival of the status quo'.[1]

If war and politics provided the edge and urgency to state intervention, the facts on the ground provided its necessary context. A Royal Commission on Housing in Scotland convened in 1912, but reporting in 1917 found almost half its population living in two rooms or fewer. A Commission of Enquiry into Industrial Unrest appointed the same year described the shocking housing conditions in Barrow-in-Furness as 'a terrible indictment ... against the Rulers and Governors'.[2] Pre-war precedent and wartime practice provided a template for the 'Housing after the War' promised by Local Government Board Circular 86/1917: councils implementing approved housebuilding schemes would be offered 'substantial financial assistance from public funds'. The 1919 Housing Act fulfilled this pledge by limiting, through generous Treasury support, the financial liability of local authorities to the product of a penny on the rates (in Scotland, with its even more dire housing conditions, four-fifths of a penny). It went further by imposing for the first time a duty on councils to build housing where needs were proven.

As to the form this new housing might take, the Local Government Board led by William Hayes Fisher initially favoured the economical designs of the pre-war public housing provided for the poorer working class. The Women's Housing Subcommittee, established by the more expansive Ministry of Reconstruction under Christopher Addison, was sharply critical. In the event, the October 1918 report of the authoritative Tudor Walters Committee (which Hayes Fisher had appointed) settled the argument by advocating improved housing serving the needs of the working class as a whole. This reflected both the nature of the contemporary housing crisis and the committee's desire and expectation that housing standards should rise.

The report, principally drafted by Raymond Unwin, recommended two-storey cottage homes, generally with parlour and separate bathroom, with front and back gardens, at a density of no more than 12 per acre, eight in rural areas. Cottage flats might be more acceptable, it felt, in Scotland where they were more in keeping with local traditions. On the question of style, the report favoured the plainer and more cost-effective designs advocated by some pre-war housing reformers, concluding that 'ornament is usually out of place and necessarily costly both in first execution and upkeep'.

All this was very substantially incorporated, with perhaps even greater emphasis on simplified forms, in the Manual on the Preparation of State-Aided Housing Schemes issued by the Local Government Board in April 1919. By this time, Addison was Minister of Health and Housing, but he resigned from office two years later as the generous postwar housing programme he had championed fell victim to economising measures, formalised in the swingeing public spending cuts of the 'Geddes Axe' in July 1921. Only 213,000 houses were built in England and Wales of the 500,000 prime minister Lloyd George had promised in 1918; 176,000 by local authorities. The 1923 Housing Act introduced by a Conservative Minister of Health and Housing, Neville Chamberlain, restored a council housing programme but looked chiefly towards the private sector. The largest amount of interwar public housing – some 493,000 new council homes – was built under Labour's financially more generous 1924 Housing Act.

The ever-present tension between aspiration and cost led to an interest in the use of prefabricated and new materials that might deliver housing more cheaply and quickly. The Tudor Walters Report concluded guardedly on the matter, but the notion of a quick fix was too appealing to be discarded, and was implemented with mixed results at best.

In 1919, council housing came of age. Co-partnership societies were effectively superseded and housing associations largely marginalised, but the latter in particular persisted, and in some cases pursued an advocative and innovatory role all the more necessary as council housing became the norm.

Munitions estates

The Housing Act passed on 10 August 1914 empowered the state to provide (directly or indirectly) housing for workers in war-related industries; specifically, it aimed to secure accommodation for the employees of the new Admiralty dockyards in Rosyth on the Firth of Forth. Britain had declared war six days earlier, and it was already clear that victory or defeat depended overwhelmingly on firepower and the personnel to produce and deploy it.

Four years later, as the protracted conflict drew to its bloody conclusion, around 10,000 permanent new homes had been built under state auspices. Some had been built by munitions manufacturers. The Vickers' schemes in Crayford (Kent) and Barrow-in-Furness were two of 20 such built with heavy government subsidy. Of longer-term impact were the 13 schemes built directly by government, by the Office of Works or Ministry of Munitions.

The Treasury, mindful of expense, had initially favoured temporary housing. However, in this it was overruled by those who pointed convincingly to the false economy of such provision, and by politicians and housing reformers who believed that the state should offer a model of good practice, which in this era meant housing on Garden City lines. The Well Hall Estate in Eltham, principally the work of Frank Baines, chief architect of the Office of Works, would be its acme.

Baines was also responsible for the Roe Green Estate, built in 1917 for aircraft workers in west London. Architecturally, this was a pared-down, less ornamental version of Well Hall and unusually, while Arts and Crafts influences stayed strong in its layout and elements, around 40% of its homes were in the form of cottage flats.

However, it was the Gretna scheme, designed by Courtenay Crickmer for the Ministry of Munitions to service a huge new explosives factory set up in a remote part of Dumfries, that had greater influence on future forms. At Gretna, Crickmer, in what has been described as the 'first large-scale demonstration of simplification of design', abandoned the picturesque but complex detailing of Arts and Crafts in favour of a far plainer neo-Georgian.[3] Two of Crickmer's designs were subsequently included as exemplars of good practice in the Tudor Walters Report.

The 'standard cottages' and formal layout devised by Stanley Adshead, Stanley Ramsey and Patrick Abercrombie for the Dormanstown housing scheme of the Dorman Long iron- and steelworks in Redcar took the process a stage further.

Rosyth Garden City, Fife, Scotland

The Admiralty had first proposed building a large new naval dockyard at Rosyth on the Firth of Forth in 1903; construction began in 1909. Vociferous lobbying by the Garden City Association that the 'new town' required to accommodate its workforce should be built on Garden City lines appeared to receive some official sanction with the appointment of Raymond Unwin as Admiralty adviser on the scheme in 1913. But by 1914, when the dockyards employed some 3,500 men, no progress had been made. Neither the Admiralty nor the Local Government Board of Scotland nor Dunfermline Burgh Council (despite the latter's ambitious town planning scheme created under the 1909 Housing and Town Planning Act) wished to assume responsibility.

The Housing Act passed in August 1914 was an emergency response, sanctioning the creation of a Public Utility Society (a private housing company which agreed to limit its maximum dividend to 5%) and agreeing to increase the Treasury contribution from two-thirds of costs to nine-tenths. The Scottish National Housing Company Ltd was formed in September.

The company's first 150 houses (located within the triangle formed by Queensferry Road, Admiralty Road and Backmarch Road) were designed by Edinburgh architects Alfred Greig and Walter Fairbairn in notably Arts and Crafts and 'English' idiom. Formally opened in May 1916 by the chair of the company, he explained that due to the large number of English workers moving to Rosyth, 'the houses had been designed to a certain extent in accordance with English ideas'.[4] Subsequent developments were designed by the company's in-house architect Alfred Hugh Mottram. Mottram had trained under Unwin and assisted him at Letchworth and Hampstead, but here his emphasis was on a plainer, more economical style.

By January 1919, around 1,600 homes had been built (of an originally projected 3,000). At an overall density of around 12.6 houses per acre, gardens front and

Left
A.H. Mottram's plan of the Garden City, 1917

Right
An architectural drawing by A.H. Mottram for the Scottish National Housing Company

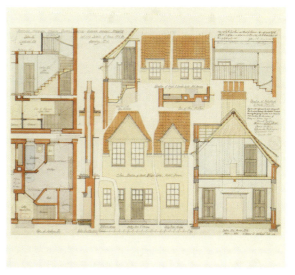

back and in a layout of curving streets and cul-de-sacs, the overall scheme merited at least a Garden Village label, though the housing itself was subject to criticism. *The Scotsman* complained that it lacked the 'uncompromising solidity of the conventional Scottish tenement'.[5] Paradoxically the (predominantly English) members of the Rosyth Ratepayers' Association argued that the 'houses should have been built after the style of those in which we are accustomed to live, prior to our transference to Rosyth' and levelled particular grievances about high rents and poor design, notably the lack of rear access. A Women's House Planning Committee appointed by the Local Government Board of Scotland criticised the small size of the houses, their distempered walls and narrow stairs.

Nevertheless, the scheme was significant in Scotland, serving as a local example of the Garden City (and non-native) ideals of the Tudor Walters Report and influential in the design of early postwar estates in Dunfermline, Kirkcaldy, Methil and – most successfully – in the Scoonie Estate in Leven.

Top left
An early postcard image of Queensferry Road

Top right
An early postcard image of Backmarch Road

Bottom
An early postcard image of Crossroads Place

Well Hall Estate, Greenwich, London

Around 11,000 men and women were employed at the Royal Arsenal in Woolwich at the outbreak of war; by 1917 there were almost 75,500. The Well Hall Estate in Eltham, some two miles to the south, was built to at least partially accommodate this enormous workforce. It was built at astonishing speed. Frank Baines was appointed by the Office of Works to design the scheme on Friday 8 January 1915. Baines and his assistant A.J. Pitcher visited the site on Saturday. A provisional plan for the layout of the estate was worked up by G.E. Phillips the following day. The first specifications for housing were sent to tender within 10 days. The estate as a whole – 1,086 houses and 212 flats – was completed by the end of the year. In this case, the pace of construction was matched by quality: Ewart Culpin, one-time secretary of the Garden Cities Association, described it as a community that was 'from the architectural standpoint, without equal in the world'.[6]

Such praise manifested the determination of Herbert Samuel, president of the Local Government Board, that the estate should be exemplary, not expedient – designed along 'the best town-planning lines'; an opportunity 'to show what a scheme of this nature should be under Government auspices'. It reflected too a willingness (under the pressures of war) to spend – the average cost per home came to £622, double the initial estimate. Of those homes, 473 included a parlour and separate bathroom; the largest number (613) were non-parlour with a bath provided in the scullery. The rest, cottage flats, were said by Baines to be surprisingly popular.

Baines's aim was that the 96-acre estate should look 'as if it had grown and not merely been dropped there'. Grass-verged and curving streets followed natural contours, and housing in terraces of 12 to 15 or smaller units of three to five was deployed pictorially to provide both vista and enclosure. This was the

Right
Ross Way photographed in 1963

ADMIRALTY ROAD, WEST, ROSYTH.

picturesque model of town planning favoured by Camillo Sitte and rooted in the more irregular look and 'organic' feel of medieval and early modern townscapes rather than Beaux-Arts symmetry and monumentalism. Ross Way, designed by Phillips, was nicknamed by his colleagues (ironically in the circumstances) the 'German village'.

This layout was accompanied by housing, in very varied but complementary form, designed in a full flowering of the 'villagey', quasi-vernacular style favoured by the Arts and Crafts movement. It had broken rooflines, overhangs and projections, and a striking range of finishes ranging from brick, stone and roughcast to tile- and slate-hung and half-timbered. At this point, versatile use of available materials counted more than economising standardisation.

The estate, initially managed by the London County Council, was sold by the Office of Works to Progress Estates Ltd, a subsidiary of the Royal Arsenal Co-operative Society, in 1925. By 1980, almost two-thirds of the estate's homes had been purchased by occupiers and the remainder were sold to what is now the Hyde Group housing association. It was declared a conservation area in 1975.

Top left
Terraced housing,
Prince Rupert Road

Top right
Terraced housing,
Dickson Road

Bottom
Terraced housing,
Well Hall Road

Homes for heroes

The Tudor Walters Report and the 1919 Addison Act set standards for council housing that would not be matched for many years – a commitment to quality signalled by the Local Government Board's official guidance that councils should employ a qualified architect to design or at least advise on their housing schemes. A number of leading practitioners were prominent in some of the best of the estates to emerge: Patrick Abercrombie in the Buddicom Park Estate in Chester; Stanley Adshead in Norwich's Mile Cross Estate and developments in Brighton and Dover; Ewart Culpin in Reading. Winchester City Council employed an architect, William Curtis Green, and a landscape architect, William Dunn, to design the housing and layout of its exemplary Stanmore Estate, opened by the Prince of Wales in 1923. The London County Council was large enough to employ its own very skilled architects in the design of its first and showpiece postwar scheme, the Dover House Estate in Roehampton. Smaller councils were generally more likely to employ the services of their own borough engineer or surveyor or commission local architects but the overall standard – closely policed by the Ministry of Health and Housing – remained high.

The Tudor Walters Committee (whose brief was only belatedly extended to Scotland in April 1918) recognised the distinctiveness of Scotland where, in the words of its report, a 'large proportion of the population have formed the habit of living in flats' and were used to living in a smaller number of (generally) larger rooms. A competition organised by the Local Government Board in Scotland and the Institute of Scottish Architects included two-storey cottage flats and three-storey tenements among its models.

In the event, of the 25,000 homes built in Scotland under the 1919 Housing and Town Planning (Scotland) Act, around 63% were – in a distinct break with Scottish tradition – two-storey cottages. But almost a third were cottage flats, and only just over a third contained the three bedrooms which were the norm in most English and Welsh schemes. The Logie Estate in Dundee, claimed as the first completed under the legislation, comprised nearly all four-in-a-block cottage flats, as did the Chasser Estate in Edinburgh, though their layouts conformed to garden suburb ideals.

Glasgow and Edinburgh were the largest builders, with 5,000 and 2,000 homes respectively. However, Scotland's 300 schemes were spread widely around the country and include notable architect-designed estates using local materials in rural areas such as Galashiels, Lockerbie and Lerwick.

South Moulsecoomb Estate, Brighton

In 1919, as part of the survey of local housing needs required of all local authorities by the 1919 Housing Act, Brighton's Medical Officer of Health estimated that some 3,152 working-class houses were needed in the town (then the second most populous county borough in the country) in the next three years. Construction of the South Moulsecoomb Estate commenced in April 1920 on land initially beyond the borough's northeastern borders but incorporated in 1923.

The local Conservative-controlled council, marking some of the idealism and ambition of the age, appointed two leading architect-planners to design the scheme, Stanley Adshead and Stanley Ramsey. Adshead, then Professor of Town Planning at University College London, had previously taught at the School of Civic Design at Liverpool University, where he was associated with the more formal Beaux-Arts planning principles favoured by Patrick Abercrombie and C.H. Reilly. In Brighton, however, the site dictated a different approach:

> *This lay-out is situated in an exceedingly beautiful hollow in the Downs, and it is due to the steepness of the hillside on which it is situated, that a very informal system of planning has been adopted.*[7]

Top
Estate plan, 1920

Bottom left
An early image of the top end of the estate; The Avenue lies further to the south

Bottom right
110–120 The Avenue; the houses themselves date from a later extension to the estate in the early 1930s

The estate's main road, The Avenue, forms an extended loop encircling an elongated village green, said by its designers to have been inspired by the 'continuous green traverses' found in a number of villages in the Sussex Downs. Other and later housing was built on hillside terraces.

The 487 houses, with spacious gardens and all with a front parlour, were designed by four local architects under Adshead's supervision, and they generally reflected the more standardised, neo-Georgian forms he

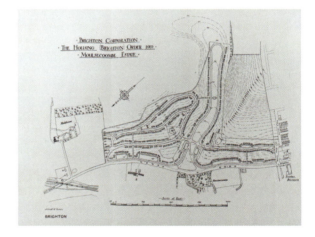

favoured. Their quality, however, in a time of postwar inflation and labour and materials shortages, ensured an average cost of £1,120 per house – around three times the pre-war norm. Calculated to repay loan charges, the rents on the South Moulsecoomb Estate ranged from 26s a week to 32s 6d (£1.30 to £1.62) – an exorbitant amount when a decent working-class wage might equate to around £3 a week. These 'homes fit for heroes', as they were unimaginatively described by one local alderman, excluded most in the class they were ostensibly intended for. Such was the difficulty in tenanting them that the council advertised vacancies in the London press. Some of the 'heroes' led a local squatting movement in protest, while middle-class tenants on the estate formed a ratepayers' association.

The council's second postwar estate, Queen's Park, built in the mid-1920s, was also designed by Adshead and Ramsey but to much-reduced specifications. It had non-parlour housing, ground-floor WCs and a density of 40 houses per acre in order to increase affordability. Later housing at North Moulsecoomb, at 12 per acre, reverted to garden suburb principles.

Top
A view of the estate as later extended from Heath Hill Avenue; the school was opened in 1951

Bottom
A contemporary aerial view of The Avenue, showing the earliest stage of the scheme towards Lewes Road

Townhill Estate, Swansea

The Borough of Swansea was an early pacesetter in council housing, building 33 infill terraced houses (though without the tunnel-back projections decried by housing reformers) on Waun Wen and Colbourne Terrace in 1905. In 1910, the town hosted the South Wales Cottage Exhibition, featuring a mix of privately built and municipal housing. Significantly, Raymond Unwin was on the judging panel, stressing the importance of a more expansive layout that would 'break the thrall of dreary terracing'.

In 1912, Unwin put his words into practice by designing, with Borough Surveyor George Bell, a new municipal estate on hilly council-owned land to the northwest of the town. Curving streets and stacked terraces followed steep contours; the ensemble was described by Ewart Culpin as 'a most remarkable example of town planning on a hillside'.[8]

The council's plans to build a scheme of 500 houses were to be scuppered by the war. However, as thoughts turned to postwar reconstruction in 1917, Swansea was far better placed than most local authorities to meet the new demand for improved working-class housing. The earlier plans were dusted off and, substantially unaltered, forwarded to the Local Government Board. From 1919, some 425 houses were built under the Addison Act on the Townhill Estate, alongside playing fields, a recreation ground and a new school completed in 1924.

Bottom
An early image of Dewi Terrace, originally labelled 'Echelon formation to overcome steep road, build to contours & obtain vistas'

Opposite left
An early image of Merlin Crescent, with the description added 'Houses sited to obtain views over the Mumbles'

Opposite right
Architectural drawings of houses in the first contract at Glyndwr Place; stepped terraces adapted to the terrain

The most immediately striking aspect of the estate was its setting, which Borough Architect Ernest Morgan exploited to the full by providing (especially along Pantycelyn Road on the southern edge of the estate) sweeping views of Swansea Bay, and in his careful deployment of a variety of housing types and forms. The houses themselves generally conformed to the neo-Georgian style then in vogue but Morgan, apprenticed in the Arts and Crafts movement, introduced variation and decoration 'in small details such as chimney caps, gable finishings, and by the introduction of Celtic patterae and ornament'.[9] Further interest was added by a variety of simple roof lines and a wide range of surface finishes and colours – all, in Morgan's words, 'with the object of avoiding monotony, rigidity and drabness'. The exposed site also demanded the high-quality construction and materials and good weatherproofing on which he insisted.

The houses, generally in blocks of six (as in the original plans) rather than the semi-detached or shorter terraces favoured after the First World War, comprised some parlour homes as well as smaller non-parlour two- and three-bedroom types, but all were provided with electric lighting and power supply and bathrooms. In 1931, Morgan spoke with some justifiable pride of his aspirations and achievement:

> I am hoping that by providing houses with every amenity, every convenience and individuality, and by creating pride of possession, slumdom will be prevented or at least very, very long deferred.

Much later, Townhill would be viewed by some as a 'rough area'; in 1996, in an era of industrial decline, it was the third most deprived area in Wales. However, the quality of its housing has sustained a resilient and strong community.

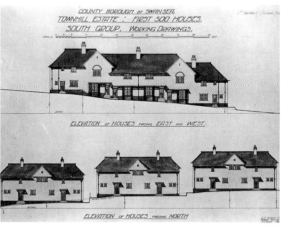

Mosspark, Glasgow

In 1919, Glasgow Corporation estimated that 57,000 new homes were required to meet the city's immediate housing needs. In the event, it would build 5,000 under the terms of the 1919 Housing Act. Among the most prestigious of these early schemes was Mosspark, built on the southwestern periphery of the city on land initially acquired by the corporation in 1909 for a golf course. War changed the nation's priorities, and in April 1919 the city submitted housing plans, approved by the Scottish Board of Health the following year. The estate was completed in 1924.

This was a garden suburb, challenging Scottish housing traditions but in line with the prescriptions of Tudor Walters. Mosspark occupies a triangular hilltop site, commanding views to the north and south. Its curving hillside streets encircle a central oval approached by wide tree-lined and grass-verged streets. Large, privet-hedged gardens, alongside a large park to the immediate north at Bellahouston, complete the semi-rustic ensemble.

The 1,510 homes of the finished estate, at a density of just under nine per acre and of 13 different types, were designed by the Glasgow Corporation Housing Department and constructed by major local contractors Mactaggart and Mickel; brick-built and roughcast save for an experimental 252 that were built of concrete in the contemporary quest to overcome shortages of traditional materials. Cottage flats formed around one-third of the total, but most were two-storey houses. The largest number – 43% of the total – were, in Scottish parlance, four-apartment homes, comprising three bedrooms, living room, scullery and bathroom; two-bedroom homes (in large numbers) and four-bedroom homes make up the remainder. Local customs didn't demand the separate parlour favoured by some south of the border, but the homes were exceptionally well equipped for their time with electric lighting, a gas cooker and a boiler.

Left
An undated early photograph of Mosspark Avenue

Opposite top
Semi-detached houses, Mosspark Drive

Opposite bottom
Cottage flats, Bellahouston Drive

All this came at a price: the houses cost an average £1,150 to build, and rents (quoted as per Scottish practice but in fact paid quarterly at the Housing Department's Trongate office in the city centre) ranged from £28 per annum for a three-apartment house to £44 per annum for a five-apartment house. These rents were simply unaffordable to all but a very few of the most highly skilled and best paid of the local working class. Zealous informal gatekeeping in the allocations process added to the estate's exclusivity. In 1926, 75% of heads of household belonged to the professional and white-collar middle classes; clerks and schoolteachers formed the two largest occupational groups. A few households had live-in maids; daily home-helps were common. It was also, in the sectarian context then powerful in Glasgow, an overwhelmingly Protestant estate: in the words of Seán Damer, 'conservative, respectable and sober ... and with more than a hint of the "unco guid" [excessive self-righteousness] which can be the hallmark of the Scots Presbyterian'.[10]

Other similar estates of the time were built to slightly lower and more economical specifications, but the social distinctions heralded in Mosspark were entrenched in Glasgow as the city went on to build cheaper and often inferior estates to rehouse the poorer working class.

Hillfields Estate, Bristol

Bristol City Council had built just 72 tenement homes before the First World War (a few survive on Mina Road) but by 1917, when its Housing of the Working Classes Sub-Committee asked the City Engineer to identify suitable sites for housebuilding, it was emerging as one of the most forward-thinking of local authorities. A rebranded Housing Extensions and Town Planning Committee was established in 1918 to develop five new garden suburbs, including one at Fishponds Park which was to become the Hillfields Estate. An architectural competition was organised to devise suitable designs for the new housing, and a Women's Advisory Committee – most concerned with suitable scullery accommodation and hot water supply to ease the housewives' burden – was appointed to help adjudicate. Ten winners out of 39 entries were announced in June 1919.

Bristol's ambition was further illustrated when it secured the support of Minister of Health and Housing Christopher Addison to create a 'Demonstration Area' at the Hillfields site to trial and showcase potential designs. It was visited in June 1920 by Addison himself, and over 500 delegates of the Inter-Allied Housing and Town Planning Congress. Addison also took the time to inaugurate the Sea Mills scheme to the west of the city by planting a commemorative oak, which stands proud to the present day.

Of the designs (all previous competition-winning entries), some were deemed unsuitable for further take-up. Two-bedroom houses were judged too small for growing families (subsequently, 96% of Bristol's interwar council housing

Left
An aerial photograph of the estate dating from the late 1920s

Opposite left
Forest Avenue, a postcard image from the 1920s

Opposite right
Plans of three-bedroom parlour 'model cottages' by Arnold Mitchell, November 1919

would be three-bedroom). Meanwhile some designs, such as W.H. Watkins's two-bed, non-parlour design lacking front-facing windows on the upper floors, were seen as too unconventional. A short terrace of three-bedroom, non-parlour houses designed by local architectural partnership Harry Heathman and Eveline Blacker – a notable early female architect – was more successful and featured, in adapted form, in many later schemes, as was a similar design by a Mr Wakefield. A similar design by S.S. Reay, at £900, was judged too expensive and not replicated. A plaque situated between numbers 64 and 66 Beechen Drive commemorates the first houses 'to be erected in Bristol under the National Housing Scheme in 1919'.

About half the estate was built when the Addison programme was axed in 1921 and, while a few more houses were built under existing contracts the following year, the rest of the development was completed under the 1923 and 1924 Housing Acts. Over half the homes on the earliest estates such as Hillfields and Sea Mills are parlour houses; a far larger proportion than in later schemes. Typically, and avowedly when the council declared in 1920 'housing first, then town planning', community facilities followed more slowly – the first junior school in 1927 and the first shops in the late 1920s and early 1930s.

By 1930, almost 1,500 houses had been built at Hillfields. Marking its unique early role as a testbed of later schemes, there are 20 individual types, mostly designed by the original competition winners alongside a few blocks designed by the City Engineer's Department that formed a larger share in later developments.

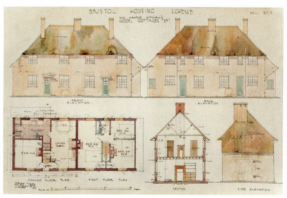

Becontree Estate, Barking and Dagenham, London

Becontree was plausibly claimed to be the largest public housing estate in the world – a site of over four square miles which, when major works were complete in 1934, contained 25,039 homes and a population of 112,570. Such scale of ambition attracted criticism as well as praise.

Its form lay ostensibly in the garden suburb movement of the day; its scale originated in the pressing housing needs of the capital where, in the estimate of the Ministry of Health in 1920, some 75,000 new homes were required within three years. Of those people in greatest need, some 40% lived in east London. A low-lying area of market gardens, cottages and country lanes beyond London's eastern borders in Essex, enjoying rail access provided by stations in Barking and Dagenham, seemed an ideal location.

The early plans were full of good intentions and included churches, shops, no less than 25 schools and a new civic centre. A flat site, in the planners' words lacking 'attractive natural features', would be offset by 600 acres of open space and parkland and a carefully designed and tree-lined streetscape. Among the notable features were the short cul-de-sacs (locally nicknamed 'banjos') that abounded on the estate. There were more innovative proposals to provide an early iteration of the neighbourhood units that would become fashionable after the Second World War, and a mixed community including larger and more expensive homes for middle-class habitation. In the event, much of this was stymied by later economies and local administration, which saw the vast estate divided between three urban district councils, none of which wished to assume heavy financial costs.

Only 8,282 houses were built under the terms of the Addison Act, and the majority – over 19,000 – followed under the terms of the 1924 Housing Act. Of the first 2,876 houses, 2,200 were built of concrete using the Winget pier and panel system. (The first, conventionally brick-built, completed in November 1921 on Chittys Lane are marked by a plaque.) There are overall 91 housing types, some weatherboarded and rendered, providing a disregarded variety to what has been condemned as a monolithic scheme.

Bottom left
Becontree – just a part of the vast estate, photographed in 1970

Bottom right
A Becontree 'banjo', photographed in the early 1930s

Opposite clockwise from top left
Housing on Chittys Lane, the first completed on the estate in November 1921

Weatherboarded homes on Lymington Road

A rendered terrace on Lymington Road

A 'banjo' off Parsloes Avenue

A History of Council Housing in 100 Estates

The estate's demographics, however, were far more uniform. Terence Young's 1934 social survey of the estate estimated some 80% of heads of household were manual workers, with a large majority working in manufacturing or transport and communications, most defined as 'skilled'. You needed to be both respectable and, in working-class terms, relatively affluent to live on Becontree. It was also overwhelmingly an estate of young families; half the population was under 18 and the average age was just 23.[11]

This 'one-class' community – they meant working class, of course – occasioned some alarm among middle-class reformers who saw it as a dangerous portent of an emerging 'mass society', lacking true culture and leadership. Attempts to forge community, spearheaded by the New Estates Community Committee, made little headway among a new, more domesticated working class generally more interested in gardening and leisure than intellectual self-improvement. For some who moved in, it was nevertheless 'heaven with the gates off'.[12]

Early forms of prefabrication

Modern methods of construction – prefabricated and non-traditional construction – might be better described as 'architecture's oldest new idea'.[13] 'Portable colonial cottages' had been manufactured for Australian settlers from the late 1830s; John Brodie, Liverpool City Engineer, had built 'Labourers' Concrete Dwellings' in Eldon Street in the city in 1905. Henry Ford's first car assembly line in 1913 seemed to portend new possibilities for the mass manufacture of housing.

To this end, the 1919 Housing Act offered additional financial support for houses of non-traditional construction. Of 90 proposals submitted to a newly created Standardisation and New Methods of Construction Committee, some 75 were approved. A Board of Building Research was established in 1921; it became the Building Research Station and, in expanded form, moved to its present site near Watford in 1925.

Steel and concrete were to form the core components of the new designs, but they existed in bewildering variety. Of the early types, the Dorlonco system produced by the Dorman Long Company in Redcar was one of the most successful. Steel-framed but completed conventionally with an external finish of brick or render and conforming readily to the contemporary neo-Georgian style favoured, some 10,000 were erected across the country, in the munitions estate of Dormanstown in Redcar and on the Mile Cross Estate in Norwich, for example.

Around 4,000 of the Duo-Slab system of pre- and site-cast concrete devised by William Airey and Son Ltd in Leeds were also built. Another concrete form, the Unit Concrete Cottage, assembled from panels manufactured on site, was also used; notable survivals remain on the Haig Avenue/Beatty Road Estate built by Southport Borough Council in 1920.

A second push towards prefabrication occurred in the mid-1920s under Neville Chamberlain as Minister of Health and Housing, motivated in part by what he perceived as the obstructionism of the building trade unions. In 1925, the Ministry of Health allocated £34,000 to support the building of demonstration homes using non-traditional methods in 86 local authorities. Seven of these cottages were shown in the Palace of Engineering of the 1925 British Empire Exhibition, including such rarities as a timber house sheathed in slates from Ffestiniog, and a Corolite (poured concrete) house from the Netherlands. The steel-frame and brick- or block-wall Dennis-Wild houses devised in Blackpool were more widely adopted, with 10,000 built nationally. More local forms in Nottingham and Yeovil are discussed later in the text.

In all, of some 4.5 million new homes built in Britain in the interwar period, it's estimated that only around 250,000 were of non-traditional construction.

Wollaton Park Estate, Nottingham

The Wollaton Park Estate is, unusually, predominantly an estate of bungalows – and bungalows with an unusual backstory. Nottingham City Council had been a pacesetter in postwar council housing. It began the Stockhill Lane Estate in October 1919; by 1924, it had built around 1,500 council homes in 20 separate schemes. The council's purchase that year of the 744 acres of Lord Middleton's Wollaton Hall and grounds, 2.5 miles west of the city centre, offered new possibilities.

Top
Wollaton Park layout

Bottom left
Shops on Farndon Green

Bottom right
A Crane bungalow

The hall became a museum, and much of the land was set aside for a public park and municipal golf course, but 93 acres on its eastern fringe were allocated to housing. City Architect Thomas Cecil Howitt – one of the most significant architects of interwar council housing – devised the layout of the new estate; essentially a sweeping semicircle with streets radiating from an attractive and treed open space, Farndon Green. Six shops, in a hipped-roofed Arts and Crafts style, were also provided at this central core. The 36m-wide tree-lined and grass-verged dual-carriageway Middleton Boulevard runs through the bottom end of the estate.

Its homes were effectively the creation of William Crane, the Conservative chair of the Housing Committee, an office he held from 1919 to 1957. Crane was also a building trades businessman, a role that offered some useful expertise but also made for a potential conflict of interest, which seems to have generated surprisingly little comment.

Nottingham had already investigated prefabricated housing in Glasgow and Blackpool and when the Ministry of Health convened a conference of local authorities inviting them to submit plans for their own steel houses in January 1925, Crane was

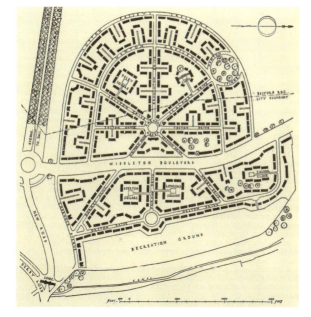

eager to respond. His solution was a steel-framed bungalow with walls formed of precast concrete slabs. A demonstration pair were erected, and received Ministry of Health approval. The Housing Committee agreed to build 500 (Crane had hoped for a 1,000) at Wollaton Park. The mostly semi-detached bungalows, in alternative north- and south-facing forms, offered a living room, kitchen, bathroom, two bedrooms and a third room adaptable as bedroom or parlour. The second innovation was that these were homes were built for sale. At a price of £490, they could be purchased with a £40 deposit and a council-provided, 20-year mortgage with weekly payments of 14s 6d (75p). This was in effect council-built housing largely intended for lower-middle-class occupation.

Building was rapidly and successfully completed within two years, but the public were reluctant to buy, presumably concerned – although it appears to have been largely trouble-free – by their non-traditional construction. As labour and materials costs fell for brick-built housing and, unable to sell the Crane bungalows (many of which were subsequently absorbed into its rented stock), the Housing Committee determined that the rest of the estate – some 313 homes in all – should be completed in traditional form.

Top
Crane bungalows; note the traditional street signage, which has been retained in some Nottingham estates

Bottom
Traditionally constructed housing in full tile-hung Arts and Crafts form

A History of Council Housing in 100 Estates

Nissen-Petren Houses, Yeovil, Somerset

Of all the attempts to use non-traditional methods to build housing more quickly and cheaply, perhaps the most eccentric were the Nissen-Petren houses built predominantly in the West Country in the mid-1920s. Engineer Major Peter Norman Nissen designed the first Nissen hut in 1916 to serve military needs; 100,000 had been built by war's end.

While prefabrication was still being promoted as a potential housing fix by central government, its adoption in Somerset owed most to the powerful figure of Sir Ernest Petter, head of the Westland Company in Yeovil which, having manufactured 1,000 aircraft for military use in the First World War, was looking to diversify in peacetime. The prototype houses were designed by a local architectural practice, John Petter and Percy J. Warren, appointed Borough Architects to Yeovil Town Council in 1911. Nissen-Petren Houses Ltd was established to market the new design to local authorities, with Nissen himself and Ernest Petter as board members.

The essential design was familiar, marked by its semicircular steel ribbed roof bolted on to concrete foundations and completed, in its first iteration, with precast concrete cavity walls. The company's publicity made much of its advantages: it required only half the skilled labour needed to build traditional brick-built homes and could be erected in half the time, while the early erection of the roof enabled 'the work of filling in the walls and building the fireplaces and chimney backs to be proceeded with independently of weather conditions'.[14] Crucially, it was claimed the houses would cost £350 to build, a saving of £100 on traditional housing.

Bottom left
The first Nissen-Petren houses, Goldcroft, Yeovil

Bottom right
Ryme Intrinseca

In 1925, Yeovil Town Council, attracted by an estimated and very affordable 5s (30p) per week rent, commissioned two Nissen-Petren houses, which remain on Goldcroft in the town. These were non-parlour homes with a living room, bedroom, scullery, bathroom, larder and coal store on the ground floor, and two bedrooms and two box rooms on the upper floor. In March 1925, the town was visited 'by a large and distinguished company' including 'representatives of the War Office, the Air Ministry, various municipalities and members of the London Press'.[15] Ernest Petter, who believed it might be possible to produce 100,000

homes a year using the design, stated his hope that the experimental houses 'would prove to be the solution of the housing problem of the country'. Yeovil Rural District Council commissioned 16 Nissen-Petren houses, parlour and non-parlour, shortly after. In all around 24 were built in and around Yeovil, and 50 more across the country.

The unconventional appearance of the homes, though their rooms were described by one observer, as 'wide and airy ... well lit and properly ventilated', attracted adverse comment. The chair of Tiverton Rural District Council, which commissioned 16 of the houses, asked 'the members to set aside prejudice ... the houses were not obnoxious and the people would be delighted to occupy them and pay an economic rent'.[16]

What ultimately did for the experiment, however, was its expense: the final cost of the Yeovil pair was £513 apiece – dearer than conventionally brick-built homes at the time. Nissen-Petren Houses Ltd was wound up in 1928 and a bankruptcy notice issued in 1930. Numbers 172 and 174 Goldcroft were Grade II listed in 1983.

Top
Nissen-Petren homes, West Camel, glimpsed from the A303

Bottom
Mixed housing at Higher Bullen, Barwick

A History of Council Housing in 100 Estates

'Boot Houses', Norris Green Estate, Liverpool

The Norris Green Estate began life in the 1920s as a Liverpool showpiece; by the 1980s, with parts of it rebranded unofficially the 'Boot Estate', it suffered unwanted notoriety. In its inception, the estate captures the municipal ambition of one of the most ill-housed cities in the country where, in 1919, 11,000 families (6% of the population) lived in one-room dwellings. To fulfil its commitment to building 5,000 council homes, Liverpool Corporation purchased 680 acres of agricultural land (470 acres beyond its then boundaries), 3.5 miles northeast of the city centre in 1926. Groundwork began the same year and when complete the estate comprised 7,689 homes and housed a population of around 37,000.

This was the garden suburb at scale, 12 houses to the acre, but its curving streets arrayed in more formal style and its housing squarely neo-Georgian in form and plain in finish. A generous 37% of homes benefited from a front parlour; all but six were three-bed family houses, built in blocks of two, four or six. Front and back gardens, electric lighting, gas cookers and a hot water supply pointed to similarly higher standards, though this was somewhat offset by the more old-fashioned practice of placing WCs outside the back door. As usual, infrastructure in the way of shops and community facilities followed some years later.

The rush to build had one, longer-term consequence, however, in the decision to commission some 3,000 precast concrete houses, awarded in two large contracts of 1,500 each to M.A. Boswell of Wolverhampton and the Henry Boot company. Both were to prove problematic – but the Boot houses, made with cheap sulphur clinker from power stations, which started corroding non-stainless steel tie wires almost immediately, were defective from the outset. Within two years, the concrete showed signs of cracking and shrinkage, causing water penetration and structural weakness. The homes' poor thermal efficiency added to the problems.

Bottom
An aerial view of the Norris Green Estate, c.1930

A renewed investigation of prefabricated housing sparked by the anticipated needs of a new postwar era in 1944 claimed the Boot houses of the LCC's Castelnau Estate, built by skilled labour, had proved less troublesome. However, evidence from the Saffron Lane Estate in Leicester – where 1,000 Boot houses were built – suggests problems were inherent and widespread. The 1984 Housing Defects Act declared the houses 'defective by reason of their design or construction', requiring local

authority remediation and rendering the homes themselves unmortgageable. The Boot houses were found unfit for habitation and beyond economic repair.

In Liverpool, politics and finance combined to slow redress. In 1971, the Norris Green Estate was still described as one of the city's 'most stable and respectable' communities, but it suffered long-term blight as its empty and derelict properties mounted. By the summer of 2006, just over half its 1,500 Boot houses had been demolished, but it took stock transfer and a fragmented nexus of housing associations, property developers and 'affordable homes' for purchase to complete the job in creating 'Ellergreen' and the new 'Norris Green Village'. Of Norris Green's 1,600 new and refurbished homes, just 37% were for social rent – a form of social engineering also intended to remodel the estate.

Top
Boot houses awaiting demolition in 2010

Bottom left
Traditionally built interwar housing, Gayhurst Crescent

Bottom right
Newbuild replacing Boot houses on Stalisfield Avenue/ Chicory Way in the new Norris Green Village

Housing associations

Housing associations in the more modern sense did not emerge until the 1930s, and even then their first representative body, the National Federation of Housing Societies formed in 1935, abjured the term. There were, of course, forerunners – charities, the limited companies of five per cent philanthropy, and the industrial and provident societies formed by co-partnership organisations. A more generic definition was provided by government (which made public finance available to a range of such bodies) in the public utility societies legally required to limit their dividends to a 5% maximum.

Some of the model dwellings companies continued to build, though on a smaller scale, in the years before the First World War; public utility societies in general formed an important element of the government's putative housebuilding programme before and into the war. Although the 1919 legislation increased the level of permitted borrowing for the societies from 66% of capital costs to 75%, the sector as a whole built just 4,545 homes under its terms. In troubled economic times, and lacking the resources and guaranteed income of local authorities, even the 25% of capital required, allied with the uncertainty of future revenues, proved too demanding for most societies. By the mid-1930s, the sector had provided hardly more than 29,000 homes in an era when councils were building around 50,000 annually.

The 10 Scottish societies active in the early postwar years built just 500 homes. However, the Scottish Veterans' Garden City Association – founded in 1915 to support disabled ex-servicemen and initially funded entirely by voluntary contributions – built a number of architecturally distinguished estates in Arts and Crafts style, including those at Longniddry and the Earl Haig Gardens in Edinburgh, both now listed.

While state housing policy and a developing system of social security limited the scope of what the sector might achieve in general, some newer housing associations, particularly in London such as the St Pancras House Improvement Society, found a new role in activist campaigning. They were critical of local government's failure to tackle inner-city slumdom, and its policy focus on garden suburbs catering overwhelmingly for the better-off working class. In this respect, these organisations foreshadow the revival of the housing association sector that occurred in the 1960s.

St Pancras Housing Association, Camden, London

The St Pancras House Improvement Society was founded in 1924 by a group, led by charismatic Anglo-Catholic priest Father Basil Jellicoe, linked to the Magdalen College Mission in Somers Town. Women were prominent in its work: Edith Neville, secretary of the Saint Pancras Council of Social Service, and Norah Hill, a voluntary social worker with the Charity Organisation Society were founding members. Better known are Irene Barclay and Eileen Perry, the first two women to qualify as chartered surveyors in Britain, employed by the society as estate managers and surveyors but significant too for their surveys exposing the shocking housing conditions of the capital. This propaganda work played an important role in the society's fundraising. Though eligible for support under housing legislation, Jellicoe preferred to use his elite connections and campaigning work to raise funds privately.

An initial experiment with reconditioning was soon abandoned, stymied by recalcitrant bed bugs and dry rot, and the practical necessity of rehousing existing residents on site. The society aimed to rehouse the poorest and maintain existing communities and was critical, on both counts, of the failings of contemporary council housebuilding programmes and model dwellings companies.

The society's interwar housing was principally designed by Ian Hamilton, who adopted a by now traditional form – the walk-up, balcony-access tenement block, neo-Georgian in style, generally arranged in formal style around an inner court. London stock brick was complemented by concrete

Figure 3.45: St Nicholas Flats, Werrington Street

Figure 3.46: St Nicholas Flats, Werrington Street

Figure 3.47: Ceramic mural, St Nicholas Flats, Werrington Street

Figure 3.48: Restored Gilbert Bayes ceramics adorning washing line posts at St Anthony's Flats, Aldenham Street

access balconies cantilevered from the floor slabs, and concrete refuse chutes to communal waste chambers. What provided the blocks' unusual quality was Hamilton's skilful detailing and their quality of workmanship. This was a 'relentless cost-consciousness achieved without meanness' according to one commentator.[17] What rendered them charming were the ceramic decorations created by Gilbert Bayes to adorn entrances, windows and even the posts for washing lines.

The Drummond Estate on Doric Way was completed in 1928. But the society's showpiece scheme was the Sidney Street Estate (now plain Sidney), begun in 1930 – 250 flats in six mansard-roofed, five-storey blocks named after saints (as was all its housing) and arranged around a central courtyard of shared green space and play areas. Some called it the 'Garden Estate'. The St Christopher's block was claimed as the first low-cost housing in London wholly fuelled electrically, even to the extent of portable electric fires.

Essentially similar blocks designed by Hamilton were built on Drummond Crescent and, on a larger scale, in the Eversholt Estate at the southern end of Werrington Street in the later 1930s. Kent House on Ferdinand Street in Chalk Farm to the north was an unusual departure – an early, 1935, example of concrete frame Modern movement architecture, designed by Connell, Ward and Lucas and now Grade II-listed.

Jellicoe's mantra was famously that 'housing is not enough', and the society also provided children's nurseries, clubs for mothers and the elderly, welfare support, and holiday and loans clubs. Jellicoe himself, who died aged just 36 in 1935, also supported The Anchor in Somers Town, a pub designed to promote convivial but moderate drinking.

CHAPTER 4

1930–1939: Slum Clearance and Rehousing

The rate and quality of council house construction had ebbed and flowed since the heady days of 1919, but one factor remained more or less constant: that those in greatest need – the poorest and those in the worst housing – were disproportionately excluded from the new council homes being built. High rents, calculated to repay construction loans and therefore particularly high in the case of the earliest and best interwar council homes, and the expectation that they would be paid regularly without fail were factors in this. Another factor was the moral and practical impossibility of building down to the standards of the worst slum housing, which might have allowed some rental equivalence. The filtering up theory, which proposed that the worst-housed private tenants might move to the slightly superior homes vacated by those moving to council housing – was the common rationale, but this was manifestly false.

Labour's 1930 Housing Act, which granted special subsidies for slum clearance and required the rehousing of those displaced, was an attempt to deal with this problem. The permission granted to local authorities to introduce rent rebate schemes in cases of need would have greater long-term significance. This attack on the slums was amplified by the policy and legislation of a predominantly Conservative 'national' government that followed. A 1933 circular directed that public subsidy should henceforth be granted solely towards slum clearance, and the 1935 Housing Act added overcrowding to the criteria of unfit housing. The 'Clearance Areas' and more expansive 'Redevelopment Areas', authorised by the 1930 and 1935 Housing Acts respectively, also reflected this renewed ambition to demolish the worst inner-city housing.

There was, in general, no corresponding ambition to design and build to higher standards. In fact, the need to keep rents affordable to new and less affluent tenants exerted a reverse pressure seen, most powerfully, in the London County Council's 'Modified Type B' flats, which reinstated shared bathrooms in some tenement blocks built after 1931. The stigma of such inferior accommodation was often transferred, less justifiably, not only to other so-called and otherwise quite ordinary 'slum clearance' estates but also to their residents, often felt to be less 'respectable' by longer-established council tenants.

But as multi-storey living became increasingly accepted as a cost-effective and unavoidable means of providing urban housing at density, it was necessary to make it more attractive in terms of both appearance and facilities. London and Liverpool pioneered new forms; in Scotland, older tenement traditions persisted.

Modernist design was gaining traction in mainland Europe, but it made little impact despite – or perhaps because of – the number of councillor and officer delegations that toured the more celebrated European public housing schemes in Vienna, Paris, Berlin and elsewhere. The *Gemeindebauten*, or municipal tenant block complexes, of 'Red Vienna' were notable for both their scale and comprehensive community facilities, and hold a particularly storied place in left-wing thinking. However, most British councillors firmly believed that the English (if not the Scots) preferred a house and garden and held a generally less progressive attitude towards the political benefits of communal living. It was undoubtedly true that British council homes enjoyed generally superior space standards and facilities. The country's small number of Modernist architects (and an increasing band of émigrés) relied mostly on private commissions from an avant-garde elite.

The most typical council housing remained the cottage home, and its setting the garden suburb, albeit a pared-down version of that aesthetic, typically with smaller and plainer housing and less generous landscaping. Of 4 million suburban homes built in the interwar period, some 1 million were council built; central redevelopment had begun too, but was far slower. This was the beginning of a housing revolution. But it remained, for the time being, largely a conservative one.

Slum clearance estates

Not all slum clearance estates were marked out by their origins. Housing continued to be built under the slightly more expansive terms of the 1924 Wheatley Act until 1933, and many local authorities continued to use well-established design templates. However, parlour homes with a second living room, the gold standard of the generous 1919 Housing Act, became very rare, as councils sought to bring down construction costs and rents for a poorer population.

Nevertheless, slum clearance estates – defined either by form or by population, sometimes by location – were a feature of the pre-war decade. Some never escaped this designation and the stigma it entailed. The Marsh Estate in Lancaster, built literally on the wrong side of the tracks, was one such, distinguished (if that's the word) by its plain housing and unimaginative and austere layout. Meadow Well in North Shields, commenced in 1932, comprised overwhelmingly cottage flats (two-storeyed dwellings with flats top and bottom and separate ground-floor entrances), a Tyneside speciality but a contrast to the council's earlier estate at Balkwell of semi-detached and terraced housing. The Niddrie Mains Estate in Edinburgh, a peripheral estate built at density to rehouse slum dwellers between 1927 and the mid-1930s (and demolished in the early 2000s), comprised entirely three-storey tenements. Blackhill, a Glasgow equivalent, was built exclusively with another distinctively and very common Scottish form, the 'four-in-a-block' – semi-detached-style housing containing four separately accessed upper and lower cottage flats under a shared hipped roof.

Glasgow Corporation took this demarcation a stage further by classifying schemes constructed under 1919 and 1923 legislation as 'Ordinary', those under the 1924 Act as 'Intermediate' and later schemes as 'Slum Clearance and Rehousing': 'any council tenant in Glasgow could tell at a glance into which category a housing scheme fell, and to which category he or she could aspire'.[1] Norwich, which rehoused a quarter of its population in the 1930s, graded its tenants: Grade A tenants could 'obviously be left alone', Grade B were visited annually but Grade C people were 'visited frequently and rendered help and assistance wherever possible'.[2] The infamous Cutteslowe Walls in Oxford, erected across a through road by developers to separate their privately built estate from a neighbouring council scheme in 1934, carried this segregation to extremes. They survived until 1959.

Bedminster and Knowle Estate, Bristol

The Bedminster and Knowle Estate in south Bristol provides a unique guide to the evolution of interwar council housing. On its eastern fringe, Knowle Park reflected the aspirations and expenditure of the 1919 Housing Act, with almost two-thirds of its homes of the parlour type. Moving west, parlour homes become vanishingly rare: there are a few in Knowle West, built under the 1924 Housing Act, but none in Filwood Park, built in the 1930s under the slum clearance and rehousing legislation of the day.

It is Bristol's largest interwar estate (its 5,392 council homes provided well over a third of the city's total by 1939), and superficially it retains a certain homogeneity. A number of early semi-detached or terraced designs dating to the time of the Addison Act were built into the 1930s. Later, non-parlour, designs retained their fairly standard, plain neo-Georgian form. Most were redbrick; rendering and wash provided some colour variation offset somewhat by the ubiquitous and signature privet hedging of the time. Most were three-bedroom; living room, larder, scullery and bathroom completed the ensemble.

Some 69% of the almost 2,500 homes of Filwood Park were built to rehouse displaced slum dwellers who formed 'so to speak, the second wave of colonists on the new estates' according to a contemporary social survey.[3] These origins and the characteristics and alleged lifestyle that accompanied them proved – or were perceived as – problematic to older-established and generally more affluent tenants as well as housing managers. There were complaints of what we'd later call anti-social behaviour, though social workers observed that 'the better housing environment [had] undoubtedly had a great educational effect upon the population. A disgustingly dirty house is now uncommon.'[4]

Objectively, we might note that in Filwood Park in the late 1930s around a quarter of heads of household were unemployed or employed casually, and some 45% of children lived under the official poverty line. These problems

Right
Queensdale
Crescent, Knowle
Park, 1930s

were exacerbated by rents higher than those of their previous slum homes, and the additional travel and lifestyle costs of suburban living. The new tenants also generally had larger families than earlier residents, but could not be allocated to older, roomier housing due to its expense and the antipathy of potential neighbours.

Typically, shops and amenities arrived sometime after the housing though the council's impressive Filwood Social Centre, opened in 1938, with dance hall, gymnasium, meeting rooms, canteen, skittle alley, workshop and reading room. (A 1936 Housing Act, reflecting a somewhat improving middle-class concern over the lack of 'community' on the new estates, permitted councils to build centres that gave 'beneficial service' to residents.) A cinema opened the same year. In providing a loan to support the latter, the council stipulated an early and well-meaning form of 'poor door' – a rear entrance that could be used by its less well-off customers. Bedminster and Knowle provides a more complex geography of council housing than generalisations usually allow.

Top
Three-bedroom, semi-detached parlour corner houses, Daventry Road, designed by the City Engineer

Bottom left
Three-bedroom non-parlour terraced housing on Kenmare Road, designed by the City Architect

Bottom right
Three-bedroom parlour houses, Throgmorton Road, designed by Mr B. Mitchell

Deckham Hall Estate, Gateshead

The Great Depression of the 1930s hit the Northeast with unprecedented severity. Alongside South Wales, Cumberland and central Scotland, it was one of several districts identified in legislation of 1934 as a 'Special Area' eligible for direct infrastructure support from central government. The North-Eastern Housing Association, founded in 1935, which constructed the Deckham Hall Estate, was one initiative which emerged. This was a body with direct Treasury funding to build housing. (The Scottish Special Housing Association was formed two years later to replicate this role north of the border.) By the outbreak of war, the North-Eastern Housing Association had built some 7,500 houses in the local area; Gateshead embraced the provision, while some other councils were wary of this usurpation of their traditional housebuilding role.

The Deckham Hall Estate reflected its origins. Gateshead had built fine council homes conforming to Tudor Walters standards and layout at Sheriff Hill and Carr Hill to the south in the early 1920s. Deckham Hall, by contrast, oozed austerity. Its layout was its most distinctive feature – a series of irregular concentric rings which earned it the local nickname the 'Frying Pan' or, less politically correctly, the 'African Village'. There were few open spaces and little in the way of greenery.

Left
Chiswick Gardens

Right
Superior corner housing, Chiswick Gardens

The utilitarian houses, constructed of industrial orange brick, were unusually plain; semi-detached boxes save for a few L-shaped pairs built around the estate's limited green space. Hipped-roof pairs with timber panelling gracing gable ends on prominent corners represented a modest aesthetic concession. Overall density, at some 30 houses per acre, is notably higher than earlier schemes, as is the proportion of smaller two-bedroom homes. It's an estate which retains the traces of its birth, still stigmatised by some as a 'bad area' but characterised objectively by higher-than-average unemployment and low take-up of Right to Buy.

Wythenshawe Estate, Manchester

The Wythenshawe Estate was Manchester City Council's largest building project of the interwar period, and the municipal scheme which came closest to emulating the Garden City ideals of Ebenezer Howard. Its driving forces were the Liberal industrialist Ernest Simon and his wife Shena, and Labour alderman W.T. Jackson. Simon provided the initial donation of land six miles to the south of the city in 1926; Shena, much of the vision; and Jackson, the municipal heft which made possible a 5,500-acre scheme comprising 8,145 homes and a population of 40,000 by 1939.

In Shena Simon's words, 'it was never intended to be merely a site for working-class municipal housing' but 'a new sort of development where uniformity would be avoided and the development would be a harmonious whole'.[5] Barry Parker, business partner (and brother-in-law) to Raymond Unwin, with whom he worked on Letchworth Garden City, had been appointed in 1927 to implement this model.

Parker's plan introduced several key features. Industrial zones were intended to provide local employment, although only catering for around 15% of the estate's workforce before the Second World War. Parkways – taken up by Parker after a visit to the US in the 1920s – were wide, landscaped highways planned to smooth traffic flow but, more importantly, to preserve existing open space and prevent ribbon development. Neighbourhood units, another American import, which would be much more widely adopted after the war, were an attempt to

Left
Barry Parker's plan of the Wythenshawe Estate

Right top
Terraced housing, Overton Road

Right bottom
Semi-detached cottages, Woodhouse Lane

Opposite left
Semi-detached housing, Longhey Road

Opposite right
Semi-detached housing, Broadoak Road

A History of Council Housing in 100 Estates

create smaller neighbourhoods within the larger development provided with the amenities to sustain more-or-less self-contained communities. In Wythenshawe, Parker placed shops peripherally rather than centrally, as was later practice in order to reduce walking distances.

However, the housing was typical of its time, as Alderman Jackson made clear: 'We are not emulating Vienna and I have not been there ... In general we favour the cottage type of dwelling.'[6] These were indeed the cottage homes favoured by Tudor Walters at the 12 houses per acre or fewer recommended in that report. The suggestion of Labour's Women's Advisory Committee that 'all windows shall be without glazing bars and therefore easy to clean' was rejected to maintain the 'cottagey' feel that Shena Simon favoured. Land was also set aside for private development but, with only around 700 houses for middle-class occupation, by the later 1930s, this early iteration fell some way short of the mixed development ideal.

And, while Manchester had declared almost 40% of its inner-city housing unfit for human habitation at the time, this was in practice decidedly not a slum clearance estate. Average rents of around 13s to 15s (65p to 75p) equated to half the typical working-class wage of the day. An affluent working class, carefully vetted by the town hall, ensured that the 'Wythenshawe ethos' as it was called became known for its self-conscious and domesticated respectability. Ironically, after further expansion and in a more troubled era, Wythenshawe was the site of David Cameron's 2007 attack on what he dubbed 'Broken Britain'.

New-style tenements

The five-storey, walk-up, balcony-access tenement block had long been an inner-London staple. By the 1930s, as central slum clearance took off and councils across the country sought high-density replacement housing, it had come to be seen as both more necessary but problematic. The problem lay, in part, in that very ubiquity; it was a common, repetitive form widely viewed as inferior to what remained the ideal, a house with garden. Practically, the access galleries were criticised for creating shadow and a lack of privacy.

Various attempts were made to modernise at least the appearance of such tenement blocks, most dramatically in the Oaklands Estate in Clapham, an LCC scheme characterised by the curving forms and long horizontal lines of an Art Deco Moderne style owing something to the grand ocean liners of the day. A boxier Modernism is seen in Constant and Holmsdale Houses (complemented by impressive International Style staircase-towers) built by Poplar Metropolitan Borough Council in the late 1930s and John Scurr House by Stepney Council, opened in 1937 and reputedly the first council scheme accepted for inclusion at the annual exhibition of the Royal Academy. The Edward Street Flats, part of a Sheffield slum clearance scheme of the same era, echo this style and featured the private balconies now increasingly included in such schemes. Efforts to improve tenement form were seen most notably in the LCC's 'New Flat' of 1937, pioneered on the White City Estate.

Their advocates also argued that multi-storey schemes could provide better communal facilities than those to be found in the garden suburbs; some argued that they might also promote communal living in the way exemplified by the great municipal estates of Red Vienna. The latter ideal gained little traction in the UK, but Lancelot Keay in Liverpool sought to implement the former.

In the event, tenements – even when rebranded as new-style flats – generally remained a second-best solution in most English eyes and a native tradition in Scottish ones. This was largely the case even in the two English cities to embrace multi-storey housing; London, where 40% of LCC newbuild in the interwar period was flatted accommodation, and Liverpool, where one in five new homes were flatted.

White City Estate, Hammersmith and Fulham, London

In 1939, *The Times* described the London County Council's new White City Estate as 'the largest and finest estate of flats which the council has yet built'. The *Architects' Journal*, less enamoured, asked 'why all 5-storey blocks? Why the soulless mechanism of the layout?'[7] The estate was a mix of old and new.

The 'old' was seen in the predominant form of the 23 blocks completed by 1939 – five-storey, walk-up, balcony-access tenement housing on well-established lines. (The finished estate, completed in 1953, comprised 35 blocks serving a population of around 8,885.) The 'new' was seen in the determined attempt to modernise and incentivise flat living represented by the New Flat design and other features reflecting Modernist influence.

Left
An aerial view of the White City Estate in 1939, with the former White City stadium shown at top left

Right
Proposed elevation of flats facing the Westway, as featured in the LCC's *London's Housing* (1937)

Labour took over the LCC in 1934 (and remained in control until its abolition in 1965). Having previously firmly opposed multi-storey housing in favour of the cottage flat, the party had by now concluded that tenement living was an inner-city necessity. Its priority, therefore, was to reverse economising measures introduced by the previous Conservative administration and to bring the design of flats 'more to accord with the modern outlook in housing provision'. Staircase access, which 'secures greater privacy for the tenants and tends to make a flat more homely, better lighted and more attractive internally', was the chief means.[8] Some 312 of the New Flats, the first to be built, were erected prominently on the northern fringe of the estate.

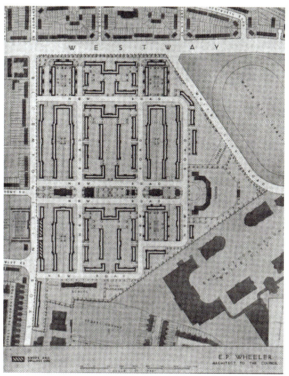

Private balconies (with concrete window boxes) were another innovation alongside the sliding doors linking kitchen to living room. Naturally, all flats had their own bathroom; the larger enjoyed 'a lavatory in a separate compartment'. The additional 6s (30p) rent paid by the lucky tenants of what *The Times* called these 'luxury flats' excluded most of those being rehoused under slum clearance measures.

Continental influence – drawn from an extensive study tour of the best European schemes undertaken by a council delegation in 1935 – was seen in the gently horizontal Moderne styling of some blocks and in an adoption of *Zeilenbau* principles (maximising sunlight) of north–south layout, though the latter was challenged by the open courtyard form favoured at White City. The delegation to Europe had also noted the superior community facilities provided in many Continental schemes, and some effort was made to emulate these in the allocation of space and buildings to shops, schools, health clinics and playgrounds.

The White City Estate would soon come to be seen as old-fashioned, less a breath of the future and more an echo of the past, but it marked a step towards the multi-storey revolution to come.

Left
Axonometric illustration of the New Flat

Right top
Older-style tenement form in Champlain House

Right bottom
Commonwealth Avenue, shopping parade and housing

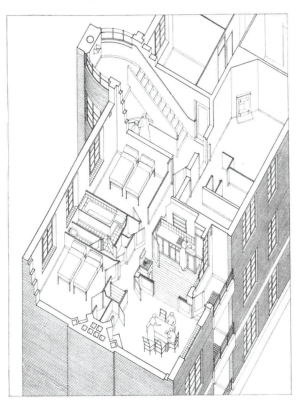

A History of Council Housing in 100 Estates

St Andrew's Gardens, Copperas Hill, Liverpool

Liverpool had been one of the pacesetters in council housing before the First World War, and was among the most ambitious and innovative councils in the interwar period. There was, among politicians and professionals alike, an unusual sympathy towards multi-storey construction propelled partly by the severity of the city's inner-city slum problem and the requirement that a casualised docks labour force be accommodated close to its place of work. A conscious urbanism also played its part.

A council delegation to Amsterdam in 1924 to view the city's cottage flats had returned more impressed by its new tenement blocks. The decision in 1925 to appoint Lancelot Keay – later the city's Director of Housing – strengthened the commitment to flatted solutions. However, Keay himself returned disappointed by the small size and poor internal facilities of the flats in Vienna's celebrated tenement blocks one year later; it was Bruno Taut's grand Hufeisensiedlung ('Horseshoe Estate') in Berlin on a 1931 trip to the International Housing and Town Planning Congress which captured his imagination. In an address to a presumably unsympathetic audience at the Garden Cities and Town Planning Association that year, Keay asserted that tenements at 50 dwellings per acre were to be preferred to the 'semi-detached respectability' of 12 to the acre, and offered housing 'with all the privacy of the small cottage and the added amenities of open spaces, playgrounds and communal gardens'.[9]

Left
St Andrew's Gardens, architectural drawing, 1935

Right
View of St Andrew's Gardens, showing the inner court and playground, 1935

This vision first took shape at St Andrew's Gardens, designed by John Hughes (recruited for the purpose) and constructed between 1932 and 1935. This was a huge tenement complex, of which only the large D-shaped block (providing its nickname, the Bullring) remains, and that now is student accommodation. The estate's basic form – five-storey, walk-up balcony-access – remained traditional; the flats themselves with solid-fuel ranges and back boilers and gas coppers (for heating water) were of their time, though each enjoyed a fully equipped bathroom. Private balconies – optimistically described as 'sun balconies' – were an innovation.

CITY OF LIVERPOOL HOUSING - ST. ANDREWS GARDENS

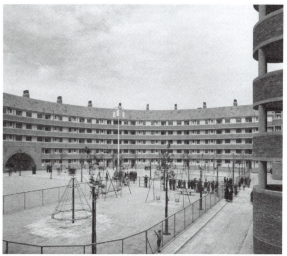

What catches the eye, however, is the scale and Modernist design of the estate, the latter only slightly mitigated by its conventional brick construction. Modernist principles are seen in the strong horizontal lines of the fenestration and brickwork banding of the design, in the estate's overall geometry (a mix of rectangular and semicircular) and in its clean, unembellished lines. Even the pitched roof is disguised by a parapet, giving the appearance at least of the flat roofing that Modernists favoured. Later estates – all since demolished – took Keay's belief in 'an A1 community in a properly planned township of flats' further in their range of community facilities.[10] By the later 1930s, he had embraced Modernism's *Zeilenbau* layout for the enhanced light and air it offered.

Crucially, the new blocks were affordable and convenient, and housed the city's poorer working class; over 80% were rehoused under slum clearance programmes. It's a sad irony that by the 1970s the interwar tenements had come to seem old-fashioned and were increasingly allocated to those the Housing Department viewed as problem tenants. It was principally this reputational shift which paved the way for their clearance.

Top
'The Bullring' – a contemporary view of the surviving part of St Andrew's Gardens, now student housing

Bottom
St Andrew's Gardens: grand main entrance

A History of Council Housing in 100 Estates

Lennox House, Cresset Road, Hackney, London

In conception and form, Lennox House in Hackney is unique in interwar Britain, though it is said to have inspired the design of the much later Brunswick Centre in Bloomsbury. What is innovative though not obvious (due to the use of yellow-brown brick cladding and facing) is its reinforced concrete frame. What is both innovative and obvious is its stepped, ziggurat shape.

That shape was intended to overcome 'a common objection to balcony flats ... by stepping each floor back 6 ft from the one below it, thus giving each the maximum of air and light'.[11] It also enabled the provision of unusually large, 15m^2, private balconies lined with permanent concrete planters accessed from the living room, which at least approximated the cottage home garden ideal. The design also allowed the creation of a large indoor space at the centre of the block, originally intended as a market hall (which might cross-subsidise rents) until the London County Council's zoning regulations stymied the plan. It later served as an air raid precautions and decontamination centre in the Second World War.

The block, opened in 1937, contained 35 flats – three-bedroom on the first floor, one-bedroom on the top, two-bedroom on intermediate levels – at a density of 75 persons per acre. External metal staircases provided access, generally to a pair of flats on each level; their recesses provided additional privacy to the balconies either side. Internally, a living room stove with vent to the main bedroom was said to be a popular feature. Sloping chimneys converged at roof level.

Lennox House was the project of the Bethnal Green and East London Housing Association formed 10 years earlier by an (Anglican) Industrial Housing Fellowship Group. The Association took the enterprising decision to appoint the architect J.E.M. Macgregor to design the new scheme. Macgregor is best

Left
Sectional view of Lennox House

Right
End elevation with entrance to intended market hall

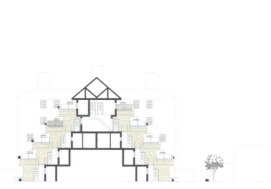

known as a conservation architect and active member of the Society for the Protection of Old Buildings, but this apparently traditionalist concern masked a deep interest in engineering and new materials, particularly concrete, and their application to design. In his Hackney scheme, he is said to have been inspired by the Apartments Rue des Amiraux in Paris designed by Henri Sauvage in the mid-1920s, though their stepbacks and balconies are far more modest.

At Lennox House, Macgregor set out to design a 'building composed of many separate homes, each having as much fresh air and light as possible, and a real substitute for the garden and yard ... together with a sense of privacy'.[12] Though his design acquired few emulators until the 1960s, when its A-frame form became more widely adopted, in Hackney he appears to have achieved this with some flair. Grade-II listed, it is now managed by the locally based Gateway Housing Association.

Left
Axonometric illustration of Lennox House

Right
A plaque near one of the entrances marks the origins of the building

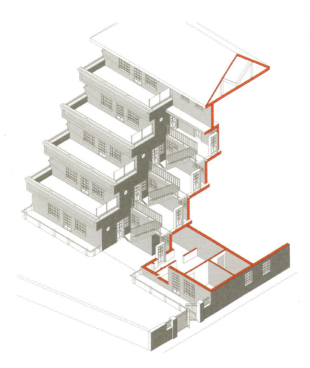

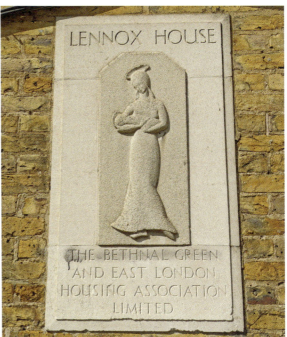

Modernist design

Modernist architecture – also described in the 1930s as the International Style – might best be distinguished by its embrace of new materials and technologies, its belief that form should follow function, and its rejection of ornament. For all this cool rationalism, to its growing band of advocates it was also a Humanist form springing, in the words of Le Corbusier, its foremost protagonist, 'from the depths of the human heart'.[13]

The Congrès Internationaux d'Architecture Moderne (CIAM) had been founded in Switzerland in 1928; its British offshoot, the Modern Architectural Research (MARS) Group – an association of 'architects and allied technicians united by a common belief in the necessity for a new conception of architecture and its relation to society' – five years later. In reviewing the MARS Group's celebrated 1938 London exhibition, Le Corbusier urged that:

> *The benefits of the New Architecture must not be confined to the homes of the few who enjoy the privilege of taste or money. They must be widely diffused so as to brighten the homes, and thus the lives, of millions upon millions of workers.*[14]

Though both Kensal House and Quarry Hill were featured in the exhibition, he would be disappointed by the UK's efforts, at least in the short term. (In the longer term, many of council housing's later woes would be unfairly ascribed to the malign influence of Modernism.) Berthold Lubetkin was celebrated for his London Zoo pool for penguins and Highpoint 1 in Highgate, the best-regarded larger Modernist housing scheme but catering for only middle-class humans. Finsbury Council's Spa Green Estate, designed by Lubetkin and the Tecton Group, though commissioned in 1938, wasn't built until 1946. However, the nearby Finsbury Health Centre was completed in 1938, and is deservedly centre-stage in any Modernist pantheon.

For the moment, a combination of architectural school and municipal conservatism ensured the new ideas had little impact. The national and local state *were* attracted by the apparent cost-saving possibilities of Modernism's first precept – the use of new methods of construction – but bricks and mortar remained, for good reason, a tried-and-trusted preference. Aesthetically, an increasingly plain neo-Georgian style ruled, despite the largely cosmetic changes noted in the newer tenement blocks. Modernism's time was yet to come.

Kensal House, Ladbrook Grove, Kensington and Chelsea, London

In a narrow sense, the driving force behind Kensal House, completed in 1937, was growing competition between gas and electric utilities for market share. The intention of the Gas, Light and Coke Company was to build a tenement block that would demonstrate how 'working-class tenants could be provided with an all-gas service offering every amenity that a reasonable middle-class family might demand'.[15] Fortunately for Modernists, the company appointed an architects' committee with far greater ambition, manifest in both the construction and the social purpose of the scheme.

The estate of 68 two- and three-bedroom flats, chiefly designed by Maxwell Fry, comprised three staircase-access, five-storey blocks of reinforced concrete frame. Set amid shared green open space, the two main blocks were disposed north–south in an early British application of *Zeilenbau* principles. Cantilevered private balconies and smaller recessed drying balconies punctuate the white-faced inner facade featured in Abram Games's famous 1942 Army Bureau of Current Affairs poster promoting the better Britain – 'clean, airy and well-planned dwellings' – that would reward wartime sacrifice.

The same planning went into the flats themselves, with each containing a large living/dining room plus kitchen, bathroom and toilet as a standardised unit. The small but well-equipped kitchen was the work of Elizabeth Denby, the housing consultant whose earlier investigation of low-cost European housing influenced her input into Kensal House – a labour-saving feature designed to ease the housewife's burden.

Denby's other key contribution and in some respects the most distinctive feature of the estate was her vision of Kensal House as 'an urban village'. Each family belonged to a staircase committee from which were elected representatives to serve on a wider tenants' body. Social clubs – one for adults and one for children – and an onsite nursery school (whose curved, large-windowed frontage is one of the most attractive features of the scheme) completed this attempt to create what Fry called 'a community in action'.

Left
Nursery and courtyard, photographed in 1937

Right
Kensal House courtyard view

Opposite
The kitchen designed by Elizabeth Denby, 1937

The ensemble has been described as a 'symbiosis of society and machine, a social and architectural response to the problems associated with bad housing'.[16]

The estate was lavished with praise by architectural commentators and housing reformers alike and was popular with early tenants, principally poorer working-class families who came from substandard and overcrowded housing. But there were grumbles, particularly in relation to the small kitchen, which hindered an unreconstructed working-class preference for taking meals there. 'The machine for living in' met unmalleable tradition.

As to the ideal of community, its later failure is generally laid at the door of the London County Council, which took over the estate when the gas industry was nationalised after the war (the estate is now run by the Borough of Kensington and Chelsea). Community was also, however, perhaps not so easily engineered. None of this detracts from the iconic status of Kensal House, Grade II*-listed in 1981.

Quarry Hill Flats, Leeds

According to R.A.H. Livett, the architect of the Quarry Hill Flats, their origin 'went back to one summer morning in 1932, when ... he saw the great blocks at Vienna with their unrivalled social amenities'.[17] In construction terms, a later visit to the Cité de la Muette, a grand apartment complex built by the Département de la Seine in Drancy, northeast of Paris, had greater impact. It was here that Livett witnessed the light steel frame and precast concrete system of prefabrication devised by Eugène Mopin that he hoped would provide the means to realise his ambitious new project in Leeds.

Livett, having previously designed the multi-storey Kennet House scheme in Manchester (since demolished), had been appointed Leeds' Director of Housing by an incoming Labour administration in 1934. The new council planned to demolish and replace 30,000 slums in five years, the largest clearance programme in the country. Inner-city Quarry Hill, first declared an 'unhealthy area' in 1901, was to be his stage.

An awkward site dictated in part Livett's adoption of Vienna's preferred perimeter layout and the sweeping curved blocks that characterised the Leeds estate. The blocks themselves ranged from three storeys (serving an elderly population) to eight. They were staircase-access in form but the taller blocks – almost uniquely in British working-class housing at the time and in contrast to Vienna – were provided with lifts, 88 in all. The range of *planned* facilities – playgrounds, bowling greens, tennis courts, a community centre, radio substation, even a mortuary – reflected Vienna's communal ambitions. However, their full extent was scuppered by the failure of anticipated cost savings from the Mopin system, plagued by ultimately terminal problems of logistics and implementation in adapted British form. The innovative Garchey system of waste disposal (another French import), by which domestic refuse was flushed by wastewater from an under-sink unit to a central incinerator and district heating system, also proved flawed.

Left
A scale model of the flats, created in 1934

Right
Lupton House with Kitson House at the rear

Opposite left top
The entrance to Kitson House; William Holmes, an unemployed coalminer, sits to the right

Opposite left bottom
A Quarry Hill living room, 1939

Opposite right
A kitchen showing the Garchey waste disposal system

Internally, the estate's 938 flats – mostly two- and three-bedroom, but including 35 five-bedroom homes for larger families – were a mix of old and new. Space standards matched those of Tudor Walters; they were generous, and each flat benefited from a private balcony. The scullery was small, but Livett intended meals to be taken in the combined living/dining room. Coal-fired ranges for heating, hot water and cooking survived, even a baking oven that Livett believed an essential tool for the Yorkshire housewife. Still, 'the details of design and fittings made these the most advanced dwellings that had then been built for working-class populations'.[18]

Overall, the scheme delivered a housing density of 36 dwellings (125 persons) per acre while still offering the plentiful open space – fully 59% of its 26-acre site – that Livett believed a key benefit of the vertical form he espoused. The 'modern' flat roofs provided additional playground space for Quarry Hill's many youngsters.

Sadly, by 1960 it was concluded that systemic construction failings outweighed the benefits of continued repair, though the estate was patched up until its demolition in the late 1970s. It remains, however, the one outstanding example of Continental forms and Modernist techniques applied in Britain.

1940–1955: Wartime Planning and Postwar Recovery

In 1945, war was once more the great locomotive of housing history. In March, a Coalition Government White Paper estimated that the country required 750,000 new homes to make good those destroyed or damaged by wartime bombing. And, as in 1919, the political emphasis was on building back better; the White Paper projected a further 500,000 new homes needed to replace existing slums. The 1944 Dudley Committee report on the 'Design of Dwellings' had previously recommended increased space standards and other modern enhancements in the shape of gas and electric cookers and through lounges.

However, the immediate housing crisis demanded an emergency response, seen most memorably in the programme of temporary prefabricated bungalows inaugurated in 1944, but manifested also in the range of permanent prefabricated designs that politicians hoped might increase the pace and scale of construction in the longer term.

Much of this new housing replicated traditional forms, and the conventional two-storey, brick-built house in a suburban setting remained the favoured solution to housing needs. It was built in huge numbers in large peripheral estates across the country. But there were significant shifts too, intended to rectify the perceived failings of interwar construction and adapt council housing to the needs of groups not previously catered for. 'Neighbourhood units' were an attempt to restore the community structures and feeling allegedly lost in the inner-city slum clearance and the new cottage suburbs of the 1920s and 1930s. 'Mixed development' provided council homes for individuals and couples. As motor transport grew, there was an increased emphasis on layouts which separated pedestrians and traffic for both safety and environmental reasons.

The postwar programme of New Towns represented the culmination of this aspiration to build a new Britain along more rational and socially just lines.

Popular support for such ambition was reflected in Labour's landslide victory in the 1945 general election. The party's socialist principles, alongside an unparalleled machinery of state control and regulation inherited from wartime necessity, were crucial to its at least partial fulfilment. In housing terms, Aneurin 'Nye' Bevan, Minister of Health and Housing from 1945 to 1951, was its personification. Labour built, in a period of genuine economic austerity, almost 805,000 new council homes during his term of office. But Bevan was committed not merely to quantity but to quality and, famously, to the belief that council housing should serve general needs – the 'living tapestry of a mixed community'.[1] The 1949 Housing Act was the first to remove the stipulation that council housing be specifically designated working-class housing.

But this apparent victory for social democratic egalitarianism was short-lived. While the incoming Conservative government maintained and even expanded the public housing drive, it prioritised home ownership in its 1953 White Paper, and the 1954 Housing Act reserved Treasury subsidy for homes for the elderly and redevelopment rather than general needs.

There was no avowed shift to high-rise housing in this period, but its seeds were sown in the population densities expected in cleared inner-city areas. The 1943 *County of London Plan* envisaged that up to two-thirds of a central population might be housed in flats, and concluded that 'a certain number of high blocks up to ten storeys might prove popular, in particular for single people and childless couples'.[2]

Temporary and permanent prefabs

In June 1943, the *Architects' Journal* asserted that there was 'one solution only to the problem of postwar housing. It can be expressed in three words – use the machine'.[3] This was a view shared to a significant degree by a coalition government anticipating similar problems to those which bedevilled the post-First World War housing drive. In September 1942, it established the Interdepartmental Committee on House Construction with Sir George Burt (head of the Mowlem construction company) as chair; its remit was 'to consider materials and methods of construction suitable for the building of houses and flats, having regard to efficiency, economy and speed of erection'.[4] Prefabrication also promised continued work to those wartime industries able to adapt to peacetime demands; the Ministry of Aircraft Production set up its own Aircraft Industries Research Organisation on Housing (AIROH) in the same year.

The Burt Committee received some 1,400 design proposals and tested a few of the most promising at a demonstration site in Northolt. Its report published in 1944 provided a thoroughly technical evaluation of the large range – categorised Concrete, Framed and Solid Timber, Steel-Framed and Metal Clad – on offer.

It was the £150 million programme of temporary prefabs inaugurated by the 1944 Housing (Temporary Accommodation) Act, however, that received most early attention. Some 156,623 were built before the scheme ended in March 1949. The most widely built were the aluminium-based AIROH bungalows; around 54,500 in total. The Arcon Mark V, constructed of asbestos cement panels on a steel frame (of which 38,859 were erected) and the Uni-Seco (numbering 28,999), asbestos cement panels on a timber frame, followed in popularity.

Contrary to later perceptions of their quaintness, the temporary prefabs, with their fitted kitchens and contemporary mod cons, represented advanced engineering: 'their architects and designers ... steeped in modernist ideas of standardisation and systematisation'.[5] The bungalows themselves generally proved popular with early residents, though some complained they could be cold in winter months, and many were to last far longer than their allotted 10-year lifespan.

Concrete was the most widely used material in the construction of permanent, non-traditional housing. Some 60,000 precast reinforced concrete panel Wates houses were built, and around 26,000 Airey houses based on the 1925 design of Leeds industrialist Sir Edwin Airey, which used smaller precast concrete blocks. The steel industry competed with its British Iron and Steel Federation (BISF) steel-frame, steel-clad houses, of which 40,000 were built.

Most proved serviceable in the short-term, though some designs were designated defective in the 1980s. Promised cost and efficiency savings were elusive, however; as more normal economic conditions resumed, the Labour government withdrew its special subsidies for permanent prefabricated housing in 1948. The sector received a later boost as Harold Macmillan sought to accelerate housebuilding in the early 1950s.

Inverness Road and Humber Doucy Lane, Ipswich

Over 140 temporary prefabricated bungalows were erected in Ipswich in 1947 in a single large scheme in Rushmere on the northeastern fringes of the town. These formed part of the approximately 19,000 bungalows built across the country designed by Tarran Industries in Hull, comprising external walls formed of a wooden frame overclad with precast concrete panels and light steel trussed roofs finished with asbestos cement sheeting. Robert Greenwood Tarran, the head of the company, had been an early advocate of non-traditional construction. He was a contractor for the Quarry Hill Flats in Leeds and was described journalistically in 1943 as 'a Henry Ford when it comes to large-scale, speedy construction'.[6]

Early residents of the estate were overwhelmingly young families. They were not always initially impressed with the homes; June Kapitan 'thought it was like a rabbit hutch when [she] first saw it' but the prefabs' facilities were good – 'a fridge, a copper [for heating water], and a sink – great for washing nappies … a big lawn' – and a friendly, close-knit community developed.[7] The prefabs survived far beyond their allotted span, and that community grew older but it remained fond of its unconventional homes, bungalows now judged ideal for a settled, predominantly elderly population. A Conservative councillor's suggestion in 2013 that the prefabs might be cleared and the area redeveloped ignited widespread opposition. In 2014, the Labour-controlled borough council announced a £600,000 scheme to renovate 127 of the bungalows (15 had been bought by tenants) with new roofs, kitchens and bathrooms, and improved insulation. The new lease of life granted the prefabs has proved popular with residents and reminds us of the resilience of this sometimes unfairly derided form of housing.

Left and right
Prefab bungalows on Sidegate Lane and Humber Doucy Lane

Non-traditional housing, Bilborough Estate, Nottingham

The Bilborough Estate, three miles to the northwest of Nottingham's city centre, offers a significant perspective on Britain's early postwar council housebuilding programme and its emphasis on prefabrication and non-traditional construction. Nottingham's western estates began life as slum clearance housing in the 1930s, but a huge postwar expansion was agreed in 1946 with the shopping parade, library and health centre on Bracebridge Drive in Bilborough reflecting the new commitment to neighbourhood self-sufficiency.

With around 11,000 on the council house waiting list, the city council was keen to build and, in a reflection of the strategic importance of two local collieries to postwar economic recovery for central government, was allocated 1,000 temporary prefab bungalows in November 1944. The city became among the first in the country to erect them six months later. A number of the AIROH B2 type were built on land to the south of Bracebridge Drive. Popular with residents, these survived into the 1980s. The innovative approach to their replacement here was to construct new bungalows on the footprint of the prefabs, retaining the intimate network of homes and footpaths that today straddles Monkton Drive.

The council showed similar ambition in its embrace of permanent prefabrication when in November 1946 it sought loan approval from the Ministry of Health and Housing to build some 1,100 BISF houses in Bilborough and the adjacent Strelley

Left
A prefab (and winner of the best-kept garden competition) on Staverton Road

Opposite clockwise from top left
'Tin tops'; BISF houses on the estate

An example of the estate's 'No Fines' housing

An unmodified Tarran Newland house on Stotfield Road

Traditionally built housing on Byley Road

Estate, and 1,000 Tarran Newland houses (with an option for a further 1,000) across the city.

You'll see unmodified steel-framed BISF houses with their characteristic steel-trussed sheeting panels on the upper storey (hence their 'tin top' nickname) dotted across the estate. Tarran Newland, comprising a concrete and steel frame with infill precast reinforced concrete panels, can be viewed in Stotfield Road, for example. Many have been thoroughly rebuilt, but unaltered originals can be distinguished by the narrow storey-height concrete panels that form their exterior walls. Wimpey 'No Fines' houses, typified by smooth painted finishes concealing the concrete beneath, are another common non-traditional housing type found on the estate, around Burnside Green and Westwick Road, for example.

Typically, here and elsewhere, it is properties purchased under Right to Buy that retain their original form, while councils have thoroughly renovated prefabs for remaining tenants. Some of the permanent prefabs have stood the test of time quite well, but a large number of types – 52 in all – were designated defective under the 1984 Housing Defects Act and declared eligible for a 90% grant towards the cost of repair.

Early postwar

Given the severity and urgency of the postwar housing crisis, immediate priorities focused on the repair of existing properties damaged in the Blitz. The power to requisition empty properties granted to councils in 1939 continued to be heavily used to rehouse those in greatest need and remained in place until 1955. But new housing was desperately needed, both practically and politically, given the public demands expressed most sharply in the squatting movement which swept the country in 1946.

The Labour government's commitment to public housing was demonstrated in a 1946 Housing Act requiring that privately built homes should form no more than one in five of total newbuild. Speculative building was rigorously curtailed by rationing, though the same shortages of building materials and skilled labour also affected local authority efforts. Given the extreme postwar balance of payments crisis, government support was sometimes granted to towns and cities best able to boost the export drive, such as Derby; its Mackworth Estate, begun in 1948 and designed to fulfil the latest neighbourhood ideals, was an unusually ambitious and extensive scheme for its time.

The early housebuilding of many councils, however, represented a continuation or delayed implementation of plans halted by war and, relying on these pre-war models, was rarely innovative. Suburban housing in a slightly more modern idiom dominated, as did by-now traditional tenement forms in inner-city areas. Legislation in 1946 granting a special subsidy to lifts in working-class housing above four storeys in height enabled an initially cautious increase in height.

In London, where the postwar council housing waiting list comprised around 100,000 families, the London County Council attempted to accelerate housebuilding by concentrating its efforts under the control of the Chief Valuer. The Woodberry Down Estate in Hackney, planned just before the war and built to new specifications soon after it, was its showpiece project. However, it proved unpopular with architectural critics, as did the contemporaneously built Minerva Estate.

Minerva Estate, Old Bethnal Green Road, Tower Hamlets, London

Officially opened in 1949, the Minerva Estate was the first estate to be completed by the London County Council after the war, but it had been conceived (as the Bethnal Green No. 1 Redevelopment Area) as far back as 1936. Wartime destruction added urgency and opportunity to this scheme of slum clearance.

Building began in 1946. Its architect described 'a nice flat site', which influenced his decision 'to set the blocks facing east and west and the principal rooms open to the best of the sun' on *Zeilenbau* lines.[8] Eight balcony-access, four-storey blocks (dropping to three at their Old Bethnal Green Road end) ensued, providing in total 261 new flats housing a population of 950, their Modernist appearance enhanced by flat roofs and white facades. On six of the blocks, the flat roofs contained playgrounds and 'sun playrooms with fitted blackboards and play apparatus for the children's interest and amusement'. Internally, the flats with their coal fires remained more conventional.

The estate's monolithic concrete construction – a cellular system pioneered by contractors Holland and Hannen, in which concrete slab floors were supported

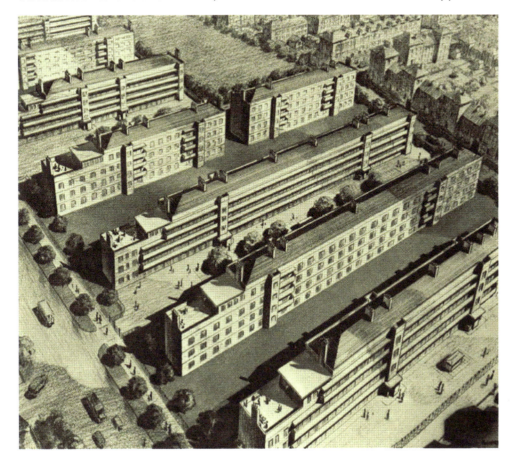

Right
An artist's impression of the planned estate

by load-carrying walls – was genuinely innovative, though it lacked the grace and daring being applied contemporarily by structural engineer Ove Arup to projects designed by the Tecton Group. By such methods (and by dispensing with skilled bricklayers, then in short supply), the LCC Valuer's Department hoped to build quickly and cheaply. On site, management and trade unions aimed to harness what they called 'the Minerva team spirit' by weekly production meetings convened to overcome 'bottlenecks and snags'. Shop steward Charlie Riddell spoke of 'a new social and political consciousness that we've got to carry out' but lamented 'the serious problem of loss of time in the morning and afternoon tea breaks on the site'.

While Londoners desperate for new homes were undoubtedly grateful for such efforts, architectural opinion was almost uniformly more critical. The Minerva Estate was panned by J.M. Richards, editor of the *Architectural Review*, for whom it reflected nothing less than 'one of the biggest tragedies of our time that the great rebuilding opportunity we were faced with after the war is being frittered away by the substitution of a policy of mere expedience for proper planning and by sheer bad architecture'.[9] An article, 'LCC housing: the need for a critical assessment', weighed in in similar fashion, and in 1951 the LCC returned primary responsibility for the design of housing to the Architect's Department.

Lysander House, a genuine expression of concrete and glass Modernism, was added to the estate in 1955, and the estate as a whole was thoroughly refurbished in 2003, offering a clean white aesthetic mellowed by developed foliage that might do more justice to original intentions.

Left
Rear view showing balcony access

Right
Mature landscaping

Pollok, Glasgow

Pollok, lying around five miles to the southwest of Glasgow's city centre, evolved as one of the four large postwar peripheral housing estates (alongside Castlemilk, Drumchapel and Easterhouse) developed by the then Glasgow Corporation as it sought to rehouse a population living in some of the worst and most overcrowded housing in the UK.

The land was acquired in 1935 and smaller-scale development began before the war, now referred to locally as 'Old Pollok'. By the time the scheme was completed in 1951, it had grown to encompass 9,159 homes and a population of some 50,000. The housing was broadly uniform across most of the scheme: some two-storey houses and a larger number of tenements in two- or three-storey blocks or terraces, generally (in Scottish terms) three- or four-apartment; that is, two- or three-bedroom.

One distinguishing feature of postwar Glasgow housing developments was the widespread use of foamslag, a lightweight aggregate derived from blast furnace slag in slabs manufactured by Glasgow Corporation's Housing Department. This was one of the more unsuccessful experiments in prefabricated construction. A roughcast finish made the houses themselves very similar in appearance to traditional brick-built homes, but their permeability to water and poor sound insulation soon proved problematic.

Another distinguishing feature – a hangover from interwar policy that continued to mark (and stigmatise) some postwar schemes – was the Housing Department's very public social categorisation of its various schemes discussed in the previous chapter. Within Pollok, to take two examples, the Craigbank area of the scheme was labelled 'Ordinary' – in fact, a superior scheme differentiated by its experimental district heating system and significantly higher rents, with

Right
Terraced housing,
Langton Road

carefully selected tenants to match. Conversely, the now-demolished South Pollok (colloquially known as 'the Bundy') – with otherwise similar housing – was judged an 'Intermediate' scheme and intended for poorer tenants. Most were relocated from the worst of Glasgow's southside slums in the Gorbals and Govan, and some 26% of the first tenants suffered from tuberculosis. South Pollok acquired the unhappy nickname 'the White Man's Graveyard'.[10]

Of course, to most early residents this was far superior accommodation than any they had known before. As one recalled:

> It was like heaven! It was like a palace, even without anything in it ... We'd got this lovely, lovely house. Well, it was lovely to me! When I got into that big empty house and the weans were running up and doon mad and – it was just like walking into Buckingham Palace because I had a bath.[11]

In the longer term, however, the poor reputation of South Pollok contributed to the decision in 1973 to demolish it and replace it with the large Pollok shopping centre, today called Silverburn, that now occupies its former site.

Top
Corner housing, Levernside Road/ Langton Road

Bottom
Flats on Waterfoot Avenue

Creggan Estate, Derry/Londonderry, Northern Ireland

The Creggan Estate lies on the upland western fringes of Derry/Londonderry, and is what might in other circumstances have been a rather typical peripheral suburban estate of its day. The Londonderry Corporation approved initial proposals for 250 new homes as early as December 1944, the first instalment of a projected 1,000 to 1,250 in what it projected as 'a self-contained community [with] its own shopping centre'.[12] Housing – varying by location but otherwise indistinguishable – would be provided both by the corporation and the Northern Ireland Housing Trust. Construction began in 1945 but proceeded slowly; by 1950, 613 homes had been built, 350 by the corporation, the rest by the housing trust. Eventually, the estate would comprise around 3,000 homes and house at peak a population of some 15,000.

Initial plans – enabled by the government's release of brick and timber for domestic building – were for short terraces of two-storey housing with three to four bedrooms and gardens front and rear. In broad terms, the estate was completed along these lines, though postwar shortages of traditional labour and materials and the desire to build at pace led to experiments in non-traditional construction. Most notably this included the permanent aluminium bungalows designed by an English company, A.W. Hawkesley Ltd, with some components manufactured locally by the Harland and Wolfe shipyards.

Given that so many were moving from appalling inner-city housing, the new homes were generally well regarded. Doris Kyle moved into Greenwalk in 1949, and thought:

> *The new houses were like palaces ... I was brought up in a two-up, two-down in Sloan's Terrace with eight other children. But Creggan was like paradise. People would come from all over Derry to see the houses. They'd knock on your door and ask you: 'Please show us around'.[13]*

Left
Housing renovated under the Northern Ireland Housing Executive's multi-element improvement programme, photographed in 1985

Right
Newly renovated housing, photographed in 1992

The *Londonderry Sentinel* described Creggan as 'one of the most beautiful housing estates in Ulster'.[14] A Unionist newspaper, it disingenuously went on to point out that 'some ninety-five percent of the houses have been given to Roman Catholics' (who apparently showed little gratitude for the corporation's beneficence). And here, of course, lay the cardinal fact of the Creggan Estate's existence: it was built in the old South electoral ward (also containing the Catholic Bogside) as a deliberate means of congregating and isolating Republican voters and maintaining minority Unionist control of Londonderry council – 'a Catholic, Nationalist enclave within a partitioned state' in Republican eyes.[15]

The sense of embattlement created a strong community quick to mobilise against perceived injustices. The additional expense of peripheral housing was a grievance found across the UK but gained extra traction in Creggan, where the corporation demanded down payments of over £5 from new residents before granting tenancies and charged a 6-foot square scullery as an extra room. In 1954, 876 Creggan tenants, mobilised by the Creggan Welfare Association, withheld the additional fee due but their legal action against it was unsuccessful. 'They took us out of rooms in congested districts because of the T.B. scare and brought us up here to starve with hunger', in the words of one disgruntled local resident.[16]

As Northern Ireland's sectarian politics descended into bloodshed, Creggan stood at the front line, occupied militarily under Operation Motorman in 1972 in the aftermath of Bloody Sunday, in which six of the 13 victims of army gunfire hailed from the estate. The peace dividend more recently has seen significant improvements to the estate in the form of new recreational and play facilities. The death of journalist Lyra McKee (accidentally shot by dissident Republicans) in Fanad Drive on the estate in 2019 reminds us that work remains to be done.

Left
Some of the small number of three-storey flatted blocks on the estate, shown after renovation in 1992

Right
Republican mural, Linsfort Drive, 2019

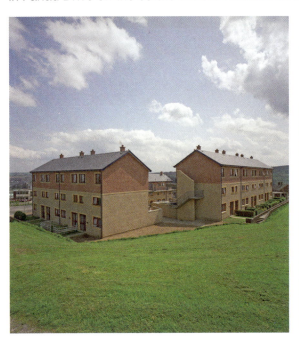

A History of Council Housing in 100 Estates

Bevan houses

While Conservative governments, despite building council housing on a large scale between the wars, tended to view it as housing for those who could afford or aspire to no better, Labour held a more positive view. The party's first majority government, and its Housing Minister Nye Bevan in particular, wanted council housing to serve a cross-section of the community; Bevan was insistent that estates serving only the poorest of the community would be 'castrated communities' and believed the 'segregation of the different income groups … a wholly evil thing'.[17]

For Bevan, this social mixing would be achieved primarily by the *quality* of new council homes. In his speech introducing the 1949 Housing Act, he insisted that 'we can only get the aesthetics of good modern architecture into a township which has the most variegated kind of housing in it'.[18] Under the harsh economic conditions prevailing, such ideals were not always fulfilled, but by 1949 the average new three-bedroom council home occupied 1,055 square feet, over a third more than the average of the 1930s and exceeding the recommendations of the Dudley Committee.

On some estates, councils built larger homes for middle-class rental or purchase; on Derby's Mackworth Estate, for example, nearly 300 houses were built for private leasehold and over 200 for private sale. In the New Towns, middle-class professionals happily occupied good-quality homes built by the Development Corporations.

In 1951, however, Labour's housing record was judged harshly by the electorate, who voted in a Conservative government committed to building 300,000 new homes a year. Macmillan, aided by economic recovery, successfully increased council house production by promoting economies in design and space standards. While the reduction of quality of Macmillan's so-called 'People's Houses' is sometimes criticised, these were largely measures anticipated by Hugh Dalton, who had succeeded Bevan as minister responsible for housing in the Labour administration's final months.

Moorlands Estate, Bath

The Second World War contributed to a housing crisis in Bath as it had in superficially far less well-favoured towns and cities across the country. A so-called 'Baedeker Raid' (targeting Britain's historic cities) in April 1942 destroyed some 1,029 homes, exacerbating severe housing pressures caused by the Admiralty's relocation of its headquarters to the city in 1939. Patrick Abercrombie's 1945 *Plan for Bath* envisaged significant modernisation and renewal of central areas and – maintaining a by now well-established theme – neighbourhood units in the suburbs.

Typically, the council began its work in more piecemeal fashion by fulfilling pre-war housing plans in Whiteway and dotting temporary prefabs across the city. The Moorlands Estate, the first phase of which went out to tender in May 1946, was to be its first wholly postwar scheme. In all, 211 houses were planned, to the design of City Engineer and Surveyor John Owens.

The quality of the estate was manifest, firstly, in the decision to build in Bath stone. This may have reflected a desire to respect the *genius loci* – the spirit and appearance of an ancient city – but the houses themselves were designed on modern lines with a clean, unembellished aesthetic that has aged well. Modernity was seen too in an open-plan layout, eschewing the fussy fencing and privet hedges characteristic of interwar schemes. Semi-detached and terraced housing, stepped to conform to a hilly terrain, was typically set back from the road line, providing plentiful green space and giving the estate as a whole an open and expansive feel.

The *Bath Chronicle* was effusive in its praise for this generous scheme, which offered each home a 'sun terrace', a south-facing living room and an upstairs bathroom as well as, more unusually, garden and fuel stores to the rear – 'an example to the whole of the West Country'.[19]

The first homes, on Cotswold Road, were ready by October 1947 and the first phase completed in February 1949, when Bevan formally presented the keys to Mr and Mrs Hector and their three children, the proud new tenants of

Left
Cotswold Road, 1962

Right
Cotswold Road, 2022 – marked by the rise of private car ownership but otherwise substantially unaltered

Opposite top
Cotswold Road, 2022

Opposite bottom
Cotswold Road, 2022

39 Chantry Mead Road. To Bevan himself, the estate represented in conception and execution something close to his ideals:

> *These houses at Moorlands are fit for everybody, and not only the working classes, or rather the low income groups. It shows we want all the different families of the community to be living with each other and we do not want those snobbish villages we had before. We want everybody, whatever their occupation may be, to be living in the same community with all the others, and thereby having reciprocal enjoyment.*[20]

'When I come across local authorities that are not paying sufficient regard to the design of their houses and the use of materials,' he concluded, 'I will tell them to visit Bath and see a real example of what they should do.'

Ermine Estate, Lincoln

The industrial county town of Lincoln typified the wartime and postwar housing dynamics of the wider country. Planning for improved peacetime conditions began in 1943 when the city council prepared a scheme for a new estate of 341 council homes. The council requested 250 prefab bungalows in 1944 but was allocated 100. In 1946, when the council housing waiting list stood at 3,000, squatters occupied War Department property in the city and received support from the Labour-controlled council, which laid on essential services.

The pressing need for permanent housing was first met by the Hartsholme Estate to the southwest of the city. The Ermine Estate, to the north, was begun in 1952 but marked by the idealism of the Bevan era and planned by a now Conservative-controlled council committed to building for general needs. Initial plans envisaged 1,350 new homes – 1,050 on what would become Ermine East, lying to the east of Riseholme Road, and 300 on Ermine West. A few of these – along Edendale Gardens in the west and Broxholme Gardens in the east – were permanent prefab Cornish houses; some of 30,000 built nationally of precast reinforced concrete panel walls and most distinguishable through the large mansard roofs that formed the upper storey. Most, however, were conventionally constructed red- or yellow-brick two-storey houses, semi-detached or in short terraces, and all with decent-sized front and back gardens. The prevailing style is 1950s Modernist, with little decorative detailing save the odd example of brick patterning on some of the flatted blocks.

Layout and landscaping provides the context in which this modest housing flourishes. Here the two estates differ slightly. Ermine East is characterised by a number of long, curving roads; in Ermine West cul-de-sacs are the predominant form. On both estates, houses are set back behind wide verges and tree-lined footpaths, and both are interspersed with open spaces and 'village greens'.

Churches were (after shops) the first community facilities to be provided on many estates. Sam Scorer's Grade II*-listed St John the Baptist, completed in 1963, is a marvellous building, marked out by its hyperbolic paraboloid (saddle-

Left
Typical family housing and green surrounds on the Ermine Estate

Right
Flatted housing on Laughton Way, Ermine West

Opposite top
Shopping parade, Woodhall Drive

Opposite bottom
St John the Baptist Church

shaped) concrete roof designed in conjunction with structural engineer Hajnal Konyi. As Owen Hatherley suggests, 'the estate is determinedly mild and moderate, far from the avant-garde; its parish church is quite the opposite'.[21]

Nevertheless, to its priest, the Reverend John Hodgkinson, 'the emphasis was very much on church as people rather than a building'.[22] The parish newsletter, the *Ermine News*, published from 1957 to 1965, provided monthly updates on a wide array of community groups and activities, and the church played a significant role in forging the community identity sought by postwar planners.

By 1963, the estate housed 10,000 – a number added to by the 17-storey Trent View tower block built the following year. To Adrian Jones and Chris Matthews, all this was 'social housing as it was meant to be, and it has survived for fifty years, not pristine, but evidently a place that works'.[23]

Gaer Estate, Newport, South Wales

The Gaer Estate (properly Gaer-Stelvio) to the west of Newport, designed by Newport Borough Architect Johnson Blackett and job architect Alfred Williams, comprises, in the words of John Newman, 'extensive and remarkably self-confident and convincing Modernist housing'.[24] Occupying a site of 163 acres and housing 4,300, it was built between 1946 and 1951, one of four large postwar estates developed by an unusually ambitious local authority.

That ambition and Blackett's skill is seen, firstly, in the use made of a superb location overlooking open country, industrial Newport and the Bristol Channel. Housing curves to follow contours and a sloping site is exploited to the full to provide vistas and open space. In this respect, though designed in a very different tradition, the layout emulates the work, built to a similar topography, of Sidney Colwyn Foulkes in North Wales (see page 121).

Some of the first homes – temporary Arcon bungalows, BISF houses and apprentice-built Ministry of Works duplexes – reflected the stringencies of the

Left
The estate under construction, 1950

Opposite
Three-storey flatted blocks, Shakespeare Crescent

A History of Council Housing in 100 Estates

postwar housing crisis. For Blackett, it 'behove[d] architects ... to keep awake to the possibilities of logically using these mediums out of which a new building art must arise!'[25]

His Modernism is seen most obviously in the flat roofs that predominate across the estate's housing, most strikingly in the two-storey homes, brick-built, sometimes colour-washed, deployed in the long hillside terraces harnessing the local terrain in the Groves and Drives (all named after British literary figures) that form most of the estate. Elsewhere, in Macauley Gardens for example, semi-detached pairs of housing offer contrast while still conforming to Blackett's Modernist idiom. Three-storey flatted blocks along Shakespeare Crescent are notable for their full-length, International Style glazed stairways. (Hillview, an 11-storey tower block on the northeastern fringe of the estate, was added in 1971.)

The residents themselves were probably more impressed by the generous living accommodation – three-bedroom in most cases, and offering large working kitchens and living rooms, as well as the bathrooms and WCs (sometimes two) – that some at least could begin to take for granted.

Like other postwar estates, Gaer was also planned as a neighbourhood with sites set aside for community and health centres, shops, church, school and cinema. Not all of that was fulfilled, though Gaer Junior School (1950–1), also designed by Blackett, is noteworthy.

The estate received a Festival of Britain's Special Architectural Award for Civic and Landscape Design in 1951. If you visit today, you should also see the Duffryn Estate (page 197), a later and very innovative Newport Borough scheme, immediately to the south.

Neighbourhood units

In 1946, the Town Planning and Development Committee of Preston Borough Council declared that:

> Housing between the two world wars failed because most of the estates were not planned as small communities within the town, and provided for only one class of tenant and lacked many of the basic amenities that were available in the centre of the town.[26]

By the late 1930s, planners and sociologists were vocal in their criticism of the peripheral cottage estates that characterised much interwar council housing. Corporation suburbia was held to be monotonous in form, lacking facilities and bereft of community feeling. Ruth Durant (better known later as Ruth Glass) condemned the north London Watling Estate as essentially a dormitory – 'not much more than a huge hotel without a roof'.[27] Later writers counterposed this alleged sterility with a much-romanticised vision of the neighbourliness of the inner-city slums being cleared. Preston's new Larches Estate, in contrast, was designed as a self-contained community of 600 houses and flats with 'bungalows and a hostel for old people, a community centre, a health clinic, library and a church'.

The committee was echoing what was rapidly becoming the established wisdom of the day. The concept of the 'neighbourhood unit' had emerged in America in the 1920s and had informed Barry Parker's planning of Wythenshawe in the 1930s. It was taken up by the UK's foremost town planner, Patrick Abercrombie, in his 1943 *Plan for Plymouth* and *The County of London Plan* of the same year. It was given some mathematical precision by a study group of the newly formed Ministry of Town and Country Planning in an appendix to the Dudley Report in 1944. In London, Abercrombie proposed 'neighbourhood units, each equipped with its own schools, local shops, community buildings and smaller amenity open spaces' with populations of between 6,000 and 10,000 based on the catchment area of the local elementary school.[28]

The Lansbury Estate in Poplar was intended to showcase the concept, but it was an idea adopted enthusiastically across the country. In Derby, for example, the Mackworth Estate was designed as 'a residential neighbourhood in full accordance with contemporary town planning principles'.[29] In Norwich, the 1945 *City of Norwich Plan* envisaged 25 neighbourhood units across the city. In Glasgow, the large postwar Castlemilk and Drumchapel estates were subdivided into neighbourhoods, each with its own shops, schools and churches. The 'village greens' promoted by Sir Charles Reilly in the Black Country were a smaller, more bucolic version of the same.

The good intentions were not always fulfilled; stymied by financial difficulties but, ultimately and more tellingly, challenged by real-world dynamics that didn't conform to drawing board visions. A more affluent working class would choose its own forms of sociability.

Lansbury Estate, Tower Hamlets, London

The Lansbury Estate in Poplar was the venue for the 1951 Festival of Britain's Live Architecture Exhibition, and it was intended to provide a practical demonstration of the quality of housing and planning principles which would distinguish a 'new Britain' set to emerge from the destruction of war. Almost a quarter of Poplar's buildings were destroyed or seriously damaged in the Second World War. The Stepney and Poplar Reconstruction Area was authorised by the Minister of Town and Country Planning in December 1947. In line with the recommendations of *The County of London Plan*, the LCC proposed a 42% reduction of population and projected 11 new neighbourhood units, of which the Lansbury Estate would form Neighbourhood 9.

Overseeing the project, architect-planner Frederick Gibberd provided not only the usual complement of schools, community buildings and churches but also, innovatively, the country's first pedestrianised shopping precinct and (since demolished) the LCC's first purpose-built old people's home. Its housing was deployed in a generally conventional streetscape with a few courts and setbacks to provide variety and greenery.

The exhibition area itself comprised some 478 new homes. To meet required inner-city densities, just over half of these were in three- and six-storey blocks; mixed blocks of houses, maisonettes and flats and terraced housing made up the rest. Designed by some of the better-known architects of the day, including Gibberd himself, Geoffrey Jellicoe and Norman & Dawbarn, the style was generally what was termed New Humanist, based on the Scandinavian model favoured by many contemporary designers. The yellow stock brick and grey slate roofs which predominated were intended to harmonise with established local housing.

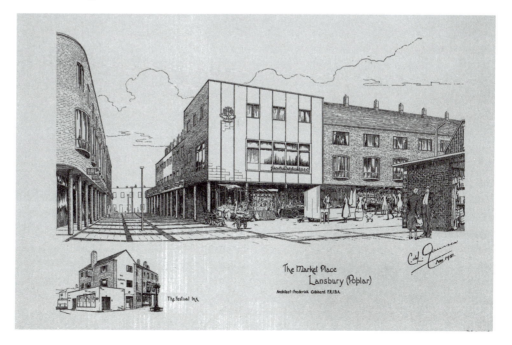

Right
Perspective view of the marketplace, Chrisp Street, 1951

To some critics, this was a lost opportunity. Sandy Wilson (then working in the LCC Architect's Department, later the architect of the British Library) berated Lansbury's 'pitched roofs, peep-hole windows, and "folksy" details of the current Swedish revival' as the architecture of 'cold feet'.[30] J.M. Richards, the influential editor of the *Architectural Review*, described 'the general run of the small-scale housing at Lansbury as worthy, dull and somewhat skimpy'.[31]

Sociologists – one such, Margaret Willis, had been a member of the LCC's Reconstruction Group, the first so employed – were generally more positive. Ruth Glass and John Westergaard concluded that an 'an environment has been created – or re-created – that is neither a pale imitation of suburban boredom, nor an apologia for city life'.[32]

New residents, a cross-section of the local working-class East End, were more effusive. One woman, who had moved from her mother's home in Millwall where her family of five had lived in two rooms, said simply 'I never thought I'd see such luxury'.[33] Around two-thirds had moved from shared accommodation and homes lacking inside sanitation.

The estate was declared a conservation area in 1998 and transferred to the Poplar Housing and Regeneration Community Association (Poplar Harca) with a brief to renew the area in the following year.

Clockwise from top left
West site housing, 1951

The old people's home, 1951

Baring House, designed by the LCC's Housing Architect and completed in 1951

Flat and maisonette block on Ricardo Street designed by Geoffrey Jellicoe, 1951

A History of Council Housing in 100 Estates

The Stowlawn Estate, Bilston, West Midlands

The superficially unassuming Stowlawn Estate in the Black Country town of Bilston evokes a richer cast of characters than probably any other in the UK. The town itself, almost literally benighted in these earlier years, may itself seem an unlikely setting for what it was planned as an almost utopian experiment in community building. But it was precisely its disregarded squalor – in 1943, 1,400 tons of smoke particles per square mile fell on Bilston annually; a 1944 survey revealed that 2,655 of its 7,700 homes were in disrepair or lacked proper sanitation – that led to such necessary ambition.

A key figure was Arthur Vivian Williams, appointed Town Clerk of the Borough in 1941. Williams, an active Labour Party member with a voracious interest in planning and sociology, met the émigré Austrian polymath Otto Neurath in 1944. Neurath believed that sensitive planning and good-quality housing, delivered in full and sympathetic consultation with its intended recipients, could promote contentment and wellbeing. The council appointed Neurath a consultant in the hope that he might 'make Bilston happy'.[34]

Neurath had a particular interest in mixed communities and communal provision and, before his untimely death in December 1945, was able to influence the plan commissioned by the council from architect-planner Thomas Alwyn Lloyd for the development of Stowlawn in this direction. Shortly after, Williams invited another Viennese émigré settled in Britain, Ella Briggs, to design 160 houses for Stowlawn; her work can be seen on Church Green and Lawnside Green.

Bottom
A sketch by Sir Charles Reilly entitled 'A Reilly Community at Bilston'

Meanwhile Sir Charles Reilly, who had retired as a Liverpool University Professor of Architecture in 1933 but remained active and influential in the field, was engaged in a very public controversy over the design of the Woodchurch

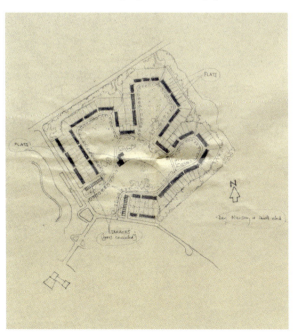

Estate in Birkenhead. He was promoting his conception of what became known as 'Reilly Greens' based, in his words, on 'the English Village Green and the small squares of the country town, where children can play and neighbours see one another and retain the friendliness of the little streets and slums'.[35] His plans were defeated in Birkenhead but given new life when Reilly was appointed consultant to Bilston in 1946.

Reilly's original vision expanded to encompass all-purpose community centres providing not only the standard facilities of clubrooms but also nurseries, laundries, cafeterias and a meals delivery service as well as a district heating system and communal waste disposal scheme. By this time, there were some – not disabused by Reilly – who believed his plan offered 'a New Way of Life'.[36]

Life, however, in the shape of the Ministry of Health and Housing, believed these plans too expensive and profligate of land. Modified proposals were accepted, with the 'Reilly Greens' remaining but community provision removed. Reilly died in 1948, and Williams moved on the same year – initially to Dudley, where a modified version of the greens was implemented in the Old Park Farm Estate. What emerged in Bilston were 'low-density housing estates with large open spaces rather than the socialist-inspired models of community living for which [Reilly] had worked'.[37] Even that has been eroded by the infill housing built on most of the greens in the 1960s, though the thinner, more sinuous Lawnside Green remains intact.

Clockwise from top left
Terraced housing designed by Ella Briggs, Lawnside Green

Semi-detached housing designed by Ella Briggs, Lawnside Green

A plainer terrace, Lawnside Green

Rathcoole Estate, Newtonabbey, Northern Ireland

Rathcoole in Newtownabbey, six miles north of Belfast, was conceived in 1945 by the Northern Ireland Housing Trust, established that year as a technocratic solution to the political obstacles impeding the development of public housing in the province. Belfast was the most overcrowded city in the UK, and the trust estimated that 44% of its homes were in need of repair. Slum clearance and redevelopment had been resisted by both Unionist politicians and the Catholic church in the interwar period for fear it might disrupt existing power bases. The trust estimated that the Province required 100,000 new homes; it would build 25,000, principally in a range of peripheral suburban estates of which Rathcoole, with a planned population of 10,000 in 3,800 homes, was one of the largest.

Construction began on Rathcoole's 366-acre site in 1952. It was envisaged as a self-contained neighbourhood with the full range of community facilities, though no pubs were permitted and none have been built subsequently. Housing allocation was to be determined on a strictly, non-sectarian, needs-based points system. People suffering from tuberculosis (rife in Belfast), ex-servicemen and those lacking inside toilets were prioritised. In the words of M.A. Neill, 'the primary objective of the planners was to create a balanced neighbourhood within a new urban community'.[38]

Left
A view of Rathcoole from Cave Hill, 1995

Right
Housing and multis, 1988

The housing itself was superficially very similar in layout and design to contemporary mainland schemes, but marked by local conditions. Much of it was system-built – No-Fines, Easiform and Orlit – in an economising attempt to keep rents close to the far lower rents of the Belfast slums, and it tended to be slightly smaller than its British equivalent. Plain three- and four-storey flatted blocks also featured prominently. A cluster of four 15-storey point blocks was added along Rosslea Way in 1965, built by John Laing using the French 'Sectra' steel formwork and poured concrete system of prefabrication.

Problems emerged. The 'single skin' prefabricated homes proved difficult to heat and prone to condensation and damp. Few of the promised community facilities were built, and Rathcoole's proximity to Belfast ensured that most residents looked to the larger city for employment, shopping and entertainment.

Such difficulties contributed to but were overshadowed by the sectarian conflict that emerged in the wake of the 1968 Civil Rights movement. As the Troubles erupted, many Protestant families fled Belfast for Rathcoole as Catholic families on the estate were forced out to seek their own safe havens. For a while from 1971, the estate was effectively under the control of the Loyalist Rathcoole Defence Association.

As the political climate eased in the 1990s, the Northern Ireland Housing Executive (formed in 1971 to remove all public housing from sectarian influence) began to improve the estate, demolishing some of the worst-built housing (notably the three- and four-storey maisonette so-called 'banana flats', named for their shape) and thoroughly renovating other homes. Community and shopping facilities were also improved. Against local opposition, two of the four tower blocks, Monkscoole House and Abbotscoole House, are currently scheduled for demolition.

Left
A renovated maisonette block on Ardmillan Drive, 1996 – a straight version of the so-called 'banana flats'

Right
Three of the four multis, 1996

New Parks Estate, Leicester

Leicester City Council had built 9,100 council homes between the wars, but a 1946 survey estimated that 1,000 new homes were required to meet immediate needs, and a further 13,000 within 10 years. The first project of its Reconstruction Committee, established in 1944, was the New Parks Estate to be built on land acquired in the northwest of the city in the 1930s. It was described by City Engineer and Surveyor John L. Beckett as an 'experiment in the new conception of estate planning'.[39]

Beckett laid out the council's principles of postwar planning: good transport links to estates divided into 'precincts' and, within those, a neighbourhood centre containing 'health centre, library, communal buildings, churches, cinema and shops'. The new estates would be mixed development, catering not just for families but, in his words, providing 'a large colony for aged person's homes and a hostel for single persons'. Beckett spoke also of an 'intermixture of classes'.

Contemporary housing pressures led to familiar solutions: 120 temporary prefabricated bungalows on Aikman Avenue, the estate's main thoroughfare, and the widespread construction of permanent prefabs – principally Easiform and BISF – across the estate. It was claimed that 162 houses of this new type were built in 162 days. At New Parks, construction began in late 1945, with the first groundwork carried out by parties of Italian prisoners of war under armed guard, and the first phase of building was completed by October 1947. (The first bus services arrived one month later.) Around 3,100 houses were built by the early 1950s.

Left
Renovated and unrenovated BISF housing, Glazebrook Road

Right
The roundabout off Aikman Avenue captures some of the open, expansive feel that City Engineer Beckett aimed for

The layout of curving streets and the occasional roundabout is typical of its time as are, to a lesser extent, the concrete-surfaced roads which predominate in the estate. The grass verges and generous open space remain, though there is less sign of another of Beckett's aspirations, unfenced communal gardens. Most of the housing – semi-detached or in short terraces, in boxy form – is also unexceptionally of its time. The seven distinctively shaped three- and five-storey blocks of flats along Aikman Avenue were more innovative, inspired by council delegations to Scandinavia.

At the top end of Aikman Avenue, note also the attractive curved and porticoed mid-1950s shopping parade, still anchored by the local Co-op, and the very typical estate pub adjacent. Across the road, St Aidan's Church, designed by Sir Basil Spence in unashamedly Modernist style and opened in 1959, offers more spiritual sustenance.

There won't seem much about the New Parks Estate that is obviously 'experimental' to a contemporary visitor, but it remains a gentle and humane expression of the planning ideals of its day. To Tom Murtha, born on the estate in 1952, it was 'a young estate full of young people creating a community and a future' – a future that Tom sought for others in his own later career in social housing.[40]

Top
The Scandinavian-inspired flats off Aikman Avenue

Bottom left
Homes for elderly people, Piper Way

Bottom right
The shopping parade, Aikman Avenue

Mixed development

The 1944 Dudley Report looking to the postwar era declared that 'there is a need for a mixed development of family houses mingled with blocks of flats for smaller households'.[41] While, for the moment, most new permanent council housing was built on pre-war lines, often according to pre-war plans, the Ministry of Health's 1949 *Housing Manual* returned to the theme with greater force, while Frederick Gibberd's Somerford Grove Estate in Hackney of the same year provided a model.

An important practical driver of this change was the simple fact that many on council housing waiting lists – single- and two-person households, most notably – were not served by the family housing built overwhelmingly between the wars. In Norwich, for example, not atypically, 70% of council homes built to date had been three-bedroom family houses. Of those on Hackney's waiting list in 1948, one-third required only a single bedroom. There was also greater emphasis on the provision of suitable housing for elderly people.

In essence, therefore, mixed development aimed to provide homes appropriate to a range of people and households in different stages of life. Sometimes, less often in practice even than theory, there was a hope that 'mixed' schemes would also mix classes by providing usually 'superior' and more expensive accommodation for middle-class renters and owner-occupiers.

Perhaps as importantly, the concept excited planners and architects. It offered them more leeway than the very uniform cottage suburbs had. Aesthetically, it allowed schemes with far greater visual interest – a mix of forms, a range of heights and more varied layouts that provided point and contrast in otherwise potentially monotonous public housing schemes. Cleeve Barr's 1958 book *Public Authority Housing* spoke positively of mixed development's 'variety of architectural form and silhouette'.[42]

Mixed development, therefore, became commonplace in postwar estate planning, sometimes applied with finesse but often more indiscriminately, particularly in the new peripheral estates where tall point blocks were planted incongruously amid low-rise suburbia. The concept was one, more minor, cause of the spate of high-rise building that would emerge from the mid-1950s.

A weakness that would later become apparent was the flawed belief that tenants would willingly move from one housing type to another as their life circumstances altered, whereas most preferred to stay in established homes. The 2013 Bedroom Tax (financially penalising tenants judged to have an 'excess' of bedrooms) was a brutal means of addressing this issue.

Somerford Grove, Hackney, London

To Nicholas Bullock, the architecture and layout of Somerford Grove was 'both clearly English and clearly modern'; its combination of traditional elements of London architecture and modern forms answering 'the hopes of the *Architectural Review* for a modern architecture rooted in a regional identity'.[43] In the more prosaic language of George Downing, Hackney Metropolitan Borough Council's Surveyor, it offered 'more interesting and open lay-outs ... and, with attention paid to landscape gardening', something 'far removed from the general pre-war conception of "council flats"'.[44]

Hackney commissioned Frederick Gibberd to design the scheme in 1944 on a nine-acre site of straight streets and bomb-damaged terraced housing. His finished scheme, completed in 1949, was radically different. Gibberd joined two key postwar concepts. The first of these was what Gibberd termed 'precinctual theory' – a modified form of Radburn; a largely traffic-free environment achieved, in his words, by 'a series of closes, each with its own character' with their buildings 'arranged to give vistas across the site'.[45] The second was 'mixed development', seen here in the estate's mix of three- and four-storey blocks of two- and three-bedroom flats, two-storey blocks of one-bedroom flats and bedsits, two-storey terraced family housing, and a terrace of single-storey bungalows for elderly residents.

The practical value of that mix was obvious to the range of new residents but Gibberd, from a design perspective, also pointed to the 'contrast and variety' that enhanced its overall composition. Gibberd had apparently been influenced

Left
A housing mix at Somerford Grove, photographed in 1950

Opposite top
A terrace of family homes

Oppostie bottom left
Four-storey flats

Opposite bottom right
Bungalows for elderly people

by his wartime study of British cities, including Bath. It is a British version of Scandinavian New Humanism, but most obviously it typifies what became known as Festival of Britain style (seen equally in the architecture of the Lansbury Estate, overseen by Gibberd – see page 101) marked by picturesque detail in its use of colour and ceramic tiles, delicate porches and Regency-inspired curved balconies.

Completed to a density of 100 persons per acre, as recommended in *The County of London Plan*, it was to *The Times*, 'encouraging proof that even dense housing need not be inhuman'.[46] The estate received an Award of Merit from the Festival of Britain's architectural committee, and Gibberd received two further commissions from Hackney – the Beecholme Estate in Clapton, completed in spacious surrounds in similar style in 1950, and the Beckers, completed in 1958, another mixed development scheme but marked of its time by the inclusion of two 11-storey point blocks.

Orlando Estate, Newhall Street, Walsall, West Midlands

The Orlando Estate in Walsall, opened in November 1961, was regarded by the borough council 'as something of a "showpiece"'. Replacing, in the words of the local press, a 'ramshackle mass of "two-up, two-down" property' where tenants, many still reliant on a communal water pump, 'were living under conditions reminiscent of Dickens' day', its well-equipped modern homes were unsurprisingly if unoriginally described by one happy resident as 'a housewife's dream'.[47]

In practical terms, that dream was a classic mixed development scheme comprising four blocks of eight-storey flats, one three-storey block of flats, two blocks of three-storey terraced houses and 11 two-storey terraced houses. Its architects referred to the severe local housing shortage and the necessity to 'redevelop at high density without giving an impression of overcrowding'; in all, some 169 new homes were provided, housing around 500 people.[48] An arched entrance to the estate within the three-storey blocks is reminiscent of Geoffrey Jellicoe's better-known St Matthew's Close scheme nearby, completed in 1953.

A previous through road was closed, replaced by pedestrian walkways, ornamental gardens and a children's playground. Each flat was provided with a bike and pram store, and around 50 garages were provided for a newly affluent working class.

Left
Low-rise and multi-storey flats

Opposite left top
A terrace of family housing

Opposite left bottom
Three-storey townhouses and block, Newhall Street

Opposite right
An eight-storey block of flats

A History of Council Housing in 100 Estates

Visiting the estate, one is struck by the detailing applied to the lower blocks in particular – seen in the tile-hung facades of the terraced housing and the coloured panelling and tiling of the three-storey blocks. It was all lovingly detailed in a properly self-congratulatory piece supplied to the trade press, listing the proprietary products applied ('Stramit' and 'Prodoglaze' are mentioned) and the West African mahogany used in the blocks' public areas. The whole scheme was finished seven months ahead of schedule, as the article mentions twice.[49]

On this occasion, credit goes to the large-scale building contractors Wates with whom the council had a close working relationship. The design of the scheme is credited jointly to Borough Engineer M.E. Habershon, Borough Architect A.T. Parrot, and G.F. Elliott, Divisional Architect for Wates. This was a custom-made, conventionally built scheme, with the eight-storey blocks of reinforced concrete frame construction.

In 1961, the hope was expressed that the Orlando Estate 'should set the pattern for future development' in the town.[50] By 1965, however, as the council's ambitions grew during the unprecedented public housing drive of the era, the Sandbank Estate in Bloxwich featured one 16-storey and three 12-storey blocks built by Wates using its own patented form of prefabricated construction. The Orlando Estate, as described to me by one resident, remains a 'time capsule' of the early 1960s.

Churchill Gardens Estate, Westminster, London

In 2000, the Civic Trust voted the Churchill Gardens Estate in Westminster the outstanding building scheme of the previous 40 years. It was the only major scheme completed to the parameters of *The County of London Plan*. When constructed, it was the largest urban area built to the plans of a single firm of architects. And those architects were young: Philip Powell and Hidalgo Moya were aged just 24 and 25 respectively when they won an international competition organised by Westminster City Council in 1946 to design what was then the Pimlico Housing Scheme on a 30-acre Thameside site of decayed and bomb-damaged terraced housing.

So Churchill Gardens earns its superlatives, but it succeeds most of all as an attractive and humane place to live. Its scale – 1661 homes, 36 blocks, a population of around 5,000 – might at first make that seem unlikely, but Powell later wrote of his 'mistrust of conscious struggling after originality ... of the monumental approach'.[51]

Nevertheless, it was a consciously Modernist scheme – as seen in the estate's overall design, laid out to the *Zeilenbau* principles. But the scheme's main road meanders through the estate and the blocks are deployed in a seemingly informal manner, which avoids the rigidity of some such schemes.

The first four blocks completed towards the eastern edge of the estate – Chaucer, Coleridge, Keats and Shelley Houses (all received Festival of Britain architectural awards in 1950 and are now Grade II-listed) – were also unashamedly modern in their concrete cross-frame construction and eye-catching full-height, glazed staircases.

In a second phase of construction, moving westwards, staircases were replaced by gallery access, which allowed a larger number of smaller flats and larger windows. This generous glazing and the piloti of some of the central blocks open and lighten

Left
The estate under construction in 1950

Right
Sullivan House in the foreground, Gilbert House to the rear in 1962

Opposite top
Children at play in the estate in 1960

Opposite bottom left
Bramwell House

Opposite bottom right
Stairwell, Chaucer House

A History of Council Housing in 100 Estates

the overall appearance of the estate. The final and easternmost phase, faced with white glazed brick, echoes the stuccoed 19th-century terraces of Claverton Street opposite. Unfussy landscaping – 'small quadrangles with neat hedges or foot-high railings ... careful patterns of paving and grass' – provided by the architects in consultation with a former head gardener at Kew completes the ensemble.[52]

This was mixed development *par excellence* – a mix of three-, five-, seven- and nine-storey blocks and, along its Thameside frontage, a terrace of townhouses intended for middle-class occupation. Neighbourhood ideals were fulfilled in the provision of a community centre, nurseries, shops and schools – and (long-gone) concrete playgrounds. The UK's first district heating scheme is marked by the striking accumulator tower in the centre of the estate, which collected surplus heat from Battersea Power Station via a tunnel under the Thames.

To some of the early residents, 'it was like moving into heaven', while residents in the private Dolphin Square flats nearby complained that 'many of the flats are not as nice as those put up by the Council in Churchill Gardens opposite'.[53]

Radburn

The Radburn system (or 'service cul-de-sac' system, as it was sometimes called in the early technical literature) was first pioneered by architect-planner Clarence Stein in the rapidly motorising United States of America. Stein devised Radburn, New Jersey, as a 'town for the motor age' in 1928. His concept, party inspired by the British Garden Cities, sought to create a safe and healthy environment by separating cars and people: motor traffic was confined to service roads, predominantly cul-de-sacs to the rear of the homes, while the housing itself, in the form of so-called 'superblocks', was served by pedestrian footpaths and located around green open space.

In Britain, the concept was noted in the 1944 Dudley Report and 1949 *Housing Manual* and recommended in the latter's 1953 revision. It was implemented with varying skill and thoroughness, and became a standard form in the later 1950s and 1960s. Its first full-scale application occurred at the Queen's Park South Estate in Wrexham in 1950. Borough architect J. Lewis Womersley trialled Radburn first on the Eastfield Estate in Northampton, begun in 1953, and, having moved on to Sheffield, in that city's Greenhill Estate in 1954. The Walshes' Farm Estate built by Stourport Urban District Council, completed in 1957, was judged one of its fullest and most successful applications.

All of these, and more so, later such schemes were variations on a theme rooted in the apparently commmonsense notion that 'the direct daily contact of people with grass and trees and gardens' contributed to health and wellbeing, particularly for the young.[54] The schemes' advocates also pointed, more practically, to the savings achieved in road and sewerage construction costs even after extra expenditure incurred on landscaping and play facilities. The homes were generally the conventional two-storey housing of the day, usually in short terraces, though low-rise flatted blocks might be added to provide greater density.

The fashion for Radburn faded, however, as apparent problems emerged: it 'was difficult to distinguish the backs from the front of houses: in a conventional sense they had neither, and the ubiquitous footpaths effectively deprived them of all privacy. Visitors, even residents themselves, had difficulty locating addresses'.[55] Garaging, often located out of eyesight, was prone to neglect or worse as conditions deteriorated on some estates in the 1970s. By the 1980s, newly fashionable theories of 'defensible space' called for a clear demarcation of public and private space and lauded the 'natural surveillance of the street'.

In truth, later criticisms often reflected issues far broader than those thrown up by any one form of estate design. In general, Radburn deserves to be remembered more kindly; for its good intentions and apparently sound reasoning certainly but, above all, for the decent housing and attractive environments that were created for so many new and later residents.

Queen's Park South, Wrexham, North Wales

The Queen's Park South Estate, developed north of the River Gwenfro about a mile to the east of the town centre, was dubbed 'the Wrexham Experiment'. It was a full-scale application of Radburn principles implemented by a 'courageous council', Borough Surveyor, Engineer and Architect J.M. Davies, and Gordon Stephenson, Lever Professor of Civic Design in the University of Liverpool, who acted as consultant and later proselytiser.[56]

The estate was planned from 1950 on, and its housing – brick-built, pebble-dashed in the first phases, largely constructed in economical terraced form – conformed to earlier postwar forms and standards. Stephenson was at pains to point out that the homes' front and rear access (footpaths to the front, service roads to the rear) was a common feature of earlier bye-law housing and some forms of Garden City development.

The breakthrough element of the estate was, of course, its Radburn-style layout inspired by the pioneering work of Stein. The undulating site and adapted design didn't allow for the internal parks Stein recommended for his own 'superblocks', but the estate's eight-feet-wide footpaths ('to give children with their wheeled toys and mothers with perambulators plenty of room to manoeuvre') were a direct recommendation from Stein, who had found the six-feet width implemented at Radburn too narrow.[57] In Wrexham, private front gardens – which saved on maintenance and provided 'a greater degree of urbanity' – bordered the expansive green open space, which remains the estate's most striking feature. Thirteen-feet-wide service cul-de-sacs to the rear were judged practically sufficient to accommodate vehicular traffic, but were found too long and narrow 'and therefore rather squalid' by some observers.[58]

Writing in 1954, Stephenson was able to comment on how residents adapted to the design. He lamented that the fronts were still regarded as too much 'the "best" side of the house' and noted that many of the children were playing in the estate's service roads, perhaps following their mothers' admonitions since

Left
Terraced housing and footway, Coad Aben

Right
Semi-detached housing, Gwenfro

these were on the housing's kitchen side.[59] He was pleased, however, that front gardens were being adapted and, in this way, some genuine 'ownership' was being practised on the part of the new residents.

The finished estate, best appreciated along Anthony Eden Drive, Gwenfro and Y Wern, comprised nine sections and around 1,500 homes, and was completed in the later 1950s. Writing contemporarily, Stephenson noted its 'separation of pedestrian ways and traffic ways giving greater safety and convenience to all, but especially to children' and its 'remarkable feeling of spaciousness'. He hoped it was a 'first step towards a more realistic housing policy'.[60] In fact Caia Park, the much larger estate of which Queen's Park South forms part – the largest council estate in Wales – comprises a far more traditional streetscape, though one still notable for its greenery and open space.

Top
Terraced housing at the junction of Coed Aben and Anthony Eden Drive

Bottom
Flats and terraced housing, Y-Wern

A History of Council Housing in 100 Estates

Middlefield Lane Estate, Gainsborough, Lincolnshire

Planning for the Middlefield Lane Estate in Gainsborough began in discussions between the Housing Committee of Gainsborough Urban District Council and council architects Fisher, Hollingsworth and Partners, project architect Neil Taylor, in February 1962. A contract with Wimpey to build '327 dwellings, six shops, 1 community hall and 143 garages at a cost of £829,007' was agreed in June 1963, and the first tenants moved in just under a year later.[61]

This was a small-scale but skilled application of Radburn principles, comprising principally terraced blocks of eight to 12 houses set in 'courts' located around pedestrianised green spaces to the front with service roads to the rear. Three-storey, walk-up blocks of flats provided greater density in the centre of the estate. Around 40% of the homes were provided with a garage, generally located close to the rear of the housing.

The housing itself was of a conventional appearance largely dictated by the constraints imposed by Wimpey's chosen method of 'No-Fines' concrete construction. Taylor's plea for higher space standards was rejected by the council on financial grounds, but he was more successful in securing additional electrical sockets and immersion heaters (supplanting back boilers), both a direct reflection of the rising living standards and new modes of living signalled in the 1962 Parker Morris Report, 'Homes for today and tomorrow', on housing standards.

The architect's vision was most fully played out in 'his stylistically modernist centrepiece of the estate, the complex of shops and maisonettes known as The Precinct' – both a nod to that postwar staple, the neighbourhood centre, and a deliberate symbol of Gainsborough's 'image as a modern, forward-thinking, local

Bottom
Family homes,
The Walk

authority'. The naming of the estate's roads and housing, complicated by its Radburn layout, also captured that moment. While some advocated traditional nomenclature, 'the architects wanted crisp, sophisticated, and modishly functional names: "The Walk", "North Parade", "South Parade", "The Lawn", and "The Precinct"'.

The *Gainsborough Evening News* recorded 'The Likes and Dislikes' of some of this new wave of residents. The estate's 'fresh-air feeling' was most praised; one mother commented 'she could think of few better places for her children to grow up'. The poor bus service was the biggest gripe, though this was soon rectified.

Time took its toll on the estate as economic decline superseded 1960s affluence. The shopping precinct was demolished in 2008, replaced by conventional low-rise housing. The flats, prone to social problems, were boarded up when I visited in 2020. The 'greens' and most of the low-rise housing have stood up better. Middlefield is a rare example of a modest estate having found its worthy chronicler, someone who both grew up on the estate and can write its history knowledgeably. As Ian Waites concludes, 'in its time, the Middlefield Lane estate clearly gave the people of Gainsborough a chance to live in a good, modern home in a thoughtfully planned, spacious and pleasant estate'.

Top
Family houses, Dunstall Walk

Bottom
Flats in North Parade, 2011; since demolished

A History of Council Housing in 100 Estates

Elwy Road Estate, Rhos-on-Sea, North Wales

The Elwy Road Estate (now known as Bryn Eglwys) in Rhos-on-Sea is a rather magical and, in parts, whimsical place. The housing needs were, as ever, pressing – there were 1,000 names on the council house waiting list of Colwyn Bay Borough Council in the late 1940s. However, the council's response, in the scheme designed by local architect Sidney Colwyn Foulkes and built between 1952 and 1956, was anything but routine.

Simple topography was one explanation. Commenting on Colwyn Foulkes's Caes Bricks (now Bryn Hyfryd) scheme in Beaumaris, which would provide a model for Elwy Road, the *Architects' Journal* noted how, 'as it is invariably necessary in Wales to build on a hill, the conventional pairs of houses 12 ft. apart are inordinately expensive ... and a satisfactory grouping of the individual units, when separated in pairs, is almost impossible'.[62]

Another part of the explanation was the vogue for Radburn layouts in the Queen's Park South Estate in Wrexham, not far away (see page 117). Elwy Road's large open greens and rear service roads represented a version of the same. But in most respects, Elwy Road was unique, perhaps rooted in what some described as the 'Celtic romanticism' of Colwyn Foulkes's design aesthetic.[63]

Left
Terraced housing, Maes Glas

Right
Terraced housing, Bryn Eglwys

The least romantic of the estate's 238 homes – despite their pitched roofs and smattering of Celtic cross-style porthole windows – are the six three-storey blocks of flats situated at the higher, southern end of the estate. Elsewhere, the dominant features are two long curved two-storey terraces of cottage housing, rendered in shades of white and stepped along Bryn Eglwys, with a plainer brown render and level along Maes Glas. Here the Radburn influence

comes to the fore in the spacious green setting of the terraces and the now rather narrow service roads to the rear, though even the latter are dignified by brick and metal-arched entrances. Contrast and variety are introduced by the 15 or so brick houses which stand out, literally and figuratively, offset at the end of the terraces.

Elwy Road is striking, first of all, for its open, airy feel and the distant views offered by its sloping site of the sea to the north. A closer look reveals picturesque detail. Those long terraces are enlivened by a mix of curved and pointed pedimented porchways; the end-of-terrace houses have their own rather grander broken pediment entrances featuring the arms of the borough council. Colwyn Foulkes allegedly had some money left over from the building work and commissioned his friend George Thomas Capstick, a Liverpool sculptor, to create the figures based on characters from Lewis Carroll and Edward Lear which adorn some of the homes. In 1956, Frank Lloyd Wright, in North Wales to receive an honorary degree from Bangor University, met Colwyn Foulkes and visited Elwy Road. He declared it 'perfectly charming'.[64]

Left top
A corner house at the junction of Maes Glas and Bryn Eglwys

Left bottom
The Mad Hatter, a George Thomas Capstick ceramic

Right
Entrance to rear service road

New Towns and expanded towns

The origins of the postwar programme of New Towns are found in the Garden City ideals of Ebenezer Howard, but the latter were given sharp focus by the economic blight and environmental squalor of the Great Depression. The report of the Barlow Commission on the Distribution of the Industrial Population in 1940 advocated the decentralisation of industry, with new and more diverse employment provided in new towns planned on Garden City lines. Three years later, *The County of London Plan* urged that half a million of the capital's congested population be resettled, some to an expansion of the existing programme of 'out-of-county' estates but around 380,000 to a ring of satellite towns located beyond the Green Belt. Social democracy, in the form of the Labour Party's first majority government, passed the 1946 New Towns Act and created the apparatus of quangos – development corporations – that would implement the programme.

Sociologically, the great goal was mixed community. As the Minister of Town and Country Planning, Lewis Silkin, declared in 1946, 'we must not make them towns inhabited by people of one income level and that the lowest. A new series of Becontrees would be fatal'.[65]

In planning terms, the early New Towns incorporated the conventional wisdom of the day, notably in their zoning of different functional areas and the neighbourhood units into which were most were divided. Their housing was typically low-rise and low-density – a suburbanism that was harshly criticised by some contemporary architectural commentators. Harlow was the subject of particular criticism for what Gordon Cullen called its 'prairie planning'.[66] J.M. Richards concluded that the New Towns were 'little more than housing estates', comprising 'for the most part of scattered two-storey dwellings, separated by great spaces'.[67]

The Conservative governments of the 1950s were in any case hostile to what they viewed as the corporatist and statist nature of the New Town programme and instead promoted, in their 1952 Town Development Act, a system of 'expanded towns' resting on bilateral agreements between 'exporting' authorities (principally London) and 'importing'. Swindon, Aylesbury and Bletchley were among the first expanded towns.

As inner-city slum clearance and redevelopment grew apace in the 1960s, a second – Mark II – generation of New Towns was designated, including Telford and Redditch in the Midlands, and Milton Keynes – the largest – in the Home Counties. In Northern Ireland, where sectarian politics had previously hindered progress, Craigavon was designated in 1965.

The New Town programme limped on, but by the 1970s, as the political focus shifted to the regeneration of the inner cities, its star was waning. Surviving Development Corporations were wound up in the 1980s and their assets controversially divested.

Crawley New Town, West Sussex

Crawley was the second of the postwar New Towns to be designated, in January 1947, on a 6,047-acre site well placed on strategic communications routes 30 miles south of London. The goal, in the words of its masterplanner, Anthony Minoprio, was to 'build a socially and economically balanced town of 50,000 inhabitants within the short space of fifteen years'.[68] Construction began in 1950; by the end of 1962, 13,596 houses had been completed, of which 10,968 had been built by Crawley Development Corporation.

In most respects, the overall vision for Crawley replicated that of most of its generation of New Towns. The town, for example, was divided into nine neighbourhood centres, though these – with an average population of 5,250 – were smaller than the norm. It was, as Minoprio said, 'an advantage of these comparatively small neighbourhoods that the distance from the perimeter to the neighbourhood centre is rarely more than 10 minutes' walk'. The local centres typically comprised 'a row of shops, or shops on two sides of a square, with a public house at one end and a church at the other, and the primary school either opposite or nearby'.[69] A new town centre was constructed adjacent to that of old Crawley. A 264-acre industrial zone was located to the north of the town.

The layout of the residential areas and the housing itself, overseen by Chief Architect A.G. Sheppard Fidler, was also fairly typical. So-called Group I houses, terraced and semi-detached, for rental only, formed 80% of the early stock; semi-detached Group II houses, for rental or sale to the middle classes, formed 15%. A smaller number of detached homes were built for sale to managers and executives. Most of the housing was built along curving streets or cul-de-sacs, or sometimes set back around green squares. Sheppard Fidler's housing closes in West Green received a Ministry of Housing award in 1952.

Left
Weald Drive,
Furnace Green,
1967

Opposite top
The Twittens, West
Green, 1961

**Opposite bottom
left**
Flats in the
Northgate
neighbourhood,
1952

**Opposite bottom
right**
Shrublands,
Furnace Green,
1970

Three-quarters of homes were three-bedroom family houses and just 3% were flats, reflecting the development corporation's research, finding that tenants moving 'to the country to live … almost universally prefer a house with a garden'.[70] This was, therefore, low-density suburban housing, generally at no more than 10 to 16 homes to the acre.

Crawley grew rapidly and prospered. Its light engineering and service industries expanded at a rate that at times threatened to outpace its population growth, and very few of the new residents – 82% had moved from Greater London – wished to return to old haunts. With the middle classes forming around 17% of the town's overall population (compared to 20% nationally), it broadly achieved its goal of a socially mixed population. The development corporation was wound up in 1962, a mark of its early success.

Now Crawley boasts 14 neighbourhoods and a population of around 110,000. The present town stands as a testimony to the ambition and expertise of an earlier generation of planners given the power and means to implement an idealistic vision that many would now judge utopian.

Cwmbran New Town, South Wales

In 1951, as the draft plan for the New Town of Cwmbran was published, Thomas Henry Huxley-Turner, the chair of its development corporation, declared its intention 'to provide a self-contained town with a character of its own, and not a glorified housing estate'.[71] It should be 'a happy, friendly and pleasing place which will set a standard of what an industrial town should be'.[72]

In that regard, Cwmbran, in the South Wales valleys, was distinct among most of the early New Towns in having an existing industrial base, employing within its designated 3,160-acre site alone some 6,500 people. A major steelworks lay just beyond its borders. The primary intention here was to provide – alongside a broader range of jobs – better-quality homes and an improved environment.

That task was first entrusted to Anthony Minoprio, working with Hugh Spencely and Peter Macfarlane, who had impressed the corporation with his work at Crawley. Like Crawley, his proposed masterplan envisaged smaller neighbourhood units, seven in all, averaging 5,000 in population, each featuring the usual retail and community facilities.

Bottom
Housing at Llanfrechfa, photographed in 1960

Opposite left
Cwmbran New Town masterplan, 1951

Opposite right
The Tower, 2018

A History of Council Housing in 100 Estates

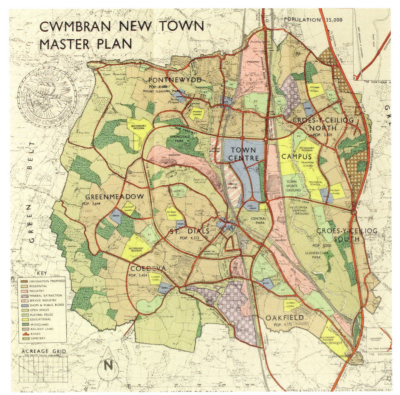

Construction began in 1952. Ten years later, 6,750 new homes had been built, 4,728 by the development corporation. As in Crawley, flats were deemed unpopular, though in Cwmbran they were to form a larger 10% of the initial housing stock. Given an often steeply sloping terrain, terraced housing following the contours was thought the most appropriate housing form in many parts of the town, as elsewhere in Wales. There were attempts to escape a stereotyped 'council estate' feel, however, notably in the mono-pitched housing of the Coed Eva neighbourhood and the flat roofs in Greenmeadow. Despite architectural acclaim at the time, neither were popular in the longer term, and flat roofs came to be judged unsuited to the Welsh climate. Nevertheless, with careful attention to providing a range of cladding and high-quality landscaping, much was achieved to create an attractive housing environment.

The civic centre designed in 1963 by Gordon Redfern, the development corporation's recently appointed Chief Architect, was another statement of intent. This was a Modernist scheme adjacent to the exiting shopping centre, comprising council offices, courts, swimming baths, a multi-storey car park and a 23-storey residential point block (called The Tower), intended very much as a local landmark though practically it provided a 64-m chimney for the local district heating scheme. As ever, for many of the early residents, basic pleasures trumped such show: 'to come down to Cwmbran and suddenly find you had a lovely inside toilet that you didn't have to go down the garden to use – we couldn't believe it'.[73]

By 2011, the town's population exceeded 48,000 and, in general, Cwmbran – with its thriving shopping centre, good-quality housing and notably green environment – has fared far better than many of its near neighbours hard hit by industrial decline.[74]

Top
Cwmbran Development Corporation housing at Hassocks Lea in the Fairwater neighbourhood

Bottom
Cwmbran Development Corporation at Teynes in the Coedeva neighbourhood

A History of Council Housing in 100 Estates

Cumbernauld New Town, North Lanarkshire, Scotland

Cumbernauld, designated in 1955, was the first of the Mark II New Towns and its design represented a decisive break from those that preceded it. This lay in part in its location, a 4,150-acre site on difficult hilly terrain 14 miles northeast of Glasgow. But more significantly, it resulted from the radically urbanist ideas of its planners.

The 1946 *Clyde Valley Regional Plan* had led to the creation of Scotland's first New Town in East Kilbride in 1947. Glasgow's continuing housing crisis led to the reconvening of the Clyde Valley Planning Advisory Committee in 1953 and its subsequent recommendation that a New Town, housing a projected population of 50,000, be built at Cumbernauld.

From the outset, the *Planning Proposals* of its largely English design team led by Hugh Wilson, published in 1958, envisaged 'a tight urban place, suitable for a hilltop' with 'a single multipurpose town centre'.[75] This was, in its embrace of urbanity, a conscious rejection of the 'villagey' neighbourhood units which until then had dominated postwar planning. A second key element, reflecting the affluence of a newly car-owning populace, was mobility. The two would be combined in the most thoroughly Modernist application of Radburn principles to date.

Left
Cumbernauld town centre in the 1960s

Right
Seafar housing glimpsed from Cumbernauld town centre, 1967

Wilson appointed two group leaders, Geoffrey Copcutt, overseeing the design of the town centre, and Derek Lyddon, in charge of housing. The 'megastructure' forming the town centre – a single building combining retail, leisure, civic offices

and housing (in the form of executive penthouses) and integrating a vertical separation of cars and pedestrians – remains Cumbernauld's signature and highly controversial landmark. Flaws in design and delivery contributed to a troubled history, and parts have since been demolished.

The New Town's housing was not unlike that of some of its predecessors. It was predominantly two-storey terraced homes (though with a greater proportion of multi-storey flatted blocks), but its 'architectural form and layout were treated in a far more dense and place-specific way ... The governing concept of space was one of enclosed space in the manner of Camillo Sitte rather than open or flowing space'.[76] The results are best seen in the high-density grid of flat-roofed, grey-rendered homes in Carbrain and the grouped blocks of Kildrum 5. Several of the tower blocks are in the same area; some – Bison system-built – since demolished. A very different, far more suburban, northern extension to Cumbernauld was created when further expansion was authorised in 1973.

In 1967, Cumbernauld was awarded the Reynolds Memorial Award for Community Architecture by the American Institute of Architects, which praised it as 'undoubtedly the most comprehensive project of community architecture to date'.[77] Though beloved by Modernists, overall opinion of the town is far more divided – though it has fared better and is generally better liked by residents than Glasgow's huge peripheral estates built in the same era.

Left
Terraced housing and play area, Kildrum 1, 1960

Right
Flatted blocks, Kildrum 5, 1960

A History of Council Housing in 100 Estates

Thetford, Norfolk

In the 1950s, Thetford in south Norfolk was a dying town. Its population of 4,447 was almost identical to that of the town in its heyday some nine centuries earlier; its major employer – the agricultural machinery and steam engine works of Charles Burrell – had closed in 1928. The borough council was desperate for the promise held out by the legislation passed in 1952 by the new Conservative government 'to encourage Town Development in County districts for the relief of congestion and overpopulation elsewhere'.

The London County Council was initially unsympathetic to the town's entreaties, put off by its small-town air and distance. But Thetford had in its favour a single large landowner (the Crown) to aid expansion, and proximity to the North Sea ports, though allegedly 'what finally won over the hearts of the London councillors was a plea by a Thetford woman councillor that "even taking on another dustman meant putting sixpence on the rates"'.[78]

In May 1957, it was agreed that the LCC would build some 1,500 new council homes in Thetford to house a population of 5,000 moving from the capital. In fact, around 3,500 new homes were built by the late 1970s.

The bedrock of this progress was employment – the 1953 Industrial Selection Scheme guaranteed some on the LCC's council housing waiting list both a job and a home. By 1966, 46 companies had set up in Thetford – some moving from London with their workforces, many occupying factories built and owned by the borough council.

Left
Kimms Belt,
Barnham Cross
Common Estate

Right
Radburn layout,
Redcastle Furze
Estate

The first housing was completed on the Barnham Cross Common Estate in April 1959 – suburban homes and low-rise flatted blocks executed in conventional form, built to the south of the town centre. The next estate, comprising some 800 homes built between 1963 and 1970, Redcastle Furze, was more innovative in both its Radburn layout and its preponderance of system-built Greater London Council 'Anglia Houses' – the latter assembled on site from factory-made concrete cross-wall units and timber panels.

Tellingly, however, in Abbey Farm to the north – the last and largest of the new estates built by the Greater London Council between 1967 and 1971, initial plans for a Radburn scheme were abandoned: 'early experience with the Redcastle Furze Estate indicated that … it had some drawbacks, e.g. visitors found difficulty in finding their way around'.[79] Instead, the estate was equipped with a spinal road, Canterbury Way, fringed by large four-storey maisonette blocks while narrow-frontage two- and three-storey houses were laid out along small cul-de-sacs leading from it.

The incomers generally adapted well; many thought 'that on the housing estate there was a much friendlier atmosphere than in London and that one got to know one's neighbours better than in a big city'.[80] Later Thetford would suffer the problems of industrial decline common to many older towns, and consequent social tensions. To some, this testament to an era of progressive modernisation has become an 'island of deprivation'.[81] The town, and its current population of around 24,500, continues to adapt.

Top
Canterbury Way,
Abbey Farm Estate

Bottom
Town houses off
Canterbury Way,
Abbey Farm Estate

A History of Council Housing in 100 Estates

Rural council housing

The housing conditions of the working class in rural areas were typically as bad, if not worse, than those in towns and cities, but rural local authorities were often less able and less willing to build council housing than their urban counterparts. While the national housing legislation of the day applied to both urban and rural districts, there had also been some efforts in the interwar period to address the specific problems of the countryside. The 1924 Housing Act provided a higher Treasury contribution to housing in 'agricultural parishes' than those in towns. The 1926 Housing (Rural Authorities) Act provided grants to rural landlords for the reconditioning of substandard properties though with little impact. The 1936 Housing Act, providing rural district councils an up to 80% subsidy on the costs of construction of housing for agricultural workers, provided a breakthrough; around 159,000 council homes were built in rural areas before 1939, many of these after 1936.

The Second World War's emphasis on domestic food production and self-sufficiency increased concern, manifest in a 1944 Hobhouse Report of the Central Housing Advisory Committee's subcommittee on rural housing. It recommended a comprehensive survey of rural housing conditions, to be completed within a year of the end of the war, and increased subsidy for agricultural workers' housing. Incomplete returns from the 476 rural districts revealed that at least 160,000 houses warranted demolition and replacement, and a further 400,000 substantial repair. Of almost a million council homes built by 1953, 22% were in rural districts, a slightly higher rate than their proportion of population, 19%.

Of the houses built before and after the war, few were of particular architectural merit. While sporadic attempts were made to build in a more vernacular style using local materials, most were brick-built in conventional boxy neo-Georgian form, often located in short terraces and cul-de-sacs on village peripheries. A programme of construction of prefabricated concrete Airey Houses was implemented in rural and mining districts to meet the immediate postwar crisis. Meanwhile the Ministry of Health's 1949 *Housing Manual* promoted best practice – in terms of well-designed and 'in-keeping' schemes carried out by, among others, Bowland and Ulverston Rural District Councils in the Lake District and Witney, Upton-upon-Severn and Sturminster in the south. The more Modernist designs of Tayler and Green in south Norfolk also featured heavily.

This brief heyday was mitigated from the 1950s by less generous housing policies and by the changing demographics of the countryside, where mechanisation contributed to rural depopulation already in train as low-paid agricultural workers and their children migrated to more affluent towns. A great deal of later council housing in rural areas took the form of housing for an elderly population.

Tayler and Green housing, South Norfolk

Between 1948 and 1974, the architects Herbert Tayler and David Green designed some 687 houses, bungalows and flats for Loddon Rural District Council in south Norfolk, and created what Ian Nairn described as 'a set of council houses unequalled in the whole country'.[82]

In many respects, Loddon was a typical rural authority with a low-paid and poorly housed population. Fifty-three per cent of its workforce laboured on the land in the 1950s; some 83% of households were reliant on pail closets. The council, initially comprising principally local gentry, tradesmen and clergymen, was also typical, but reform-minded. A growing Labour presence – in 1957 it was the first wholly rural authority to come under Labour control – cemented its progressive politics. Above all, however, the council was, in the words of Herbert Tayler, 'an excellent client in every respect, but particularly in this, that they never fussed over architectural matters, but stated their opinions freely and then left it to us'.[83]

While the council had made the usual use of prefabrication to address the immediate postwar crisis, Tayler and Green were determined that their customised designs should be based on a close 'study of rural requirements' down to the rural workers' muddy boots and likely use of a bicycle.[84] Hence, in their first commissioned schemes, Leman Grove in Loddon and College Road in Thurton, front and back doors were replaced by a single side entry and roofed passage connected to a large outside store. More schemes followed, increasingly featuring bungalows suited to an ageing population.

Bottom
Houses 1–16, The Boltons, Hales, 1955

Opposite top
Windmill Green, Ditchingham

Opposite bottom left
Corner of Kenyon Row and Forge Grove, Gillingham

Opposite bottom right
Langley Road, Chedgrave

A further innovation – or at least one, in Tayler's words, 'not used in rural districts since the 18th century' – was the use of terraces 'with their advantages of economy, warmth and restful appearance in the landscape'.[85] These are best seen in their third scheme at Windmill Green, Ditchingham in 1949, where 30 terraced houses are arranged in a horseshoe around an expansive open green.

Decorative touches were also felt important, both to add to people's enjoyment of their homes and to ensure 'each site [was] given a marked individuality'. Colour washing was initially used to disguise unattractive Fletton bricks, but implemented more expansively alongside brick patterning and wooden screens, trellises and fretted bargeboards as conditions allowed.

The quality of this unique range of rural council housing dotted around the villages and hamlets of the south Norfolk countryside was recognised by five Festival of Britain Merit Awards, three awards from the Ministries of Health and Housing, two Civic Trust awards and a RIBA Bronze Medal.

Early multi-storey

The shift to high-rise occurred in a paradoxically stealthy fashion. It was foretold in the focus on inner-city tenement construction before the war. It was implied *sotto voce* in wartime and postwar reconstruction plans that required higher central population densities. It was boosted practically and aesthetically by the new emphasis on mixed development.

A decisive shift occurred in the mid-1950s. The already questioned concentration on family housing was strengthened by the postwar rise in households and increase in smaller households as life expectancy and divorce rates rose. At the same time, there was growing criticism, codified in the Green Belt policies established by a number of conurbations and cities, of urban sprawl and consequent loss of agricultural land and open space.

The high cost of urban land – alongside improved space standards, new zoning regulations and slum clearance itself (which all reduced housing density) – combined to incentivise higher-density, multi-storey construction in the inner cities. The 1955 RIBA Symposium on High Flats, which noted the range of factors 'compelling a growing number of authorities to consider the contribution that the building of high flats can make to their housing and reconstruction programme' gave both recognition and, in its way, licence to this emerging trend.[86]

There were other, less tangible, dynamics too. High-rise blocks had an air of modernity that appealed to some planners and councillors; in some cases local authorities seemed in competition to build higher and more impressive schemes. In most cases, though not all, the assumption remained that higher blocks would not house young families, and many new residents welcomed the fresh air and views – and always improved space and conveniences – that their new flats offered.

The 1956 Housing Subsidies Act, which provided greater financial support to local authorities the higher they built over six storeys, is sometimes crudely blamed for the boom in residential high-rise construction which succeeded it, but is better understood as both a cause and consequence of this broader evolution. In 1956, only 6% of new public housing approvals were for blocks of six storeys or more. They formed just over a quarter at their peak 10 years later before a precipitous fall from grace.

Redcliffe Flats, Redcliffe Hill, Bristol

The Redcliffe district southeast of Bristol city centre, heavily bombed during the Second World War, was earmarked for redevelopment as early as 1945 when the city council agreed proposals that it be set aside as 'a housing area for key workers'. Plans were formalised for what the Housing Committee chair, Alderman Charles Gill, described as this 'tremendous and interesting project' in December 1949, though construction finally began some three years later.[87]

On this occasion, City Architect J. Nelson Meredith rejected the contemporary fashion for mixed development in favour of a scheme of flatted blocks, the deciding factor apparently being the intention to provide an innovative district heating system for the scheme as a whole. Laundries were provided in each of the main blocks. However, accommodation was mixed, with around one-fifth of the homes comprising bedsits and one-bedroom flats, and around three-fifths two- and three-bedroom flats and maisonettes.

Bottom
Waring House to the left and a distant view of St Mary Redcliffe; care was taken to preserve and enhance existing views of the medieval church

In terms of design and construction, Bristol pursued the individualistic approach that would mark the longer history of its high-rise. The six-storey Canynge House, containing the heating scheme boilers, was the first built, commended by one observer for its 'refreshingly uncompromising modernity ... an interesting foil to the medieval grandeur of St Mary Redcliffe' to the rear.[88] (Later observers

might raise an eyebrow that later phases were to commence 'after the pulling down of some adjacent streets of low grade or blighted late Georgian house property'.) It, like its successors, was essentially a balcony-access slab block, but its appearance was enlivened by alternating bands of brickwork and varnished boarding and two end walls of squared, undressed stone.

The 13-storey, three-winged Waring House followed, an imposing presence beyond the city's Bedminster Bridge and similarly distinguished by a contrasting range of brick, stone and terrazzo finishes. Seven further blocks, ranging from eight to 13 storeys in height, completed the overall scheme in the early 1960s.

Early residents, many employed centrally and some moving from more distant council suburbs, professed themselves generally happy with their new homes, though the heating scheme was said to be somewhat more expensive than its solid fuel equivalent, and some found the spaces allowed 'for the collection of pig food and inedible refuse ... unsatisfactory'.[89] The architects, for their part, regretted the unsuitably old-fashioned and bulky furniture favoured by residents.

Bristol would go on to build high-rise on a substantial scale – by 1971, 55 high blocks of 10 storeys or more formed 14% of its total housing stock – but it would generally continue to eschew the more off-the-peg and concentrated schemes of many of its counterparts.

Left
An architect's sketch of proposed garaging to the rear of Waring House

Right
Waring House today

Opposite top
The estate as planned in 1956

Opposite bottom
An architect's drawing of one of the blocks, showing the variety of materials employed

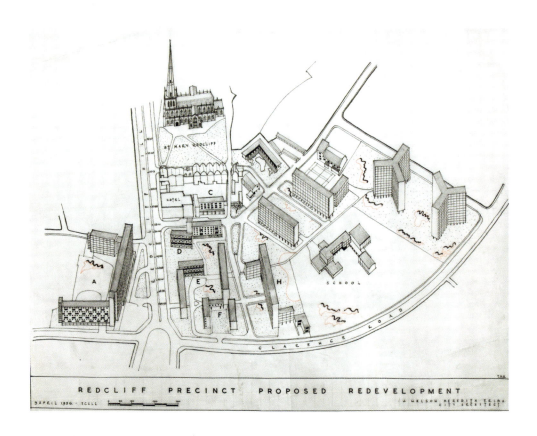

REDCLIFF   PRECINCT   PROPOSED   REDEVELOPMENT

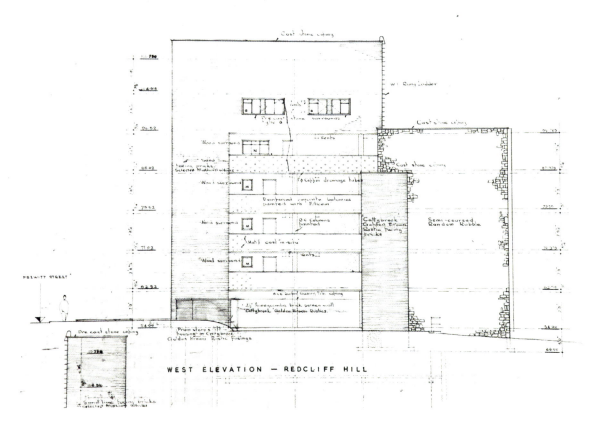

WEST ELEVATION — REDCLIFF HILL

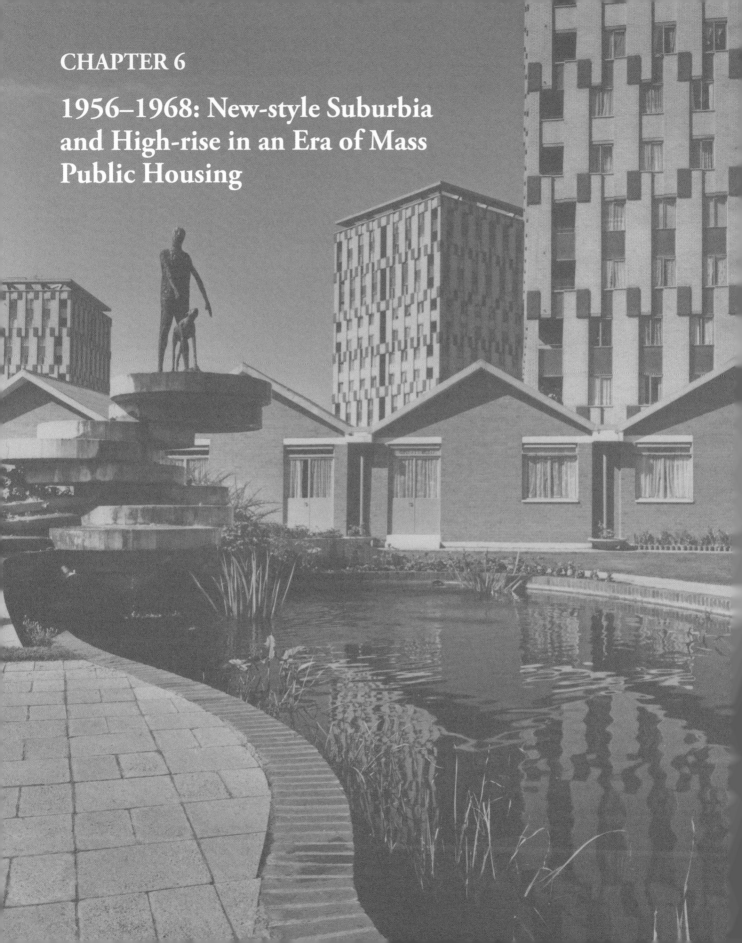

CHAPTER 6

1956–1968: New-style Suburbia and High-rise in an Era of Mass Public Housing

In 1948, a Ministry of Works survey found that 54% of British households lacked their own bathroom, 15% had no water-heating appliance and 7% lacked even piped water.[1] Early postwar efforts had necessarily focused on repairing and replacing bomb-damaged homes but, from the mid-1950s as economic conditions normalised, the drive to clear the slums and build anew was renewed and intensified.

This mass public housing drive is inextricably linked in popular perceptions with high-rise. In fact, most new council homes continued to be two-storey houses of more or less traditional form, and high-rise approvals (of blocks of five storeys or more) peaked numerically in Scotland in 1965 at 28% of the total and in England and Wales in 1966 at around 26%.[2] By the end of the decade, high-rise construction had fallen precipitately.

The environmental and planning factors that caused this more modest but nevertheless real and undoubtedly eye-catching shift to multi-storey construction were discussed in the last chapter. The 1956 subsidy regime which provided local authorities a higher subsidy the higher they built added its own impetus. A political arms race in the 1960s between the major parties to build more housing increased momentum – a Conservative White Paper of 1963 pledged 350,000 new homes a year; by 1966, Labour was promising a 500,000. Locally, councils and powerful councillors vied to build more and increasingly (until a modified subsidy regime was introduced in 1967) to build higher – blocks of

15 storeys or more formed over 8% of approvals in 1964. System building seemed to offer a modern, technocratic means towards promised ends, and 'off the peg' solutions to those in a hurry. The self-conscious modernity evinced in these new forms of prefabrication was another powerful, though less tangible, driver of the public housing forms of the era.

Architecturally, Modernism was the style of the day. Some architect-designed schemes were explicitly Brutalist in conception and design, though that descriptor was applied more widely and pejoratively by hostile observers. Mixed development remained a core planning ideal but was often implemented crudely. The quest for 'community', renewed as traditional terraces were cleared in ever greater numbers, found a new would-be solution in the 'streets in the sky' of some innovative deck-access developments.

The Central Housing Advisory Committee's Parker Morris Report of 1961, 'Homes for today and tomorrow', spoke to a less controversial modernity. Rising living standards, it concluded, were leading to 'an easier, more varied and more enjoyable home life' for much of the British population – a change it urged should be reflected and fulfilled in new, more spacious and centrally heated homes that facilitated more flexible and leisured lifestyles. Parker Morris standards were applied to new public housing in the New Towns in 1967 and council housing generally in 1969. (They were adopted voluntarily by the new London boroughs formed in 1965.) It was hoped that private developers would emulate this new standard.

New-style suburban estates (and a 'New City')

As inner-city redevelopment took off, new estates on peripheral and greenfield sites remained significant, both in resettling a displaced population that could not be rehoused centrally and in providing the conventional family homes still in great demand. But, in contrast to the characteristically low-rise, almost uniformly two-storeyed form of the interwar estates, the new generation of suburban estates were mixed in housing form and type. Low-rise housing catered mainly for families and elderly people. Point blocks were still in principle usually intended for households without young children, though waiting list pressures easily overcame such scruples. They added variety and contrast to otherwise sprawling estates and were held to increase housing density. (The latter belief, though rarely challenged, was largely mistaken due to the surrounding open space required by high-rise blocks to avoid overshadowing and overlooking.)

Such a mix could be achieved with some flair and style when planner- and architect-led, as it was when implemented by the London County Council, whose Architect's Department was then the largest architectural practice in the world, and Sheffield City Council, for example. Tellingly, the planning for both the Alton and Gleadless Valley Estates began in the early to mid-1950s. As pressures grew to build rapidly and at scale, and where councils possessed fewer resources or simply chose to prioritise quantity over quality, results could be more variable. Birmingham, working closely (corruptly in some cases) with favoured developers, focused on numbers and chose to deploy system-built blocks quite haphazardly across the city until, by 1971, almost two-thirds of the council's 464 tower blocks were located in the suburbs, along or beyond the city's ring road.

While individual homes almost invariably provided better amenities and increased space to most new residents, the estates themselves often suffered poorer facilities and weaker transport links than the areas from which most had moved. The chronological and financial priority given to housing above supporting infrastructure was a problem that afflicted even the supposed 'New City' of Craigavon in Northern Ireland.

Gleadless Valley Estate, Sheffield

When it comes to Sheffield, most architectural enthusiasts will be familiar with Park Hill (see page 167), but some have called the Gleadless Valley Estate, three miles to the southeast and built between 1955 and 1966, 'the supreme, but often overlooked achievement' of then City Architect Lewis Womersley.[3]

Both were part of Sheffield's exhilarating 1952 development plan, which estimated that the city needed 35,000 new homes; 20,000 to replace existing unfit housing, and 15,000 to cater for increased population. The council aimed to meet this objective with some panache and daring, and the city's hilly terrain provided both obstacle and opportunity. 'Sheffield's situation at the centre of a landscape of hills and slopes was to be visually integrated, united, through public housing.[4] Harold Lambert, powerful chair of the Housing Committee, envisaged the emergence of 'something of the fascination of the Italian hill towns'.[5]

This would be achieved in part by the placing of landmark tower blocks at the city's high points. In the Gleadless Valley, six point blocks were erected at Callow Point and three (two survive) in the Herdings district at either end of the valley. Here, as elsewhere, Womersley applied his favourite maxim from the landscape architect 'Capability' Brown to 'flood the valleys, plant the tops'.

As to the 'flooding' of the valley, after an aerial survey and slope analysis of the site, it was determined to preserve some 161 of its 267 acres as parkland and woods and create three neighbourhoods to emerge naturally from the topography – Hemsworth, Herdings and Rollestone, each with its own schools and shopping centre.

The housing itself had to be similarly adapted. Womersley established teams of architects with specific briefs – some to design two-storey homes, some maisonettes, some elderly people's housing and so on – to create a truly mixed development with forms appropriate to the landscape in the various parts of the estate. What emerged, according to Lionel Esher, was 'every kind of ingenious hill-climbing or adjustable dwelling capable of being entered at any level'.[6]

Left
Aerial view, early 1960s

Right
A view from Constable Road showing the three original Herdings towers, 1963

The patio houses on Spotswood Mount were nicknamed the 'upside-down houses' for their upstairs living rooms providing sweeping views of the valley below. Elsewhere, sloped terraces of more conventional two-storey housing were another means of coping with the terrain. More plainly, so were the three-storey cluster blocks adapted to existing contours and the six-storey blocks along Blackstock and Ironside Roads, where a bridged entrance at second-floor level obviated the need for lifts.

While the detail impresses, it is the ensemble that earns Gleadless Valley its superlatives. *The Times* in 1969 described it as 'touched with the English genius for country things'.[7] Keith Marriott, who grew up on the estate and was later an architect himself, remembers it as 'a fine and humane place to grow up in the 60s and 70s … the relationship between its architecture and Sheffield's topography and landscape … an inspiring one'.[8]

Top
Morland Road shopping centre and Herdings point blocks, 1963

Left
Six-storey blocks with second-floor entrance, Blackstock Road

Right
Patio ('upside-down') houses, Spotswood Mount

Alton East and West, Roehampton, Wandsworth, London

The Alton Estate was 'probably the finest low-cost housing development in the world' in the eyes of one contemporary American commentator. It epitomised the clash within the LCC's Architect's Department between the 'soft' New Humanists who, taking their inspiration from the housing of the Scandinavian welfare state, designed its eastern component and the 'hard' Brutalists, looking to Le Corbusier, who designed its western.[9] Its 130-acre site, purchased by the council in the late 1940s, comprised in the words of Nikolaus Pevsner 'fine eighteenth-century mansions in their grounds and many Victorian villas in their gardens'. Their replacement, he concluded, 'standing securely in a modern European tradition of town planning that reaches back into the early twenties, and equally securely in an English landscape tradition that goes back almost two centuries further', provided 'one of the masterpieces of post-war residential design'.[10]

Alton East (originally Portsmouth Road), designed by a team led by Rosemary Stjernstedt and including A.W. Cleeve Barr and Oliver Cox, was built between 1952 and 1955 – a mix of low-rise terraces and maisonette blocks and 10 11-storey point blocks deployed amid mature trees on the footprint of those Victorian villas, 744 homes in all. The point blocks are in situ reinforced concrete structures with a grey brick facing, located on higher ground at the southern edge of the estate, offering a benign contrast to the traditionally constructed housing below. Staggered terraces, such as those in Horndean Close with a range of brick and painted finishes and the individual detailing applied throughout to entrances and end walls, combined to fulfil the picturesque New Humanist ideal.

Left
Alton East from the air, late 1950s

Right
Alton East: 11-storey point blocks

The larger Alton West (Roehampton Lane), comprising 1,867 homes, followed between 1955 and 1959. Here the site's parkland setting encouraged a more monumentalist approach, one that in any case sat easily with its design team, led by Colin Lucas, inspired by an earlier visit to Le Corbusier's Unité d'Habitation in Marseille. The five 11-storey slab blocks ranged on the hillside above Danebury Avenue are its most obvious impact, though their present

oblique orientation owes more to Housing Minister Harold Macmillan, who rejected original plans for what he viewed as a 'continuous wall' facing Richmond Park; the result gained 'dramatically in architectural power at the expense of the residents' views'.[11] Some 15 11-storey point blocks and lower-rise housing – most notably the tiny studio-bungalows for elderly residents along Minstead Gardens – complete the ensemble.

This was, across both parts of the estate, an embodiment of the mixed development ideal – 40% houses and maisonettes, 60% flats, in a rich and contrasting range of forms and heights. And while the estate lacks any formal centre – the shopping parade at the eastern end of Danebury Avenue comes closest – a district heating system, community centre and new schools sought to bring coherence to this new estate of 9,500 residents.

Clockwise from top left
Alton East: terraced houses in Horndean Close

Alton West: 11-storey slab blocks

Alton West: a contemporary view of the Danebury Avenue slab blocks

Alton West: old people's bungalows and 12-storey point blocks

Cranbrook Estate, Roman Road, Tower Hamlets, London

The Cranbrook Estate was the last major work of Berthold Lubetkin and it remains, despite modern depredations, a fitting tribute to the Constructivist belief that technology and design could be harnessed to improve working-class lives that this left-wing Soviet émigré 'artist-engineer' brought to his work.

Bethnal Green was a decidedly poor and working-class borough, but one with a Labour-controlled council determined not only to rehouse its population but also to do so in some style. In this, it was aided by one of its more elite members, the alderman Peter Benenson, a personal friend of Lubetkin's, who persuaded the council to appoint a panel of some of the leading Modernist architectural practices of the day to design its schemes that included Powell & Moya, Yorke Rosenberg Mardall, and Fry, Drew, Drake & Lasdun. Their designs can be found dotted around the borough.

Skinner, Bailey and Lubetkin (a regrouping of the pre-war Tecton Group that had designed the Spa Green Estate in Finsbury) were appointed to design what became the Cranbrook Estate in 1955. The compulsory purchase of a 17-acre site of decayed Victorian terraces and workshops was agreed two years later. The 1,600 residents displaced were guaranteed places on the new estate.

Left
The old people's communal gardens and ornamental pond with the statue *The Blind Beggar and his Dog* by Elisabeth Frink, photographed in 1964

Right
Point blocks, 1964

Left
Two-storey flatted
blocks, Cranbrook
Estate

Right
St Gilles House
staircase

The first homes were officially opened in 1963; the scheme as a whole
was completed in 1966. John Allan describes the scheme as Lubetkin's
'most ambitious achievement in urban orchestration, an essay in controlled
complexity'.[12] That is apparent, firstly, in its scale – six high towers, five medium-
rise blocks and a range of low-rise; 529 new homes in total. The complexity is
seen in their arrangement. Set along two diagonal axes (now more a figure of
eight), the buildings progressively reduce in height from 15 storeys to 13 to 11
in the towers, to four- and five-storey in the maisonette blocks, to two-storey
terraces and finally – in a conscious *diminuendo* – to the single-storey old
people's bungalows on the estate's Roman Road frontage.

Original plans that the rear of the estate should open on to Victoria Park were
scuppered, and now only the bare vestiges of Lubetkin's compensating *trompe
l'oeil* – a tapering ramp and series of diminishing hoops to give the illusion of
a distant vista – remain. Elisabeth Frink's statue of *The Blind Beggar and his
Dog* on Roman Road survives. Lubetkin's patterned facades have also been
diminished; steel shutters cover the deep openings which originally marked
the towers, green concrete bosses and glass beads have been replaced by
aluminium boxes. But something of his unique aesthetic vision lingers – Allan
suggests a 'synthesis of the Constructivist and classical traditions' – and is seen
(if you can get inside) most powerfully in the signature towering stairwells of the
higher point blocks.

Chinbrook Estate, Lewisham, London

The Chinbrook Estate represents one of the finest examples of 1960s estate planning in the country. Earlier responses to the housing needs of the heavily bombed area had necessarily been more immediate and short-term in the form of 1,484 temporary prefab bungalows, of which 209 were erected on an area of farmland between Grove Park Road and Marvels Lane. As these were finally cleared in the early 1960s, the LCC planned a model estate integrating some of the key planning ideals of the day.

Firstly, it was a Radburn estate, not in its purest form (some of the housing faces on to the several service roads which pierce the estate) but perhaps a more successful hybrid given the compactness of the overall scheme. Around half the homes were provided with garages – a high proportion for the time, reflecting rising working-class living standards.

Bottom
The estate in pristine condition, 1963

Secondly, it embodied mixed development principles. Two 11-storey point blocks, situated on the northern and southern fringes of the estate, provided 177 homes of the scheme's 395 in total. Two-storey terraced housing supplied family accommodation, while low-rise flats were built for couples without

children and elderly people. There was recognition of neighbourhood and community ideals, with the provision of a clubroom for the elderly and a state-of-the-art youth centre.

In the event, the estate was completed, after the abolition of the LCC in 1965, by the Greater London Council (GLC) and was seen as one of its showpieces. It was featured in a delegate visit of the Housing Centre's annual conference in 1967 and celebrated in a council publication, *GLC Architecture 1965/70*. The Civic Trust offered an independent endorsement when it commended the estate in 1967. The trust noted how the 'elevations have been consistently and simply handled in red brick and white shiplap boarding' and created 'a pleasant and bright background to the well-proportioned pedestrian ways and squares formed by the layout ... the landscaping, both hard and soft, [was] well detailed and has been carried through with functional simplicity'.[13] (Right to Buy 'improvements' have unfortunately weakened the estate's overall aesthetic and appearance.)

It all, the trust concluded, illustrated 'the tremendous improvement in environment and standard of living which results through the segregated layout, open-space amenities, well-proportioned pedestrian streets and effective landscaping' – a contrast it drew with earlier and more conventional surrounding estates. The estate also bears comparison in form, layout and quality to some of the Span housing designed for middle-class owner-occupiers by architect Eric Lyons in nearby Blackheath, for example.

The estate was transferred to the London and Quadrant housing association in 2008, and the old people's clubroom was demolished shortly after. Fortunately, a tenacious local campaign has saved the Grove Park Youth Club. Incorporating Bauhaus influences and aspects of Swedish Modernism in its flexible open-plan interior, it's worth a visit in its own right.

Orchard Park, Kingston upon Hull

In 1993, the social policy and housing specialist Anne Power described the Orchard Park Estate, on the far northern fringes of Hull, as 'one of the poorest peripheral estates in Britain'.[14] Planning for the estate began in 1963 under Hull City Architect David Jenkin, who envisaged four 'villages'. The Courts, some 746 traditionally constructed two-storey houses in Radburn layout, was the first 'village' completed, in 1965. The Danes, planned afresh under a new City Architect, J.V. Wall, maintained a Radburn layout but comprised long (many said 'monotonous') terraces of Wimpey 'No Fines' housing. The Shaws, built between 1965 and 1967, saw a return to traditional brick construction. The last completed, in 1969, The Thorpes, was made up of some 500 terraced and semi-detached homes, 48 town houses and three 10-storey point blocks. Eight other tower blocks, ranging from 17 to 22 storeys in height, were dispersed around Orchard Park – a crude form of mixed development intended to add point and contrast to the otherwise low-lying and low-rise estate.

Problems soon emerged. The 'No Fines' housing suffered from condensation and mould and was provided with expensive underfloor heating that combined to make The Danes area in particular hard to let. A broader defect was the estate's crude form of Radburn layout. An early resident recalls 'footpaths that went nowhere and abruptly stopped, pedestrian underpasses that flooded in winter and "landscaping" that had to be navigated both around and over'.[15]

Left
Family homes in a Radburn setting, The Courts

Right
Terraced housing and walkway, The Courts

Orchard Park's peripheral location, compounded by its lack of community facilities, ensured a downward spiral in which Hull's poorest and most vulnerable residents, those with least housing choice, were disproportionately housed on the estate. By the early 1980s, unemployment on the estate stood at 18% and some 90% of estate households were on Housing Benefit.

This was an estate that perhaps justified the adjective 'failing', and it epitomised the defects identified by urbanist and planner Sir Peter Hall of a number of such schemes: poor housing stock, 'an impersonal and alienating physical environment', lack of variety in housing types and sizes, and geographic isolation.[16]

A plethora of regeneration initiatives followed. The earliest, the Priority Estates Project, applied remedies that would become common by implementing area-based housing management and adjustments intended to overcome 'design disadvantage' and improve (in the newly vogueish term) 'defensible space'. Modified lettings policies to alter the estate's demographics confronted housing shortage, and the legal requirement to house those in 'priority need' and were less successful. Three of the tower blocks were demolished in 2002, and the last survivor in 2016 when a thorough renovation of the 'No Fines' homes also commenced.

Orchard Park is now much changed and much improved in terms of housing quality and community provision, but it remains a scheme unusually beset by the flaws of its original conception.

Top
Tower blocks and old people's bungalows in The Danes, photographed in 1984

Bottom
The towers on Thorpepark Road, photographed in 1987

Craigavon New City, County Armagh, Northern Ireland

Craigavon, 30 miles north of Belfast, was the first Northern Irish New Town when officially designated in 1965; in fact, it was optimistically named a 'New City'. Its origins lay in Sir Robert Matthew's 1963 *Belfast Regional Survey and Plan*, which recommended a new settlement taking in the existing towns of Lurgan and Portadown as a means of relieving acute housing and transport pressures in the capital.

Early visions of Craigavon created by the New City Design Team assembled by chief architect Geoffrey Copcutt (recruited from Cumbernauld) depicted new forms of leisure and consumerism, even a monorail transit system. But Northern Ireland's history was a stronger force. The town's location, in a predominantly Protestant area rather than the more depressed, mainly Catholic, west was an initial point of controversy. Copcutt concurred and resigned. Its naming after the first (Unionist) prime minister of Northern Ireland was unpopular with the Nationalist community. The Troubles, erupting just as the town was being developed, exacerbated the sectarian divide.

Nevertheless, initial planning was innovative. Rejecting 'the Corbusier approach', the Craigavon Development Commission's 1967 report proposed a 'Rural City' based on a 'close interrelationship of urban and rural elements'.[17] 'Craigavon will be a linear town with the countryside never more than half a mile from any house, a town of parks and open spaces.'[18] Brownlow, the first (and, in the event, only) neighbourhood to be developed, was envisaged as one of 'a chain of townships of 20,000 population each' connecting Lurgan and Portadown to the new central district of Craigavon itself.

Some early housing was completed in Modernist form (the flat-roofed bungalows of the Old Rectory Park housing area received a Civic Trust award in 1968), but much of it was built hurriedly and defects – ranging from ill-fitting

Bottom
Vision sketch of integrated transport routes, 1967

doors and windows, and leaking roofs to infestations of field mice – were legion. Promised community facilities came a poor second to housing. Despite a £700 grant to move to the New City, relatively few were willing to do so.

The Craigavon Development Commission was wound up in 1973; in 1978, some 50% of the 3,000 acres compulsorily purchased remained undeveloped. The town's major success story, the heavily subsidised Goodyear tyre factory, employing 1,800 at peak, closed in 1983. Craigavon became 'the lost city', famed for its many roundabouts, boarded-up homes and bleak open spaces.[19]

Today, the town – with almost equal numbers of Protestant and Catholic residents – has a population of around 65,000 compared to the 120,000 projected by 1981 in original plans. But significant regeneration has revived the town and provided new employment; a 2017 survey identified it as Northern Ireland's 'most desirable place to live'.[20] Belatedly, and perhaps despite early planning rather than because of it, some of the New City's initial promise has been fulfilled.

Clockwise from top left
Old Rectory Park, 1967

Moylinn play area, 1970

Blocks of flats in Drumgor Heights

Family homes and derelict flats, Westacres

Chelmsley Wood, Solihull, West Midlands

The reputation of Birmingham's Chelmsley Wood Estate has suffered from Lynsey Hanley's description of it as a 'clean, wide-open prison for those who had little choice in the shape, the age or the location of the house they were given'.[21] Hanley's views softened later as she moved from her youthful angst as a teenage resident of the 'Wood'. In fact, the scheme was one of the better planned of the city's peripheral estates, and the choice it accorded its residents proved problematic to the Council's Housing Department.

Chelmsley Wood's origins lay in the fears of Birmingham's civic leaders in the early 1960s of a 'land trap' – a shortage of available building land that would prevent them building housing for the Second City's growing population. The estate, personally approved by Labour's new Housing Minister Richard Crossman in December 1964, was the council's typically colossal response. Located on greenfield land beyond the city's borders nine miles south of central Birmingham, construction of 15,590 homes began on its 1,500-acre site in 1966 and was completed in 1971.

A simplified Radburn layout was applied to parts of the estate alongside a careful deployment of housing blocks that was intended (unsuccessfully, according to Hanley) to avoid a wind-tunnelling effect. Award-winning landscaping was applied to 'act as a transition between the roads and buildings, in some cases to relieve the hardness of the buildings, and in others to stimulate interest and add to the visual pleasure of the area'.[22]

Left
Balliol House and Merton House viewed from Bosworth Drive, 1987

Right
Oriel House viewed from Nineacres Drive, 1987

The estate's 39 point blocks, most system-built using the Bison wall-frame method, form its dominant impression for some, but only 17% of its housing exceeded four storeys. Most was low-rise, predominantly two-storey brick terraces with a conscious variety of forms and finishes. It was the last of the city's estates built with tall blocks and – alongside similar style development in contemporaneous schemes – the sudden plethora of low-rise housing, preferred by tenants to high-rise and maisonette blocks, caused panic in the Housing Department: 'all of a sudden as those three estates came in there were whole swathes of empty dwellings that we struggled to get let'.[23]

The estate's distance from the city centre – a 50-minute bus journey in its early days – was problematic to many but had the positive effect of encouraging the development of more local facilities, including an indoor shopping centre opened by the Queen in 1972. Depressed economic times afflicted the estate in the 1980s but regeneration – including the demolition of some of its tower blocks – have lifted the estate in recent years. Its housing was transferred to Solihull in 1980. Revisiting Chelmsley Wood with her children, Hanley is able to recapture some of 'the paradise [her] nan saw in Chelmsley Wood when it was brand new. A place of freedom and freshness, where there is nothing to be afraid of, or to escape from'.[24]

Top
Family homes, Alder Drive

Bottom
Housing at Durham Croft

Multi-storey

For some, the characteristic form of modern public housing is the multi-storey block. The statistics belie the perception; at peak, in 1966, blocks of above five storeys formed just 26% of all public housing approvals. However, given its prominence in the inner city (and some peripheral estates), the emphasis on high-rise is understandable and reflects, in part, the focus of planners and architects of the time.

Architecturally, initial inspiration came principally from the *punkthusen* of Scandinavia. The principal advantage of such point blocks (an anglicisation of the term) was their flexibility – they were easily adaptable to varying heights, fitted well into mixed development schemes and could sit in a range of landscapes or on restricted sites. Slab blocks, the more horizontal high-rise favoured by those who looked more to Le Corbusier, were less flexible in all these aspects but lent themselves particularly to the increasingly popular maisonette form and (as a greater number of flats were accessed by corridors or decks) saved money on lifts.

The cluster block – with its central, free-standing service tower and separate but linked accommodation blocks – devised by Denys Lasdun represented an ingenious third way, intended to break up the sometimes forbidding mass of larger multi-storey blocks while allowing residents greater privacy, fresh air and light. But the model, seen at its best in Keeling House, designed by Lasdun for the Metropolitan Borough of Bethnal Green in 1959, was not widely adopted.

Landmark blocks in Brutalist style, such as Ernő Goldfinger's Balfron Tower (1967) in Poplar and Trellick Tower (1972) in North Kensington, built for the LCC, capture the attention but while some larger or more independently minded councils, such as Aberdeen or Bristol, implemented distinctively local forms of high-rise, the ready-made solutions offered by the oligopoly of major contractors increasingly came to dominate.

While in the 1960s, the media generally embraced the Brave New World modernity of high-rise, the reaction against it was rapid – from critics who questioned its suitability for younger families and from those who contrasted the drawing board visions of parkland settings with the reality of the rather bleak, underused open space that often emerged. Crucially, high-rise was an expensive option, rarely delivering the significantly higher densities promised and generally more costly than the refurbishment of existing housing stock. The 1966 Deeplish Report supported the regeneration of previously condemned terraced housing, and the 1967 Housing Subsidies Act abolished the special subsidy for high flats. In this context, the collapse of the Ronan Point tower block one year later, rather than instigating a new era of lower-rise construction, merely confirmed existing trends.

Loughborough Road Estate, Southwark, London

The LCC Architect's Department wrested back control of housing design from the Valuer's Department in 1951. The Loughborough Estate in Lambeth, designed by a team led by Gill Sarson under Chief Architect Leslie Martin and built between 1953 and 1957, marked its return with some statement Modernism and a considerable nod to Le Corbusier.

A difficult, bomb-damaged 30-acre site, bisected by two major roads and bordered by a railway viaduct, required some ingenuity. The signature feature of the estate – nine 11-storey slab blocks, 80 m long, around 10 m wide – allowed a housing density that permitted the creation of a six-acre parkland buffer between railway and estate. Five of them comprised predominantly two-bedroom maisonettes. These were the coming idea within the Architect's Department, seen, as Margaret Willis (a sociologist in its Planning Division) explained, as 'a compromise between a house and a flat'. In more homely fashion, she went on, 'people prefer this type of building to a flat because they like going upstairs to bed'.[25] At the Loughborough Estate, the architects claimed that their increased density made 'it possible to provide larger families with maisonettes or houses with gardens'.[26]

This was, then, despite the visual dominance of those tall blocks, a mixed development estate *par excellence*. It had 61% of its homes in the slab blocks, 31% in four- and six-storey maisonette blocks, and 8% in two-storeyed terraced housing – 1,029 homes in all at a density of 135 persons per acre. A clubroom, tenants' stores and garaging, and nine laundries provided community facilities, but there was no district heating system as the slender concrete chimney stacks that can be glimpsed atop the slab blocks attest.

Left
Eleven-storey slab blocks, photographed in 1957

Opposite top left
A family home and garden, photographed in 1955

Opposite top right
Block of shops and maisonettes, 1958

Opposite bottom
A contemporary view of a slab block

In other respects, this was a Modernism fully embraced. The slab blocks, of reinforced concrete cross-wall construction, were aligned along a northwest–southeast axis fulfilling *Zeilenbau* principles. Their facades' outward appearance – a repetitive rectilinear pattern of concrete and glass – and external surfaces of concrete in its natural state or faced with exposed aggregate reflect an unashamedly Brutalist credo best summed up in Reyner Banham's definition as '1, Memorability as an Image; 2, Clear exhibition of Structure; and 3, Valuation of Materials "as found"'.[27]

Kemble House, Ettleby House and Wooley House, the three slab blocks ranged against the Wyck Gardens park, make for a powerful ensemble, and Ian Nairn thought the estate 'very impressive from the air'. He added, more caustically, that 'alas at ground level there is nothing to bind the slabs together or make proper place'.[28]

Aberdeen Multis, Scotland

In applying for the listing of the eight Aberdeen slab block 'Multis' in 2021, Historic Environment Scotland described them as 'among the most coherent and architecturally distinguished group of Brutalist flats in Scotland'.[29] (After appeal, five of the eight secured official protection.) Their origins lay, firstly and more typically, in the kind of urban renewal envisaged across Britain in the early postwar era; in this case a 1952 report by W. Dobson Chapman and Charles F. Riley, *Granite City: a plan for Aberdeen*, which recommended suburban neighbourhood units and, in the inner city, the replacement of slums by new high-density, multi-storey blocks.

A visionary City Architect, George McIntosh Keith, supported by a powerful and well-respected housing convener and treasurer, Councillor Robert Lennox, ensured that the housing programme that followed was of a distinctively local and high-quality character that eschewed the off-the-peg and increasingly system-built designs favoured by many local authorities. Visits to the Alton Estate in London (see page 145) and Hutchesontown in Glasgow in 1959 provided additional inspiration.

The first block completed, in 1963, the 11-storey Gilcomstoun Land, comprised 75 maisonettes in crossover (or scissor) section. This innovative design, pioneered in the mid-1950s by the LCC, created dual-aspect homes entered from a central corridor at either bedroom or living area on their lower floor with up-and-over stairs providing access to an upper floor on the other side of the block. It is a flexible and ingenious plan but was criticised later as complex and costly and is now outlawed by building regulations.

The 19-storey Porthill Court and nine-storey Seamount Court, connected by glazed footbridges, followed in like fashion, as did the similarly connected Virginia Court and Marischal Court completed in 1966. Three later blocks, built in the 1970s – Thistle Court,

Left
Gilcomstoun Land

Right
Greig Court and Hutcheon Court

Opposite left
Seamount Court and Porthill Court

Opposite right
Virginia Court and Marischal Court

Hutcheon Court and Greig Court – were completed under Keith's successor as City Architect, Tom Watson, and contained a mix of crossover maisonettes and conventional maisonettes and flats.

In their overall form, the blocks are unashamedly Modernist and Brutalist, as evidenced by their cross-slab in situ concrete frame construction, ground-level concrete piers and sculptural concrete detailing. At the same time, the *genius loci* of the 'Granite City' is honoured by the large granite aggregate and concrete panels used to clad their monumental end elevations. (They had the additional advantage of providing necessary weatherproofing in this northerly Scottish city.) The blocks' orientation and landscaping were also used to integrate them into the wider townscape.

The listing of the Multis has predictably been criticised in some quarters but, suitably adapted to meet modern standards of hearing and insulation, the blocks have generally proved popular with local residents. To one of their foremost advocates, architectural historian Miles Glendinning, they 'stand out because architecturally and socially, they are a continuation of the civic-mindedness and pride of previous generations of great Aberdonians'.[30]

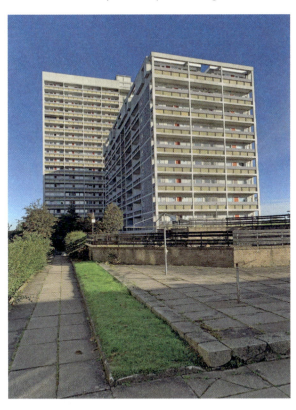

Pepys Estate, Lewisham, London

The origins of Lewisham's Pepys Estate lay in the Admiralty's sale of 11 acres of Thameside land to the LCC in 1958. Clearance of adjoining areas created a 45-acre site on which the council planned to build 1,500 homes. After 1966 the estate became one of the showpiece schemes of the new GLC, incorporating much of the planning wisdom of the day.

As a GLC brochure explained, 'one of the main themes has been the separation of pedestrian from vehicular traffic' achieved by an extensive series of elevated walkways connecting the blocks and an elevated shopping precinct.[31] Residents' parking was generally provided below ground. The estate was also another where split level 'scissors maisonettes' (see Aberdeen Multis, see page 160) were extensively employed to provide dual aspect homes in innovative form. A more recent trend was incorporated in the rehabilitation of older properties, though here the salvaged properties were sturdy Admiralty buildings rather than rundown terraces. Suitably adapted, these were let to middle-class tenants at higher rents.

Newbuild comprised 10 eight-storey and three 24-storey blocks. Larger family homes were placed in the lower-rise housing, with the planners' intention of accommodating 'as few children as possible … in the tower blocks'. Homes for elderly residents were located conveniently close to the shopping precinct. Around one-third of the estate as a whole was open space comprising a range of children's play areas and 'quiet green squares' formed by 'the grouping of the lower buildings'.

In its early years, 'people were fighting to move onto [the estate] and the lucky ones felt privileged'.[32] With weekly rents set at between £5 and £8, it housed a relatively affluent and initially overwhelmingly white working class. (GLC officers operated an informal but undeniably racist allocations policy whereby black tenants were generally placed on the nearby New Milton Estate.)

A subsequent history of economic decline and rising crime, complicated by a troubled racial politics, reminds us that popular and well-designed schemes can rapidly transform into apparently 'failing' estates as they fall on hard times. Regeneration ensued. As new theories of defensible space took hold, some

Left
An aerial view of part of the estate, 1970

Right
Upper-level walkways, shopping centre and playground, 1970

Opposite top
Children playing on raised walkway, 1970

Opposite bottom left
Aragon Tower and a converted Georgian terrace, 1973

Opposite bottom right
The privatised Aragon Tower with added penthouse storeys

of the walkways were removed. Subsequently, six of the low-rise blocks were demolished, replaced by flimsier lower-rise housing in the currently generic New London Vernacular. Aragon Tower, with riverside views, was sold to a private developer and now houses wealthy middle-class leaseholders. The overall loss of some 366 social rent homes allowed, according to Pat Hayes, Lewisham's Director of Regeneration, 'a good mix of people: tenants, leaseholders and freeholders. The Pepys Estate was a monolithic concentration of public housing and it [made] sense to break that up a bit and bring in a different mix of incomes and people with spending power'.[33]

Wyndham Court, Southampton

Wyndham Court in central Southampton causes mixed feelings. It is, in the words of Owen Hatherley, 'big city architecture, stark and hard'.[34] For some, its stark Brutalism is a little too much, 'an eyesore'; for others, its bold design represents a rare example of architectural daring in a city whose postwar reconstruction generally disappoints.

If Southampton's central redevelopment was undistinguished, its postwar housing programme under Borough Architect Leon Berger, appointed in 1948, was noteworthy. Its housing programme 'most closely approached Sheffield's in its range and vitality, thanks to its choice of private architects and a tradition of decent housing' in the view of Elain Harwood.[35] The city's 1956 Development Plan noted how 'the pressure of high land values and actual land shortage, together with trends in modern housing development, are increasing building density and are studding the townscape with tall blocks'. Eric Lyons' 14-storey Castle House built for the council in 1963 was one such product; a mixed development of maisonettes and towers in inner-city Northam another. The 16-storey Millbrook Tower was the highest residential public housing block in Britain when completed in 1966.

Wyndham Court was designed by the significant but undervalued architectural partnership Lyons Israel Ellis and completed, on a site close to Southampton's civic centre, in 1969, one of three schemes that the firm designed for the city. It comprised linked six- and seven-storey blocks ranged around a central square. The ensemble provided three cafes and restaurants, 13 shops and some 184 flats; around one-third, on the lower floors, one-bedroom, the rest two- and three-bedroom maisonettes.

Construction was of reinforced concrete with a Portland stone aggregate and board-marked finish, intended to complement the white classicism of Ernest Berry Webber's 1930s' civic centre. That effect is slightly lost given

Left and right
Viewed from Blechynden Terrace

Opposite top
Wyndham Court undergoing renovation, 2022

Opposite bottom
Viewed from Wyndham Place showing ground floor commercial premises

A History of Council Housing in 100 Estates

the current greying, grubby state of Wyndham Court's facades, but the latter are commended in Historic England's 1998 Grade II listing of the building as 'sculptural and expressive'. Prominent service towers add to the overall drama and impact of the design.

The flats were let at 'economic' rents and intended for occupation by middle-class professionals; a symbol of an era when it was still possible to imagine council housing serving 'general needs' or a broader cross-section of the population. Given contemporary housing pressures, the scheme now houses a more mixed population.

For Hatherley, an unashamed Modernist, Wyndham Court is 'by far the finest twentieth-century building in the city … [it] immediately evokes the cruise behemoths that sailed from the nearby port. A glorious concrete Cunard, impossible to ignore'.[36]

Deck access

Deck access was, in essence, an updated version of a well-established balcony-access tradition in public housing. If it was distinguished from the latter (and the distinction wasn't always clear), it was by the width of the gallery providing access to front doors and, more frequently than before, other estate amenities – and, more importantly, by its rationale. Decks, as the more informal term 'streets in the sky' suggests, were envisaged as places to socialise and sometimes, for younger residents, places to play.

One can trace the concept back to the almost science-fictional imaginings of, for example, the Italian Futurist, Antonio Sant'Elia before the First World War and some of the more innovative Modernist designs of the interwar period. M.R. Brinkman's Spangen Estate in Rotterdam, constructed in 1919 and featuring, on its second floor, a 1-km long, 2–3-m wide gallery giving access to upper-storey homes, is the first and finest example. In the UK, however, the concept was pioneered in Peter and Alison Smithson's rejected 1952 plans for the City of London's Golden Lane Estate, which envisaged, as they wrote later:

> A true street-deck in the air, each deck having a large number of people dependent on it for access, and some decks being thoroughfares leading to places ... Decks would be places, not corridors or balconies: thoroughfares where there are 'shops', post boxes, telephone kiosks.[37]

In practical terms, the great British exemplar was Park Hill in Sheffield, completed in 1961 and much admired in its earlier years.

A principal driver of the 1960s fashion for deck-access housing was that elusive postwar quest for community, criticised as lacking in interwar council estates and apparently threatened further (as the sociologists Michael Young and Peter Wilmott suggested in their influential though methodologically flawed 1957 book *Family and Kinship in East London*) as slum clearance gathered pace. Architects hoped that the 'streets in the sky' might replicate the terraced streets of yore.

Southwark's Aylesbury Estate, begun in 1963, was an ambitious example of deck-access design with 'route decks' at second-floor level for movement between blocks, which included space for shops and other community facilities, and 'local decks', with play areas, within the blocks. The estate is now undergoing a drawn-out demolition. Another Southwark deck-access estate, North Peckham (see page 185) and the Hulme Crescents in Manchester (see page 222) have also been torn down. The Smithsons' own implemented scheme of deck-access layout, Robin Hood Gardens in Poplar, is also being cleared, betrayed in part by its poor execution – narrow decks on the exposed exterior of its two blocks. As some of these estates became genuinely troubled and as ideas of defensible space became common currency, deck access was transformed perceptually (with sometimes questionable justification) from a means of neighbourly interaction to an agent of disruption, its 'streets in the sky' labelled 'rat runs' and 'escape routes' for those whose intentions were apparently far from neighbourly.

Park Hill, Sheffield

Park Hill, completed in 1961, was – alongside the Gleadless Valley Estate (see page 143) – part of the city council's postwar reimagining of Sheffield; a towering presence on a hilltop site just south of the city centre. It was the first and remained the prime British example of deck-access housing, and became a Brutalist icon loved and hated in almost equal measure.

The estate, designed by Jack Lynn and Ivor Smith under J. Lewis Womersley, Sheffield City Architect, replaced a rundown area of back-to-back housing and small works. Those displaced were moved to the new flats and, in a deliberate attempt to retain community feeling, old neighbours were housed next to each other and former street names reused. The 3-m wide decks were 'allegedly the product of close study of working-class life by [the architects] who sought to reproduce the safe and sociable streets of yore without the danger and din of traffic'.[38]

The estate was also provided with four pubs, 42 shops, a community centre, social clubs, a health centre, dental surgery and nursery and primary schools. Grenville Squires, a caretaker on the estate, says it 'was like a medieval village; you didn't have to leave'.[39] Many didn't want to; as one early resident recalled, 'it was luxury ... three bedrooms, hot water, always warm. And the view. It's lovely, especially at night, when it's all lit up'.[40] Joan Demers, the estate's resident sociologist employed by the council to help incomers settle, judged the scheme an outstanding success.

Left
Park Hill from the air, 1960

Right
Access deck and milk float, 1965

Others took more note of the estate's overall form – a sinuous series of slab blocks, linked by those decks in bridge form at every third floor, ranging from four storeys to 13 and so maintaining a flat roofline in adaptation to the sloping site. All but the topmost deck reached ground level, reducing the reliance on

lifts. Some 996 new homes were provided – one- and two-bedroom flats below deck level, and two- and three-bedroom maisonettes above it, each with a large private balcony.

In the longer term, the estate fared less well. Its vaunted 'streets in the sky' were now said to encourage crime and antisocial behaviour. The council was criticised for poor maintenance and an allocations policy that placed poorer and more troubled tenants on the estate. The latter was, of course, a reflection of a broader change in the nature of council housing taking place in the 1980s, as was a process of deindustrialisation that saw Sheffield, which lost 40,000 jobs in the steel industry, hit particularly hard. This was no longer, or far less so, a working community.

In 2003 the council outlined a new vision for the estate, Grade II*-listed in 1998 as a 'mixed use development including owner-occupation, social rented properties … and commercial usage'. Urban Splash were appointed developers the following year to create the more controversially colourful version you see today. Just 200 of the 900 refurbished homes are let at social rent.

Clockwise from top left
Shopping area, 1961

Children's play area, 1961

Park Hill renovated by Urban Splash, 2018

Park Hill with its original colour scheme, 1960

Divis Flats, Belfast, Northern Ireland

Belfast's Divis Flats complex was described even before its completion in 1972 as 'the youngest slum in Europe'.[41] The estate's problems lay in the complex motivations of its conception, in its problematic form and flawed construction and, not least, in the Troubles themselves.

A 1960 survey by Belfast's Medical Officer of Health reported 18,440 houses in the city as 'unfit and incapable of being rendered fit'. The Northern Ireland Housing Trust undertook to redevelop the Pound Loney district, a 14-acre site of decayed terraced housing at the foot of Falls Road in Catholic and Nationalist West Belfast.

In a fiercely sectarian context, local community leaders wanted above all to maintain the existing power bases – Catholic clerics their parishes and Nationalist politicians their constituencies. (Unionist politicians, for their part, were content that the non-Unionist minority be safely contained.) The trust took a delegation to visit the newly completed Park Hill Estate in Sheffield and promoted its deck-access model as the best means 'to preserve, as far as possible, the existing community with its long-established social and family relationships'.[42]

What ensued, in a scheme designed by architect Frank Robertson of the John Laing Construction Company, was a complex of 12 seven- and eight-storey 'Sectra' system-built blocks and the Divis Tower, connected by balcony walkways that enabled residents (and others) to traverse the estate end to end without ever touching ground level. Its 850 one- to six-bedroom flats were designed to accommodate a population of around 2,500.

Bottom
Divis Flats and Cave Hill, 1981

As elsewhere, the trust's preference for quick but badly implemented prefabricated construction soon proved problematic, with residents noting cracks in the cladding, poorly constructed joints and individual homes rendered cold and damp thorough cold bridging between slabs and poor insulation. The use of asbestos and calcium chloride (added to the cement to speed drying time but contributing to water penetration and corrosion of steel beams) in the construction process compounded the problems. Nevertheless, the outbreak of intercommunal violence in Northern Ireland in 1968 and the flight of families to safer sectarian enclaves it caused rapidly led to overcrowding. Within a few years of its opening, almost 30% of resident households were unofficial squatters.

In August 1969, nine-year-old Patrick Rooney became the first child fatality of the Troubles, hit by a tracer bullet fired by the Royal Ulster Constabulary into his family's home on the estate. Eighteen others would be killed on the estate as the Troubles spread and the flats themselves became a major flashpoint of the conflict, effectively under a military occupation marked most powerfully by the army observation point placed on the upper floors of the Divis Tower.

Campaigning for the flats' demolition began as early as 1973, and took more powerful form with the formation of the Divis Demolition Committee in 1979. In 1986 the decision was taken to demolish the entire complex save the tower, whose one-bedroom flats were popular with elderly residents. Low-rise housing was built in its stead. The army observation post was removed in 2005 as peace emerged.

Top
The flats photographed from the roof of Divis Tower, 1982

Bottom left
Demolition of the flats, 1984

Bottom right
New homes replacing the Divis Flats complex, 1991

A History of Council Housing in 100 Estates

Hunslet Grange, Leeds

When Leeds City Council approved the Hunslet Grange scheme (colloquially the Leek Street Flats) in 1966, it was hoped that:

A method of housing design has been developed which … should enable the maximum economic benefits to be gained from industrialisation and at the same time provide a flexible medium for creating environments adapted to the special conditions of each site.[43]

This model scheme of system building survived just 15 years.

Hunslet Grange was the first estate implemented to the designs of the Yorkshire Design Group (YDG) formed by a consortium of local authorities – Leeds, Sheffield, Hull and, later, Nottingham – with its 'Housing Mark 1' part of a projected initial contract of 4,500 such homes. The big idea of its chief architect Martin Richardson was for a kit of prefabricated components that could be adaptably assembled to meet a range of housing needs and styles.

In Hunslet, the new scheme replaced an area of predominantly back-to-back terraces, comprising 12 six-storey and six seven-storey blocks in three clusters grouped around a central park. A permitter road separated pedestrians and traffic. Around a quarter of the 350 flats and maisonettes were at ground level; the rest were accessed by wide decks, as were the estate pub and general store. The homes themselves were well equipped, spacious (on average 5% above Parker Morris standards), light and airy, and initially popular with residents. Similar schemes were built in Sheffield, Nottingham and Hull, though these were notably different in overall form and finish, such was the flexibility of the system. It was praised too for its economy – construction costs were calculated £365 per unit below the government's housing cost yardstick introduced in 1967 to limit local authority spending.

By 1970, however, one journalist was writing the epitaph of the YDG: 'Six years ago, factory production techniques were to be the panacea for the nation's housing ills. Today … "system building" is a term of disparagement'.[44] Douglas Frank commented on the difficulties in securing cooperation between disparate local authorities but in Leeds far more practical problems were emerging, chief among these issues of condensation and the expense and inadequacy of the warm air heating system. A 1976 report by a tenants' group was entitled

Bottom
A rather bleak view of Hunslet Grange, 1969

'Hunslet Grange: an experiment and its victims'. Others, as new theories of defensible space spread, criticised the deck-access system for facilitating crime and antisocial behaviour.

Some former tenants remember the estate fondly – the 'flats were great to grow up in, plenty of open spaces to knock about in and great people to know' – but the overall verdict is best summarised by the cultural historian Richard Hoggart, who grew up in Hunslet and thought it 'some of the worst, most crass and inhumane public housing I have seen in any developed country … much less human than the old back-to-back streets'.[45] Martin Richardson blamed bad construction (Leeds City Council sued the contractors in 1979) and poor maintenance.

Top
Main entrance in 1987; the flats are part occupied but awaiting demolition

Bottom left
Rear of the flats

Bottom right
This photograph of the flats' demolition in 1987 clearly shows their modular construction

Killingworth, North Tyneside

To Elain Harwood 'Killingworth is the forgotten English Cumbernauld', and to see it today there is little to remind you of the sweeping architectural and sociological vision that once actuated this Northumbrian New Town.[46] It was in essence a modest project: a town of around 20,000 people built under the 1952 Town Development Act by a partnership of Northumberland County Council, Longbenton Urban District Council and Newcastle Borough Council, and intended primarily to resettle those displaced by the latter's sweeping slum clearance programme. But Roy Gazzard, its Director of Development appointed in 1962, imagined something far greater.

Gazzard had cut his planning teeth in the early 1950s in Uganda, where he was involved in building new towns and, he hoped, new communities in the then colonial state. He brought some of that same energy to Killingworth Township (as the scheme was originally dubbed) in an unlikely combination of local heritage and futuristic design.

Northumberland's castle towns provided the overarching reference for his conceptualisation of the New Town. The high-rise town centre would be 'The Citadel' complemented by surrounding multi-storey slab blocks, 'The Towers'. Beyond these lay the 'East Bailey' and 'West Bailey', containing the town's low-rise public housing. An area of subsided land to the south was flooded to form Killingworth Lake, an attractive recreational amenity envisaged as an echo of the medieval moat.

Beyond that town centre, designed as a megastructure similar to that of Cumbernauld, The Towers were the town's most striking feature – 27 deck-access six- to 10-storey blocks built using the Swedish Skarne system of concrete panel prefabrication. Gazzard described these as a 'vertical village', with the 'streets in the sky' intended to encourage neighbourly interaction.[47] Construction of the low-rise housing, of flat-roofed, industrial form, also

Left
Killingworth Township in 1960; The Citadel and The Towers substantially complete and West Bailey housing under construction

Right
West Bailey housing, 1960

commenced to the west in the so-called 'Old Garths'. Later housing in the 'New Garths' to the east was more conventional in construction and form, though determinedly distinct in its semi-Radburn layout of sinuous cul-de-sacs.

Such high hopes were perhaps always doomed to fail, but they were not helped by the austere and grey appearance of The Towers, described in Pevsner as resembling 'nothing so much as a set from Fritz Lang's *Metropolis*[48] By 1970, they had become 'difficult-to-let, difficult-to-live-in, and sometimes difficult-to-get-out-of'.[49] The second, eastern, phase was abandoned; The Towers as a whole were demolished from 1986. The Citadel suffered the same fate in 1992, and from 1995 pitched roofs were added to the Old Garth housing and its layout modified. This was all a precipitate fall from grace but testimony to the misplaced idealism placed in Killingworth Township by its planners and would-be social engineers.

Top left
Garths Four and Six, West Bailey, 1968

Top right
The condemned Killingworth Towers, 1987

Left
Killingworth Lake and West Bailey housing today

System-building and high-rise

As we've seen, there was nothing new in the attempt to accelerate housebuilding using industrialised methods but system building – as it was now most often termed – took off in the early 1960s. A 1963 Government White Paper announced that local authorities would 'have to step up their output of houses both by rationalisation of traditional building methods and by making use of industrial systems'.[50] The Ministry of Public Building and Works was tasked in the same year with supporting the process. The then Conservative government initially proposed a target of 25% of new council housing be built using such methods; after 1964, the incoming Labour government raised the proportion to 40%. By 1966, at the peak of the system building boom, 55% of new council housing starts came in package deals with the small group of major contractors capable of delivering such schemes.

Beyond the powerful numbers game, system building was embraced by some architects and planners. A.W. Cleeve Barr, when Chief Architect to the Ministry of Housing and Local Government, thought 'the main results in using repetition and standardisation ... must surely be that relatively more money and a higher degree of skill can be put into design and working efficiency'.[51] As Muthesius and Glendinning conclude, 'one could plausibly portray "system-building" as the final, decisive realisation of the longstanding Modernist ideal of architecture as "pure construction"'. For politicians, central and local, perhaps it simply embodied a modernity befitting a more confident and go-ahead Britain.

Leeds was among the first councils to trial system building with its large-panel system Reema blocks from 1958. The London County Council applied the Danish Larsen Nielsen large-panel system in its Morris Walk scheme in Lewisham from 1962. Liverpool, using the French Camus system, followed suit in a large-scale building programme begun the following year. In Scotland, Glasgow and Dundee fully embraced system building, other municipalities less so.

The promise of such enterprise was not long-lasting. While the Continental models of the British schemes were generally soundly built, in the UK the rush to build often led to slapdash methods and poor execution, and by the end of the decade problems were emerging in a number of system-built estates across the country. Ronan Point was their most obvious manifestation. The tide was turning in any case as central government policy embraced rehabilitation of derelict areas and lower-rise alternatives.

Pendleton Estate, Salford

The Pendleton Estate was once envisaged as 'a Salford for the Space Age'.[52] If so, it became to many a dystopic one. Its good intentions lay in plans of the Borough of Salford, first promulgated in 1960, to redevelop the Ellor Street area – 89 acres of land where 'three thousand families lived in slum conditions as bad as any to be found in the country'.[53] This marked a shift in council policy. In the 1950s, the borough had proposed moving almost 40,000 of its 178,000 population to greenfield sites beyond its borders; 10,000 had been relocated to Worsley, eight miles to the west. Now, like many other comparable inner-city authorities concerned at the loss of tax revenue and supportive voters such migration represented, it wanted to rehouse its population locally. The Ellor Street scheme would 'add 2,800 families to our population, revitalise our trade, and give our rateable value its first boost since the war' according to one Salford councillor.[54]

The original plans were devised in-house by City Engineer G. Alexander McWilliam. Three 15-storey slab blocks along Belvedere Road (two remain) were built, but in 1961, on the advice of the Ministry of Housing and Local Government, the council appointed former LCC Chief Architect Robert Matthew and former LCC Senior Planner Percy Johnson-Marshall, both now based in the Architectural Research Unit of Edinburgh University, as architect-planners for the entire scheme.

Their principal proposal of Matthew and Johnson-Marshall was a new combined civic and commercial centre (containing new town hall, library, museum and gallery as well 'one of Europe's finest shopping centres') that would establish Salford as a regional satellite 'for the motor age'.[55] Housing featured less prominently, but their

Left
General view of the Pendleton Estate, 1987

Opposite top left
John Lester Court and Eddie Colman Court, 2016

Opposite top right
Briar Hill Court and Salford Shopping Centre, 2016

Opposite bottom
Fitzwarren Court, Madison Court and Bronte Court with Briar Hill Court to rear, 2016

A History of Council Housing in 100 Estates

Report on the Plan proposed a mix of medium- and high-rise development for the estate. Here the ministry flexed its muscles by insisting on the inclusion of five system-built 17-storey point blocks. In all, the completed estate would feature 20 high-rise blocks, ranging in height from seven storeys to 23.

New residents were generally positive about the size and facilities of their new homes despite their higher rents, but many felt misgivings about the loss of community: 'the demise of the traditional street, the corner shop and small local pub … a whole way of life ceased to exist'.[56] The more grandiose ideas for the new civic centre were largely abandoned and the area remains poor and troubled, by 2009 subject to a major new regeneration scheme planning to create 'a new Pendleton'.

Red Road Flats, Glasgow

In 1945 Glasgow remained the most overcrowded and poorly housed city in Britain. Two strategies presented themselves to tackle this unprecedented scale of problem. One, broadly favoured by Glasgow Corporation, was contained in a 1945 report by the council's Chief Engineer Robert Bruce, proposed so far as possible to redevelop central areas and rehouse their surplus population on peripheral estates within the city's boundaries. The other, outlined in Sir Patrick Abercrombie's Clyde Valley Regional Plan of 1946, advocated the creation of New Towns and overspill schemes beyond the city. For the former, and more so as new Green Belt policies restricted the availability of land and imposed higher-density solutions, high-rise was an inevitable corollary.

Glasgow's first high-rise scheme – three comparatively modest 10-storey slab blocks – was built at Moss Heights in the southwest of the city in 1953. But the Housing Committee's ambition would reach higher as David Gibson (then chair of a housing subcommittee on sites and buildings) suggested: 'Let the planners check that all available city land is being built on. Let them push the frontier upwards instead of outwards. Where 10 floors are planned let them build 20 instead'.[57]

This high-rise drive reached fruition under Gibson's tenure as Glasgow's Housing Convenor from 1961 until his death in 1964. Gibson was described by the planner Sir Robert Grieve as 'a white-faced, intense, driving idealist, absolutely fanatical and sincere ... He saw only the one thing – how to get as many houses up as possible, how to get as many of his beloved fellow working-class citizens decently housed as possible'.[58] In 1962, the corporation signed off contracts for 30 blocks of 20 storeys or above. The Red Road scheme, approved that year, included the UK's first blocks over 30 storeys; six slender 31-storey point blocks and two 27-storey slab blocks in all.

In one respect, however, Red Road represented a compromise for Gibson; it was a sop to the corporation's powerful Direct Labour Organisation, its directly employed building and maintenance workforce, anxious that it was losing work to private contractors. It was also an unusual scheme in construction terms for Glasgow – a steel-frame and concrete slab design devised by local architect Sam Bunton in emulation of the New York skyscrapers he admired.

Bottom
The flats under construction, 1960

Opposite top
The flats with earlier housing in the foreground in 2010

Opposite bottom
The flats in 2010

Though contemporary press reports hailed the scheme's 'space-age innovation' and Glasgow's role as a 'forward-looking city', the scheme was not a success.[59] Aside from a nursery school and a small shopping centre, community facilities were lacking. By 1968, social researcher Pearl Jephcott observed that the flats 'were already showing signs of social problems since the lifts were proving most inadequate' and the 'high proportion of child-users'. Later, '"The Red Road" ... became a byword and symbol of poverty, social problems, alienation and exclusion'.[60] Two blocks of the scheme were demolished in 2012; the rest ignominiously in 2015.

Freemasons Estate, Newham, London

When Ivy Hodge got up on 18 May 1968 to make a cup of tea in her 18th-storey flat in Ronan Point, Newham, she inadvertently triggered a gas explosion. An entire corner of the block collapsed like a house of cards. Four people died. Luckily she was an early riser, or the death toll might have been much higher.

Ronan Point had been officially opened just two months earlier (the flats above Mrs Hodge's were still unoccupied) in a year when the Borough of Newham built 15,000 new homes – a postwar record in the London boroughs. That pace of construction reflected urgent need. Roughly a quarter of the area's housing had been destroyed in the Blitz and Thomas North, Borough Architect for West Ham and then its successor authority (with East Ham) Newham, had long pressed for high-rise solutions. In 1961, West Ham finally gave approval for a programme of 16- and 21-storey blocks, and in the decade that followed around 70% of Newham's new homes were provided in tower blocks – 114 across the borough.

North looked too to system building – and the speedy delivery and lower labour costs it promised – and concluded, after a visit to the LCC's Morris Walk Estate in Woolwich, that the Danish Larsen Nielsen large-panel system offered the flexibility he desired. In Denmark, the Larsen Nielsen system had been implemented only in blocks of six storeys or fewer. Taylor Woodrow Anglian,

Left
Condemned blocks on the Freemasons Estate, 1988

Right
Freemasons Estate, with Ronan Point the furthest block, in 1984

Opposite left
Ronan Point collapse, May 1988

Opposite right
Low-rise housing built on the site of the former Freemasons Estate

A History of Council Housing in 100 Estates

the British licensees of the system, aimed far higher and, in the rush to build quickly and cheaply, paid the 10- to 12-man teams that built the Freemasons Estate blocks by their pace of work. The Freemasons Estate, of which Ronan Point formed part, was approved in 1966 and built in three stages; five of its nine 22-storey blocks were completed in 1968, the rest by 1970.

The Griffith Inquiry, appointed to investigate the causes of the disaster, concluded that the blocks' construction was inadequate; too weak to resist even a small explosion (such as had occurred), expected wind loading and fire damage. In its aftermath, similar blocks across the country were strengthened and gas fittings removed. Ronan Point itself was rebuilt to supposedly improved specifications.

Though high-rise construction briefly paused it was far from halted, but public opinion turned decisively. Residents' groups in Newham had protested against the tower blocks even as they were being built. Campaigning revived in the early 1980s under the auspices of the Newham Tower Block Tenants Campaign, which finally secured the demolition of Ronan Point in 1986. The estate as a whole was razed in the early 1990s, replaced by a low-rise Barratts estate.

Sam Webb, architect and indefatigable campaigner for high-rise safety, had criticised the Griffith Inquiry as deficient in 1968. Further investigation enabled by the block's demolition revealed just how so – large panels affixed by two rusting bolts; voids that should have been filled with cement, mortar or concrete stuffed instead with newspaper. Prefabrication is not an inherently flawed approach, but its British application in the 1960s was all too often botched and slapdash, profit-driven and inadequately supervised. Goscote House in Leicester, the last surviving tower built using the Larsen Nielsen system, awaits demolition.

CHAPTER 7

1968–1979: Alternative Models of Social Housing Design and Provision

There was no clean break in 1968 with the forms of design that characterised – most prominently if not numerically – the mass public housing drive of the mid- to late 1960s. Large-scale projects were underway or in the pipeline and worked their way to fruition. In the shorter term at least, high-rise blocks continued to be felt a necessary and workable means of providing housing at scale. System building had lost its cachet but existing schemes, often modified to address the failings revealed by Ronan Point, were maintained.

But a turning point had been reached. While increasing numbers of commentators criticised the social consequences of high building, particularly for children and young families, central government was equally alarmed by their cost and a realisation that the net housing gains promised were frequently not delivered. The Housing Cost Yardstick of 1967 (requiring local authorities to work within maximum cost guidelines set centrally) that bore particularly heavily on high-rise blocks, and the withdrawal of the special high-rise subsidy in the same year marked this changing policy. Rehabilitation of older property, typically the Victorian and Edwardian terraces that might once have been condemned, came into focus – firstly in the 1968 Government White Paper 'Old houses into new homes' and legislatively in the 1969 Housing Act's creation of General Improvement Areas that replaced the 'redevelopment areas' which had previously given the green light to wholesale clearance.

Municipalisation – the purchase and council management of mostly previously private rental homes – was another response to these changing times. Sometimes this was a political intervention by left-wing councils, but practically it was another means of rehabilitation. Increasingly, into the 1970s, it was an early sally against the gentrification that was making some areas of London in particular unaffordable to working-class residents.

Architecturally, the most important and striking shift that took place was the embrace of low-rise, high-density housing – a design form that wrested control from the volume contractors and allowed architects to design high-quality housing at densities at least equal to those offered by conventional high-rise development. It gave rise to a new but sadly quite brief golden age of council housing, though its signature schemes were created by the more ambitious local authorities that typically employed strong, sometimes visionary, in-house architectural and planning teams. The Byker Estate in Newcastle, a mix of higher-rise and low-rise housing designed by Ralph Erskine and constructed between 1968 and 1982, was unique in both its colourful design and model of public participation.

In other respects, however, this was a period of decline for council housing. Overall numbers held up and it was, in part, the very success of the mass public housing drive of the era that caused problems. Positively, large numbers of households previously on council house waiting lists had been allocated new homes. In some cases, the degree of choice created led to the rejection of estates that were deemed less desirable in form or reputation. The phenomenon of the 'hard-to-let' estate emerged and became increasingly self-fulfilling. Negatively, such hard-to-let estates were frequently the failures of the mass housing drive, suffering flaws in construction and, more subjectively, in design. High-rise, system-built estates were particularly unpopular; deck-access schemes were increasingly understood as trouble-prone.

Short-life housing – the granting of tenancies to single and younger people who might otherwise not qualify for council housing – was in part a response to this phenomenon. Sometimes, it was barely more than an official recognition of the squatting that afflicted such unpopular and often poorly managed estates. Housing cooperatives reflected a reaction to council housing departments sometimes criticised as paternalistic but by now more often as overstretched and inefficient.

High-rise and multi-storey

High-rise commanded attention. Indeed, for architects and planners that was one of its principal attractions – to provide a focal point and visual interest in otherwise low-level and largely featureless estates. Its scale and visual impact were also embraced by some local politicians anxious to demonstrate their progressive credentials. When Birmingham City Council completed the twin 32-storey Sentinel Towers in 1972, the tallest residential local authority blocks in the UK, they were deliberately planned to exceed the height of the recently completed Red Road development in Glasgow. Increasingly, however, that attention was negative.

To state the obvious, it was vital that the lifts worked reliably. All too often they didn't. While a general presumption still held that high flats were not best suited to children and younger families, waiting list pressures saw this policy relaxed and frequently ignored. In some cases, the blocks were badly built, with tenants reporting irremediable problems of damp and condensation. Post-Ronan Point, the prohibition on gas appliances forced reliance on alternative heating systems that – particularly after the fourfold increase in crude oil prices in 1973 – were prohibitively expensive. Uncontrolled access that facilitated intrusion and antisocial behaviour was an obvious weak point. Entryphones and a concierge system where feasible were commonsense improvements made as 'defensible space' ideas gained currency in the 1980s.

Those issues notwithstanding, individual homes were generally designed to a high standard, with space and amenities that few of their residents had previously enjoyed. Although not the predominant narrative, there were many who enjoyed the privacy and views their new homes afforded, and others who praised their sense of community. Robert Banks, a resident of Southwark's unfairly reviled Aylesbury Estate, recalls how he 'knew all the neighbours ... You know you would never have got that sort of community in a row of houses as you did with the landings'.[1]

While too often high-rise development reflected simply a rush to build, in many cases much thought went into planning and design intended to promote community and aesthetic appeal, though the good intentions of the former were not always fulfilled and the latter remains subjective. The North Peckham Estate was designed to encourage neighbourliness. Derwent Tower, Dawson's Heights and the futuristic Thamesmead represented in different ways architectural innovation in an era allowing it greater scope.

Nevertheless, the apparently rooted English preference for houses with gardens remained firm. In 1968, the Institute of Housing Managers concluded that only '10 per cent will live willingly in high flats'.[2] The majority were catered for; of the over five million council homes built between 1945 and 1979, well over three million were houses. There were only 400,000 flats in blocks of six storeys or more and just 45,000 in blocks of 20 storeys and above. Whether the new pressures to build high and the current fashion for privately developed high-rise for middle-class occupation allow a more nuanced attitude towards the council blocks of the past remains to be seen.

North Peckham Estate, Southwark, London

In 1972, the newly completed North Peckham Estate in Southwark was seen as a model of community planning. An enthusiastic journalist praised the deck-access walkways that were its dominant feature as a successful 'attempt to recreate the neighbourly atmosphere of old-established districts ... the housewife can open the door to the tradesman much as she does in an ordinary street. The children can also run around unmolested by traffic, just as they used to do in the days of hop-scotch and the hoop'.[3] Yet by the end of the decade, the estate was in decline and it was demolished in the later 1990s.

The 40-acre estate, of traditional construction, comprised 1,444 homes in 65 five-storey blocks of two types, residential and parking. In the latter, the three lower floors provided lock-up garages for residents and parking spaces for visitors. A wide platform at second-floor level linked the blocks and contained the estate's shops, pubs and community facilities. A celebratory account in the council's newsletter lauded these walkways that allowed residents to 'walk freely along this two and half miles of deck away from the dirt, noise and danger of London traffic'.[4] More importantly, early residents were positive; one recalled that her flat was 'beautiful ... split over five levels, huge, with a big patio at the top ... rooms for all her children, and the kitchen was so big they had a sofa and a telly in it'.[5]

This heyday appears short-lived. By the end of the decade, there were reports of wear and tear and abuse of the walkways. By the mid-1980s, the estate's walkways and open, insecure access were blamed for 'a sense of anonymity due to intrusion by non-residents' and providing 'escape routes for criminals'.[6] The UK's leading advocate of defensible space theories Alice Coleman awarded the estate 13.1 on her 16-point scale of 'design disadvantage', a verdict repeated in more sophisticated form by a 1994 'space syntax' study that concluded its design 'generated a pathological pattern of space-use by creating lacunas in the system of natural movement'.[7] It's salutary, nevertheless, to remember a wider context. A local councillor described the estate as 'brilliant' until 'unemployment knocked six kinds of shit out of people'.[8]

Left and right
The estate in 1973

In the 1990s, annual turnover of homes had reached 25% and 70% of residents wanted a transfer. Squatting of empty properties became common. Plans for radical remodelling in the 1990s proved too expensive and impracticable. A Single Regeneration Budget award of £60 million in 1994 funded the demolition of the estate and its replacement with the low-rise, suburban housing that you will find in its place.

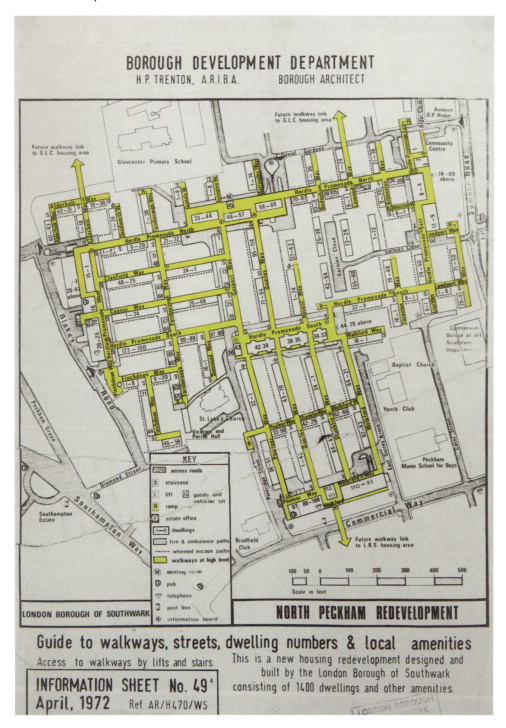

Left
The layout of the estate as described in a 'Guide to walkways, streets, dwelling numbers & local amenities' issued by Southwark Council in 1972

Derwent Tower, Whickham, Gateshead

When Whickham Urban District Council commissioned the Derwent Tower in 1967, they intended a prestige project to put the area on the map. In the 'Dunston Rocket', the nickname that stuck, they perhaps got more than they bargained for. Though loved by fans of Brutalism, the tower was never much liked by locals and Gateshead Council – Whickham's successor authority – was only too happy to demolish it in 2012. Whickham had originally planned three 22-storey towers on the 12.5-acre site of cleared terraced housing, but adverse ground conditions forced a rethink. The architects, the Owen Luder Partnership, favoured low-rise development but, on council insistence, created the 29-storey, 85-m tower and 116 maisonette scheme that was completed in 1972.

It was the angular, roughly heptagonal tower, unique in form and appearance, that naturally commanded attention – a striking reinforced concrete structure distinguished by the flying buttresses reaching from ground to fifth floor that supported its foundations, and the change in plan form between the 10th and 11th floors where the building's services, including two large water tanks, were located. The first 10 floors contained two-bedroom flats, floors 11 to 29 three-bed, 196 in all. An elevated walkway from the third floor gave residents traffic-free access to local shops and amenities. Out of sight lay the concrete caisson (a form generally used in harbour constructions) that rooted the structure, sunk 10 m deep to reach firm ground. Luder adapted it to provide an underground car park.

Many thought the tower overbearing. Over time, lift failures and service breakdowns were reported, and many flats were said to suffer from damp. The council blamed poor design and construction; its defenders pointed to inadequate upkeep and maintenance. As it became hard to let, it was used to house the statutorily homeless and refugees: 'It used to be called the Heartbreak Hotel because when blokes split up from their wives they could always get a flat in the Rocket'.[9] In this way, its failure as a desirable residence became self-fulfilling though in sometimes contradictory ways – one former resident remembers she 'hated the Rocket but it was a lovely flat'.

Bottom
Derwent Tower dominating the landscape, 2011

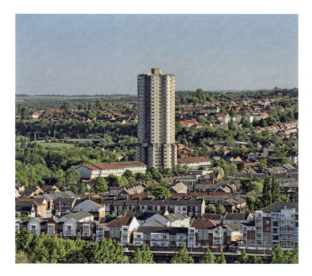

In 2007, Gateshead Council emptied the tower and looked to redevelop the area. Local polling was overwhelmingly in favour of its demolition and the council welcomed the decision in 2009 not to list it: 'we think the 95% of residents who live under its shadow and who've told us it is a blight on their landscape will agree'. Owen Luder, who would see his Trinity Square car park in Gateshead (made famous by its appearance in the 1971 film *Get Carter*) demolished the following year, argued that the council had 'allowed, indeed encouraged, deterioration' but believed the flats could 'be brought up to modern standards and the Rocket kept as the landmark in the new development'.[10]

Dawson's Heights, Southwark, London

Dawson's Heights was designed by Kate Macintosh when she was just 28 years of age. Macintosh had secured the commission through the in-house competition favoured by Southwark's Borough Architect and Planner, Frank Hayes, and brought to it a critical and ambitious eye. Looking at existing schemes, she thought London's balcony-access tenement blocks 'institutional' and its new Modernist slab and point blocks 'unrelated to the surrounding urban grain'. Even at Park Hill, which she generally admired, she lamented the 'flattening of the hill produced by the constant height of each meandering super-block'.[11]

The 12.5-acre hilltop site in East Dulwich created its own challenges, crowned by a refuse tip and ringed by interwar housing on unstable London clay slopes. This dictated the core elements of her design: two large blocks (Ladlands to the north and Bredinghurst the south) constructed on the more stable terrain overlooking a central communal space, formerly the dump. The buildings nevertheless required 60–80-feet reinforced concrete cylinder foundations. The blocks themselves were of traditional construction – loadbearing cross-wall structures of brick and concrete, softened by warm brick-textured facades. Each flat was provided with a private balcony, an amenity secured by Macintosh against contemporary economising by adapting them as fire escapes, thus justifying their inclusion on safety grounds.

Macintosh's vision was expressed most powerfully in the scheme's overall form. The blocks' ziggurat style, rising from four storeys to 12 at their central peak, ensured all the flats received sunlight even in deepest midwinter, and two-thirds had views in both directions. Their staggering created 'ever changing silhouettes which adds the beauty of surprise to a relentless suburb'.[12] English Heritage, in an application for listing that was rejected in 2012,

Left
Ladlands and the view to the north from Bredinghurst, 1973

Right
The Western Access Deck in 1973, since demolished

Opposite left
The living room of a three-bedroom maisonette, 1973

Opposite right
Ladlands and the view to the north from Bredinghurst, 2014

praised 'a striking and original massing that possesses evocative associations with ancient cities and Italian hill towns'.

Macintosh paid equal attention to her design's social aspects and conceived it as a mixed development scheme with households of different sizes and a range of ages in a way, she felt, that replicated the community of the traditional terraces. The 296 homes – all split-level, dual-aspect maisonettes – came in a complex array of one- to four-bedroom forms; a 'Chinese puzzle of differing types to be assembled in various combinations' in her words.[13]

In a complex project, there were inevitable teething problems. Damp and condensation in some flats had to be rectified. With less justification, two overhead walkways that originally connected the blocks were removed in the 1980s as ideas of 'designing out crime' took hold. Dawson's Heights remains 'a courageous and enduring large-scale experiment in British social housing design and ... continues to be much loved by its residents'.[14]

Macintosh went to work for the Borough of Lambeth shortly after her work on Dawson's Heights, where she designed a very different low-rise sheltered housing scheme at 269 Leigham Court Road, now listed and renamed Macintosh Court in her honour. She remains, as I write, a doughty defender of social housing's value and purpose.

Coralline Walk and Binsey Walk, Thamesmead, Boroughs of Greenwich and Bexley, London

The Erith and Plumstead marshes are 12 miles to the east of central London – part saturated semi-wilderness, part brownfield land, and a site of the Woolwich Arsenal since Tudor times. They weren't an initially promising site for a 'Town of Tomorrow'. But, if that initial promise wasn't entirely fulfilled, the planning and early design of Thamesmead were as visionary as any this country has seen.

Having abandoned plans for a new town of its own in Hook, Hampshire, in the mid-1950s, the thoughts of the London County Council turned to Erith and a portion of Arsenal land and 500 acres of marshland it purchased at the end of that decade.[15] Initial plans devised for this 'Town-on-Stilts' – a form necessitated by the risk of flooding and local bye-laws – were abandoned as too expensive, but they received a boost from a 1963 White Paper urging the redevelopment of surplus Ministry of Defence land around London. The purchase of 1,300 additional acres in 1964 provided the scale the project needed. By the mid-1960s, the new Greater London Council was planning a new town of some 60,000 population.

Thamesmead's 1967 masterplan proposed an urban setting formed of long spine blocks and high towers located around expanses of water (artificial lakes were created to aid drainage). There was talk of 'being able to travel by punt right across the site along four and a half miles of canals'; the town's waterways were intended to beautify and calm.[16] More conventional in contemporary terms was the separation of cars and pedestrians achieved by a network of walkways at first-floor level connecting neighbourhoods and services. System building was adopted to overcome a shortage of traditional materials and skilled labour and build at pace.

Left
Southmere Lake and Southmere Towers, 1970

Right
Coralline Walk, close-up of balconies, 1970

Opposite left
Binsey Walk, the maisonette blocks, 2017

Opposite right
Binsey Walk, 2016

Phase I of construction took place around South Mere and was planned to provide 1,500 homes of a projected 17,000. Thirteen-storey towers lined the southern edge of the lake, while a half-mile long spinal block – Binsey Walk and Coralline Walk – formed a barrier between its eastern shore and a major highway. These were essentially four-storey maisonette blocks raised on stilts, but in very distinct form. Each maisonette had a large private balcony built on the roof of the one below, 'giving the buildings an exciting diagonal, ziggurat appearance, further exaggerated by the expressive concrete staircases on the outside of the blocks'.[17] The stark white in situ poured concrete used in construction added to the drama.

In July 1968, Terry Gooch and his family moved from Peckham to Coralline Walk, Thamesmead's very first residents and the area's only residents for six months. By 1974, Thamesmead's population had reached 12,000 but its growth – hindered by contemporary cutbacks and its poor transport connections – was faltering. The same year saw the Thames riverbank raised, allowing more conventional construction closer to popular tastes. After a long period of confused and limited progress, the Peabody housing association took over the entire project in 2014. Their revival of Thamesmead has included the demolition of some of the town's signature early landmarks, including, sadly, Coralline Walk and Binsey Walk.

Low-rise, high-density

High-rise had always had its critics – the many who, in a peculiarly English context, preferred a house and garden; those who criticised its allegedly overpowering aesthetics; and, as its presence spread, those who lamented its damaging effects on children and family life. As we've seen, though, it was economics that dealt its death blow – its cost and the basic shortfall between promise and delivery in terms of housing density, at least until the more recent fashion for privately developed tower blocks. But architects and planners – and local politicians – needed an alternative that could challenge these deficits while providing the dense urban housing their constrained sites and budgets required.

In 1959, for those in the know, Atelier 5's Modernist Siedlung Halen development in Bern, Switzerland – a small, terraced scheme of 81 private homes – offered a way forward. In the UK, Michael Neylan's Bishopsfield Estate in Harlow New Town, winner of an architectural competition in 1961, was an innovative example of dense, low-rise housing. The Lillington Gardens Estate, designed for Westminster City Council by John Darbourne in 1964, is sometimes seen as a progenitor of low-rise, high-density development, though its maximum height at eight storeys precludes it for most. The North Peckham Estate might qualify, at five storeys, but its monolithic form won it few architectural plaudits.

As Mark Swenarton suggests, 'nowhere was reaction against high-rise more emphatic than at the Architectural Association' (a leading architectural school), and he marks the major competition for the Portsdown scheme in Portsmouth as a turning point.[18] The adjudicators' rejection of all low-rise, high-density solutions led to an influential special issue of the *Architectural Association Journal* championing the approach in March 1966. In the same month, the planning brief for the Dunboyne Road estate in Camden was published, where our story might conventionally begin.

What followed was a flowering of innovative and high-quality design that marks a high point in council housing design though, in the event, it would also be its swansong for several decades. Enlightened local authorities, championing their house style such as at Lambeth and Camden, or implementing the best of external thinking, such as at Newport in South Wales, would lead the way. Elsewhere, good but denser low-rise estates became more common.

Dunboyne Road Estate, Camden, London

Plans for the Dunboyne Road Estate were first approved by the Borough of Camden in 1967. Planning issues and politics pushed back the implementation of the scheme and, after further delays in construction, it was finally completed in 1977, by which time several other Camden schemes – notably the magisterial Alexandra Road Estate – had almost stolen its thunder. But it remains, in conception and design, the fountainhead of a swathe of council housing of unparalleled innovation and quality.

Formed in 1965 by an amalgamation of the Metropolitan Boroughs of St Pancras, Holborn and Hampstead, Camden combined radical politics and relative wealth and a youthful leadership committed to making their mark, in housing above all. Its Borough Architect from 1965 to 1973, Sydney Cook, recruited a talented team of young architects with the drive and ambition to fulfil this vision. One was Neave Brown. Brown thought that 'In discarding the street for the tower and the slab, we threw away a whole pattern of life with a quite inadequate understanding of its complexity and value'.[19] His solution was not only to recapture the 'traditional social and physical form and virtues of the city' but also 'to try and improve on them'.

At a 2.45-acre site off Fleet Road, Brown's design of an intimate estate of 71 homes, ensured that:

> The houses are in terraces as near traditional as possible. Every dwelling is identifiable with its own front door on an open route ... every dwelling has a paved garden, not overhung by a balcony above, and fenced for privacy. The houses are in groups so that eight or sixteen also share a communal garden, where children can play and people meet in groups.[20]

Left
Roof terraces and balconies, 1978

Right
Side elevation of one of the blocks, 1978

To this end, he created parallel, stepped section blocks of terraced homes – flats at ground level, maisonettes in the upper tier – each with its own pedestrian walkway. The blocks themselves were separated by strips of land containing the estate's individual and communal gardens. Car parking was provided below ground level. The housing, completed in what became Camden's signature house

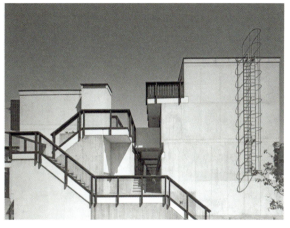

style, were of white-painted rendered concrete and dark-stained joinery. It's a dry description of a striking mix of unashamedly Modernist design and homely living, particularly as those communal and individual gardens have matured.

A 21-feet frontage for each home (much wider than that of traditional terraced housing), allowed each home two rooms across and surprisingly spacious interiors, whose lightness, flow and flexibility was enhanced by split-level design in the case of the flats and glazed stairwells and sliding partitions in the maisonettes.

Brown, in his words, sought 'new buildings that "belong" appropriate in scale and texture, and related to two traditions that I do not find incompatible: that of the immediate past ... of the Modern Movement, and that of an older formal tradition of English Housing'.[21] By the time of the estate's delayed completion, some of this thinking had become commonplace but its original creativity and successful execution was recognised when the estate was Grade II-listed in 2010. Brown was himself a resident of the estate in his later years.

Top
West elevation of the east block, 1978

Bottom left
Terraces and underground parking, 2021

Bottom right
Walkway access to maisonettes, garden terraces to right

Ladbrooke Place and St Leonard's Road, Norwich

As David Percival arrived in Norwich as City Architect in 1955, the council was approaching the end of its general needs housing programme and, like others, was looking to redevelop its areas of slum and bomb-damaged housing in the inner city. Later, Percival would echo common criticisms of 'the monotonous appearance of the earlier post-war housing estates due to the constant repetition of neat but uninspiring types of dwelling'.[22] He aimed, in his new building programme, not only 'to reflect the regional architectural traditions in housing schemes' but also 'to give individual character to each site'.[23]

In fact, a huge range of housing followed, including two 16-storey, system-built point blocks and in the Heathgate Estate a deck-access scheme likened (a little imaginatively) to Sheffield's Park Hill. But the early Alderson Place sheltered housing scheme in Finkelgate, backing unobtrusively on to the ancient St John's churchyard, winner of a Ministry of Housing and Local Government Good Housing Design award in 1961, paid closer respect in its scale and layout to the *genius loci* that Percival wished to emulate and provided a model for the best of what was to come.

The Camp Road schemes lay on hilly terrain just east of the city centre across the River Wensum. The first two phases of the development around Albert Place, Camp Grove and Saunders Court comprise a number of traditionally brick-built low-rise blocks with dark-stained joinery in an intimate warren of lanes and walkways, a deliberate replication of existing streetscapes and forms.

Right
St Leonard's Road,
2015

Top
St Leonard's Road,
2015

It is Phase III of the scheme along Ladbrooke Place and St Leonard's Road which garners most attention, however, where 87 two- and three-bedroom flats in three-storeyed terraces designed by Tayler and Green (see also page 134) make almost extravagant use of local colour and materials. Gable ends, front and back, echo traditional Norwich housing, while external walls feature 16 different types of brick and flint, cobble and colour wash. Four types of pantile adorn the roofs. This was a scheme built by the council's own workforce. Many of the others were built by trusted local contractors; the use of traditional materials was intended as a means of ensuring high-quality workmanship.

Norwich, a city which by some measures had the highest proportion of any living in council housing, built consistently well. At least eight of the central and infill schemes designed under Percival's leadership won awards from central government and the Civic Trust. This reflects an era when local authorities employed some of the country's best architects and design teams – in the mid-1970s around 49% of qualified architects worked in the public sector. And it reflects the proudly independent and progressive spirit of the city itself, part of the *genius loci* Percival served so well.

Duffryn, Newport, South Wales

Duffryn in Newport was described by one architectural critic as 'a most adventurous experiment'.[24] Comprising 977 homes on a 96-acre site, it was largest scheme of perimeter planning undertaken – and the last. Its design originated in the work of Lionel March, a mathematician, architect and digital artist, and Leslie Martin, Chief Architect at the London County Council before becoming an influential academic, at the Centre for Land Use and Built Form Studies in the University of Cambridge. Their effort, rooted in a rejection of high-rise development, was to devise forms and layouts that could deliver greater density in attractive surrounds.

Perimeter planning was predicated on the deployment of long, zig-zagged terraces, typically formed into a series of pendulous cul-de-sacs, and external access roads laid out around the edge of a large central open space, thus incorporating another key planning ideal of its time – the separation of cars and pedestrians. The concept was first applied practically by Richard MacCormac, a student of March and Martin's at Cambridge, in the Pollards Hill Estate in Merton, south London, in 1970, and subsequently in the same borough at Eastfields and, most successfully, Watermeads.

MacCormac and Peter Jamieson were commissioned by the enterprising Newport Borough Council to design Duffryn in the mid-1970s. The estate, built by 1979, was originally intended as part of a major new suburb comprising some 4,000 homes – though in the event only this first stage was completed. Its layout was characteristic of its type – a long perimeter terrace, divided into a series of

Right
Duffryn, aerial
view, 2017

octagonal courtyards or cul-de-sacs surrounded on all but one side by housing and punctuated by footpaths leading to the central open space. At Duffryn, apart from a new primary school, much of this central area was preserved as semi-wild woodland. MacCormac intended the estate to be experienced as a suburb (which he believed a popular form of housing in comparison to many public housing schemes of the day), but few community facilities were provided.

The housing itself, of prefabricated timber-frame construction, was uniform – two-storey homes with a brick ground floor and an upper level faced in cream-coloured asbestos cement with tile-hung mono-pitch roofing above. Three shades of brick, reddish-brown to mushroom, and dark-stained window framing did little to provide variety, but standardisation enabled quick and efficient construction and the layout ensured that only relatively few of the homes could be glimpsed from any one point.

The architects and the *Architects' Journal* commissioned a survey of residents in 1980. Some 'didn't like the appearance of the place and call it Stalag 15' but the survey found that its homes 'are greatly and universally liked'.[25] A majority liked the rural setting, a few missed the intimacy of their old quarters. As to neighbourliness, it concluded that Duffryn provided 'an adequate physical foundation ... for the healthy growth of a community; but whether such a future materialises will depend on other factors'.[26] In fact, the survey concluded that there were 'signs of malaise', particularly in the antisocial behaviour caused by the very high proportion of children on the estate – an astonishing 70% – and an apparently 'disproportionate number of "problem" families'. It's a reminder of the limits of architecture and planning to socially engineer our world that a majority of residents perceived Duffryn as 'just a large housing estate set on the edge of town'.[27]

Left
Duffryn in 2020

Right
Another image from 2020; the disposition of the estate belies its uniformity

Cressingham Gardens, Lambeth, London

While the Borough of Lambeth's housebuilding programme of the 1970s may have lacked the aesthetic bravura of Camden, it had in Ted Hollamby, its chief architect, an 'acknowledged leader in high density housing with low buildings'.[28] Although associated with several notable high-rise schemes in his earlier career, by this time Hollamby was championing an architecture that was 'anti-monumental, anti-stylistic, and fit for ordinary people'.[29] He sought, in housing terms, to 'create a sense of smallness inside the bigness ... and to get the kind of atmosphere in which people did not feel all herded together'.[30]

At Cressingham Gardens, begun in 1971 and finally completed after long construction delays in 1978, he achieved this both through its overall form and intricate detail. This was a small estate of some 306 homes, built in terraces of warm yellow stock brick and comprising a by now typical range of family housing and smaller units including homes for elderly and disabled people, deliberately interspersed. It rose to four storeys at its western perimeter, where a larger block acted as a barrier shielding the rest of the estate's resolutely low-rise housing from the busy Tulse Hill Road. Lead architect Charles Attwood fought for a relative low density of 100 persons per acre and carefully crafted sightlines that linked the already green estate – old trees were preserved, new ones planted, concrete flowerbeds supplied to provide colour – to Brockwell Park to the east.

Many of the larger homes also had patio gardens, and each overlooked an open space – a Hollamby signature. The neighbourliness that Hollamby desired was fostered by small design touches – front doors that faced each other and kitchen

Right
A section of the estate, 1979

windows overlooking the network of traffic-free walkways that connected the estate in intimate, almost villagey, style. The homes themselves, apparently compact but built to Parker Morris standards, were light and airy internally, with floor-to-ceiling windows and skylights, and internal walls minimised.

This was and remains an overwhelmingly popular estate, seen as friendly and attractive by almost all who live on it. At least one thought it 'like a fairy-tale, it was so beautiful'.[31] It is surprising therefore to learn that it is under threat of demolition from a council claiming (strongly disputed) heavy repair costs and wanting to build at higher density. Another fine Lambeth estate, Central Hill in Upper Norwood, designed by Rosemary Stjernstedt to similar principles and completed in 1973, is similarly imperilled. In both cases, residents have campaigned strongly to defend their homes.

Top left
A section of the estate, 1979

Top right
Scarlette Manor Way, 2014

Left
Hardel Walk with bungalows for elderly residents to the right, 2014

Dartmouth Park Hill, Camden, London

To the architect Roger Stonehouse, the Dartmouth Park Hill estate was:

a typical story of the 60s and 70s – a dramatic swing of attitude away from massive high density redevelopment in complex forms of innovative construction, towards gradual renewal at lower density in low rise, traditional forms of housing using traditional construction.[32]

It lies just next to Peter Tábori's Whittington Estate, with its white concrete stepped terraces, one of the signature schemes of Cook's Camden. That had been Highgate New Town Stage I, but by the time it was finally completed after long delays in 1978, it had already been superseded in form and ethos. Highgate New Town Stage II would take its cues from the Edwardian terraces of Dartmouth Park Hill.

Bottom
Dartmouth Park Hill, 1981

The architect Bill Forrest had proposed a scheme closer in form to Tábori's in 1974, but a revised Housing Cost Yardstick withdrew funding for underground car parking. (That may have been fortunate, as the underused subterranean garaging of the earlier scheme had been one its most troublesome aspects.)

Meanwhile government guidelines were re-emphasising renewal of rundown areas through a combination of rehabilitation and selective infill. Forrest's new plans preserved (and improved) 82 existing homes and redeveloped some 145. In another nod to emerging preoccupations, it retained some existing streets and created pedestrian through routes to enhance the 'permeability' that was held to be lacking – dangerously so in some accounts – in more traditional enclosed estates.

The finished estate in 1981 comprised a long three-storey terraced block of flats along Dartmouth Park Hill, a shorter terrace of two-storey housing on Raydon Street, and an open triangle of similar housing around Doynton Street enclosing a green open space. What is immediately obvious, however, in Stonehouse's words, is 'polychrome brickwork, some arched lintels, a facing panel or two of glazed asbestos and a few filigrees of mild steel flat and timber trellis'. The scheme retained Camden's favoured dark-stained joinery, but in all other respects it represented a stark contrast to the borough's earlier estates. It had clearer echoes of some of the Victorian and Edwardian housing it faced, particularly so in the tall arched throughways and recessed stairways that punctuate its Dartmouth Park Hill facade.

Top left and right
Dartmouth Park
Hill, 1981

Opposite
Dartmouth Park
Hill, Doynton
Street, 2015

A Civic Trust commendation in 1983 highlighted just this in praising the estate's evocation of 'memories of Edwardian villas and the welcoming scale of a delightful suburbia'. 'It is not often that nineteenth century housing appears at a disadvantage in comparison with new-build, but this scheme enhances the surroundings', it enthused.[33]

This was, in attractive and well-executed form, a return to a more traditional streetscape and scale and one deliberately more 'in keeping' with its surrounds: 'even the Camden Borough architects, hitherto whiter than white, switched to yellow brick with red stripes and pretty ironwork'.[34] In that sense, it was a rejection of much recent planning – but by 1981 council housing was facing a far more existential threat.

Rehabilitation

At a time when the powers or, excepting very rare cases, the will to build new council housing were non-existent, the rehabilitation of unfit properties was the favoured strategy of housing reform. From the mid-19th century, discretionary powers acquired by councils in private Acts of Parliament or granted in national legislation allowed councils to require landlords to improve homes 'represented' as unfit for human habitation. In general, such powers were used sparingly unless the local Medical Officer of Health was particularly zealous or councils unusually activist. Into the 1920s, some typically Conservative-run local authorities pursued vigorous programmes of reconditioning (as it was usually termed) in their rundown inner-city areas; for example Birmingham and Lambeth, though both also built council housing at scale in their suburbs.

The 1949 Housing Act made cash grants available for the first time to private owners towards the cost of the repair and improvement of their homes. At first, such powers were little used; around 4,000 grants were provided annually in the years to 1954. Conservative reforms, which loosened terms and conditions and allowed landlords to raise rents, increased the average number to around 42,000 annually in the later 1950s.

Despite the scale of redevelopment in the 1960s, housing conditions remained dire for many millions. The first comprehensive house condition survey in 1967 categorised 7.8 million English and Welsh homes (of 15.7 million in total) as unfit, requiring major repair or lacking at least one basic amenity. Fewer of these were in declared clearance areas and more were owner-occupied. As criticisms of the form, impact and expense of contemporary redevelopment intensified, rehabilitation emerged as a favoured option. At the same time, the necessity of *area* regeneration was increasingly recognised, both as a means of general uplift and as an incentive to the improvement of individual homes.

Labour's 1969 Housing Act marked this sea-change in its creation of General Improvement Areas – areas designated by local authorities comprising structurally sound but poor-quality housing, for which the Treasury would provide councils financial support to aid home improvement and environmental upgrades. Compulsory purchase powers were added to strengthen their operation but, in the event, take-up was disappointingly slow, particularly in the areas of greatest housing need.

The Conservatives' 1974 Housing Act addressed these shortfalls by concentrating resources on areas of greatest housing stress, raising grants and increasing powers of compulsory purchase in newly designated Housing Action Areas (HAA). A secondary policy aim, important to government thinking, was to enhance the role of housing associations, still at this point a very minor player in the social housing field. Of the first 81 HAAs declared in England and Wales, 55 were run by councils in cooperation with local housing associations. By mid-1977, some 219 HAAs had been established. That they contained just 80,000 homes is a reminder of the relatively small-scale impact of this intervention.

Arthur's Hill Housing Action Area, Newcastle upon Tyne

Arthur's Hill, northeast of Newcastle city centre and designated a General Improvement Area in 1973, became subsequently the first HAA to be declared in the country. A very different fate had been ordained under the grandiose city-wide redevelopment plans of T. Dan Smith (Labour leader of the city council from 1959 to 1965) and Wilfred Burns (Chief Planning Officer from 1960 to 1968). The city's 1963 Development Plan envisaged the clearance of its dense terraces and newbuild housing in their stead, part of a scheme which would see around a quarter of the city's older housing demolished.

Newcastle had made considerable (and controversial) progress in Smith and Burns' grand reimagining of the city by 1970, even if it wasn't yet the 'Brasilia of the North' they hoped for. Some 11,000 slums had been cleared and, by mid-decade, an average of 6,000 new homes were being built annually. But the mood had shifted. Burns' replacement as Planning Officer, Ken Galley, showed far more interest in the conservation of historic areas and what was termed their revitalisation. The Byker Estate, approved in 1968, was another indication of a revised approach.

The Arthur's Hill HAA, larger than most, contained 870 homes, north and south of its main through road, Stanhope Street. All but 47 of these were 'Tyneside flats' – single-storey flats upstairs and down, each with a ground floor entrance, in two-storey terraces. Eighty-eight per cent of the homes lacked an inside toilet, 62% lacked bathrooms; almost two-thirds were privately rented. It was a mostly elderly community of small households.

Left
The southern end of Arthur's Hill in a photograph taken from the Vallum Court tower block, seen here under construction, completed in 1965

Right
Renovated Tyneside Flats, Croydon Road, 2016

Left
Houses on the
junction of Croydon
Road and Tamworth
Road, 2016

Right
Mature landscaping,
Dilston Road, 2016

Having declared eight further HAAs across the city in 1975, Galley set up a 'Revitalisation Agency' within the council, while 'Housing Action Teams' were established to deal with local residents in each area. Newcastle liaised with the National Building Agency, tasked by central government to lead the programme nationally, to shape its approach and, somewhat reluctantly recognising its own lack of in-house capacity, appointed housing associations to run each scheme. In Arthur's Hill this would be North Housing, an evolution of the North Eastern Housing Association which had built the Deckham Hall Estate in Gateshead (see page 65).

The essential task, of course, was to provide inside toilets and bathrooms and, after much discussion, these were created – alongside new kitchens – in two-storey brick extensions to the rear of the homes. An average of £20,000 was spent per flat. North Housing acquired and converted around 450 of the properties.

Environmental improvement was secured by sprucing up the brickwork and lintels of existing homes, the replacement of railings, and the provision of low-level planters containing trees and shrubs on the streets. A small scheme of sheltered housing on Stanton Street represented the only newbuild.

In general, the scheme appears successful. North Housing declared itself 'very pleased'; the Department of Environment commented more guardedly that 'expectations were low and it turned out better than expected because there was a [housing association] involved'.[35] Residents' groups complained about lack of consultation and lengthy disruption, however. Demographically, the project increased the proportion of elderly residents and, conversely, the number of private student renters. Now, Arthur's Hill is a centre of Newcastle's South Asian population.

Municipalisation

In 1939, some 58% of homes were in the private rental sector; by 1991 that proportion had fallen to 9%. (It has risen more recently to around 20%.) One factor in that original precipitate decline was the rise of owner-occupation, but another was local government's acquisition and take-over of privately rented homes. The policy had deep roots on the left, where attacks on 'landlordism' had long been a staple of its rhetoric from Victorian times. Into the postwar period, Labour's 1958 housing policy pamphlet, '100 questions asked and answered' asserted 'the case [for municipalisation] in a nutshell is the failure of the private landlords ... the private landlord who owns property in order to make money must be replaced by a public landlord treating housing as a social service'.[36]

In the mid-1950s, the left-wing St Pancras Metropolitan Borough Council bought up about 1,000 houses and 'municipalised' 1,670 tenancies. At around the same time, the more moderate Birmingham City Council acquired over 30,000 privately rented homes. The difficulties caused by Birmingham's decision – which had essentially seen the council become a large slum landlord – illustrated the reasons why Labour governments approached the issue more cautiously in practical terms at a time when, in any case, the political priority was very much clearance and newbuild. In government, Labour's 1965 Rent Act focused on security of tenure and 'fair rents'.

The emphasis on redevelopment declined, as we have seen, in the later 1960s. New policies promoting the rehabilitation of rundown areas and properties provided a boost to a later wave of municipalisation, and in 1974 a new Labour government pledged an additional £350 million funding to support municipalisation. Inner London boroughs in particular, frustrated by the rate of new council housebuilding and attempting to counter the first wave of gentrification that was beginning to price out working-class locals, responded enthusiastically in purchasing 'street properties' that could be adapted to better house existing residents as well as those on the waiting list. Camden acquired the equivalent of 3,850 new homes between 1973 and 1974, and by 1983 'acquired' properties – around 12,600 homes in all – formed 36% of its total council housing stock.

However, the impetus soon slowed as a result of central government spending cuts. Whereas at peak, between 1974 and 1975, around £234 million was spent across Great Britain to purchase some 25,600 privately rented homes, by 1977/78 the figures had fallen to £56 million and 9,500 respectively. By the end of the decade, the policy was largely defunct, killed by political opposition in Westminster, not least after 1979, but hampered too by the logistical difficulties encountered by local authorities in modernising the many older properties rapidly acquired.

Islington

Islington had witnessed early controversies over the wholesale clearance of its 19th-century housing when the construction of the Packington Estate (since substantially remodelled) and Marquess Estate proceeded against local protest in the mid-1960s. In the early 1970s, however, campaigners were successful in blocking the plans of the Northampton Estate (a large corporate landlord) to redevelop parts of Canonbury. In the words of Harley Sherlock, local architect and activist, it had become 'clear that the only acceptable way of providing new housing was now through the rehabilitation of the borough's Georgian and Victorian estates, which were largely rent-controlled, dilapidated and under-occupied, and owned by big private companies'.[37] And, in fact, there was little opposition to council acquisition. There were – pre-gentrification – few owner-occupiers and landlords were often eager to sell; established residents 'positively welcomed the prospect of becoming council tenants, rather than the tenants of landlords who had neither the will nor the wherewithal to put their dilapidated properties in order'.

By this means and through negotiation rather than compulsory purchase, the Borough acquired Claremont Square from the New River Estate – three imposing (but then very rundown) Georgian terraces around a central green mound concealing a reservoir constructed by the New Rover Company. Harley Sherlock's practice was commissioned to rehabilitate most of its houses found too small to accommodate one-bedroom flats on a single floor but too large to provide a single home.

Their solution was to subdivide the houses into two units, one formed from basement and ground-floor levels, the other from the three upper storeys. Each home was provided with its own front door, a basement entrance for the lower flat that was agreed with tenants after consultation despite its elements of inconvenience. For the larger upper flats, Sherlock provided a kitchen-diner-living room in the attic storey adjacent to a roof garden created by removing the rear attic room. Three bedrooms and a bathroom were provided on lower storeys.

Left
The eastern terrace of Claremont Square

Right
The confined basement entrance to the lower flat, Claremont Square

Opposite
Tibberton Square; the estate agents' signs mark the loss of former social rent housing

A History of Council Housing in 100 Estates

Andrew Sherlock and Partners were also responsible for the rehabilitation of another Islington acquisition, Tibberton Square, around a mile to the northeast off Essex Road. The 'square' comprised two terraces of narrow three-storey houses with basements facing each other across an open space. The narrow frontages precluded the houses' conversion to family homes; here, the solution was to create upper and lower flats formed by joining pairs of houses together. The square was lowered three feet to provide better lighting and access to basement rooms and kept traffic free by the provision of new vehicular access to the rear.

Between 1971 and 1974, Islington purchased 2,012 such 'street properties'; in 1980, just 64. Central government policy dictated that decline but the policy brought its own problems, not least the ongoing difficulty and expense of maintaining such housing as purse strings tightened. Andrew Sherlock records another 'sad postscript'. The conversions proved highly popular, particularly in the Grade II-listed Claremont Square: 'The result was that, under the "right to buy" scheme, many of them eventually reached the private sector, where they fetched astronomical prices and were no longer available as social housing'.[38]

Co-operative housing and self-build

While the co-partnership schemes discussed in Chapter 2 represented an earlier (and largely unsuccessful) attempt to introduce an alternative form of housing tenure to challenge the dominance of rental and owner-occupation, the promotion of co-ownership models in the early 1960s – largely based on Scandinavian practice – was something new. Self-build projects, promoted from the 1970s, in which an individual household directly organised the design and construction of its new home, were inevitably a more niche solution to housing needs and predicated on owner-occupation or shared ownership, but found support in one notable local government experiment.

In contrast to co-partnership societies, co-ownership projects restricted share ownership and capital return to member tenants. In 1961, the Conservative government offered a £25 million grant to support cost-rent housing provided by not-for-profit housing associations and co-ownership. Its 1964 Housing Act established the Housing Corporation to provide greater financial support. It's estimated that by 1977, when this initial surge peaked, there were some 1,222 co-ownership projects in existence, owning and managing around 40,000 homes. These were generally small, averaging 40 to 50 households each; around one in five were located in newly built buildings, with most of the rest in rehabilitated terraced housing.

However, this represented just 0.2% of total housing stock; in Norway and Sweden 19% and 17% of homes were co-owned. In Britain, in contrast to Scandinavia where trade unions were major supporters, the sector had few large institutional investors. Access to finance remained a problem even after the 1975 Housing Rents and Subsidies Act allowing co-ownership schemes to register as housing associations, and support structures were generally weak.

But the biggest problem the sector faced was ideological – a British political system for which the essential choices lay, in Rob Rowlands' words, between 'market liberalism and state socialism'.[39] Labour remained committed to council housing while, conversely, from the mid-1960s also promoting owner-occupation. The Conservatives sought essentially 'to create in co-ownership a cheap form of owner occupation dressed up superficially as the more collectivist Scandinavian model'.[40]

In 2019, the Confederation of Co-operative Housing reported 180 member schemes owning and managing 74,000 homes. The sector continues to provide a lifeline of secure and low-cost rental accommodation for some, but the essential binary between social rent housing, more broadly defined, and owner-occupation remains. Despite the favourable publicity achieved by the model of self-build housing promoted by Walter Segal in the 1970s, the sector as a whole has made little headway. It is estimated that around 13,000 self- and custom-built houses are erected annually in the UK, a far lower proportion than in Continental Europe; in Germany over half of new homes are of this type.

A History of Council Housing in 100 Estates

Sanford Housing Co-operative, Lewisham, London

The Sanford Housing Co-operative in New Cross, London, was founded in 1973 – the 'first purpose-designed housing scheme for the young and mobile in the country'.[41] It emerged initially from the efforts of John Hands, one of the country's leading advocates of cooperative housing and the founder of the Society of Co-operative Dwellings in the late 1960s. Hands describes five years' campaigning before the government agreed in 1973 to support a pilot project. The Housing Corporation supplied a loan of £200,000; the Commercial Union insurance company an additional £200,000.

The scheme, 14 communal houses for 10 people each and three self-contained flats, opened in October 1974 – an inconspicuous terrace of three-storey homes tucked away on an unused parcel of land between two railway lines. One year later, collective ownership was transferred to its member-tenants. In its first full year, as members undertook many management responsibilities themselves, the co-op reported a surplus. Following a democratic vote, it was agreed to donate half the surplus to a local homelessness charity and the other half towards cooperative education. In 2013, the blocks were retrofitted to reduce their carbon footprint by 60%.

The Society of Co-operative Dwellings went on to develop a further seven newbuild cooperative schemes in London and the southeast. The Sanford Co-op itself continues to provide decent and affordable housing for its members, with those in the shared houses paying around £200 a month, less than half the rate for equivalent homes in the private rental sector locally.

Right
Sanford Housing
Co-operative

Segal Self-Build, Lewisham, London

The architect Walter Segal believed 'anyone who could saw in a straight line could build a house'.[42] The self-build model he advocated enthusiastically originated in his own 'Little House in the Garden', erected as a temporary structure while his main residence was being rebuilt in the early 1960s. It was based on a simple post-and-beam system using standard and easily acquired building materials – principally wood and woodwool for insulation – that avoided the need for bricklaying and plastering, in a modular grid format that permitted the additional advantages of greater flexibility in design and adaptability to changing needs.

Lewisham Council became an unlikely ally in promoting this model after a meeting between Segal and Brian Richardson, Assistant Borough Architect, arranged by a mutual friend, the anarchist housing reformer and educationist Colin Ward. Councillor Nicholas Taylor, another critic of mass housing, secured the Housing Committee motion that the council investigate 'alternative methods of housing such as setting up a co-operative self-build housing society'. The timing was providential; having acquired land across the borough, Lewisham found that the Housing Cost Yardstick precluded building council housing on anything but the most suitable terrain.

An initial public meeting in 1976 attracted over 168 attendees and the successful applicants, all from the council house waiting list, were selected by ballot. Land was allocated on a difficult wooded and hilly site in Brockley Park. Ironically, the radical nature of this first self-build project involved a great deal of official

Left and right
Segal Close

Opposite left
Segal Close

Opposite right
Walters Way

input; as one self-build pioneer recalled, 'meetings between officials went on and on, round and round, but in a gradually upward spiral'. Segal advised on their construction but saw himself essentially as an assistant to those building their homes. Construction finally began in 1979; the first home was completed within nine months.[43]

Segal Close emerged – a hidden and private cul-de-sac of 14 homes, described by Rowan Moore as 'delightful, faintly Japanese, faintly Tudor constructions', built on stilts to accommodate a sloping site.[44] Initially, they were purchased with the benefit of a guaranteed council mortgage on a shared ownership arrangement, but all are now owner-occupied. The success of this first trial led to a similar second scheme of 13 self-build homes in Walters Way, a kilometre to the northwest.

And there, despite the popularity of the homes themselves with residents, the matter has largely rested. Around 200 Segal-style self-build buildings have been erected across the country but, in terms of local government involvement, the Lewisham experiment was a one-off. Increased health and safety and thermal efficiency standards have imposed their own demands on new self-build; resident and exponent Alice Grahame admits Segal's houses 'are a bit draughty … he just thought you should put another sweater on if you got cold'. Conversely, a strength of the homes is their adaptability. Dave Dayes, one of the original self-builders in Walters Way and still resident, completed his three-bedroom home in 1987. In 2009, he undertook a complete rebuild – including triple glazing and thicker, better-insulated and clad walls – that brought his home to the highest environmental standards. Despite increased government support, the largest obstacle to the spread of self-build appears to remain a cultural resistance to the practice in the UK.[45]

CHAPTER 8

1980s–1990s: A Housing Counterrevolution – the Attack on Council Housing and the 'Council Estate'

With the election of a New Right Conservative government, 1979 is regularly and reasonably portrayed as a crucial watershed in British housing policy. In fact, in some respects it occurred earlier. In May 1975, Labour's Secretary of State for the Environment Anthony Crosland had declared, in the context of darkening economic times, to a gathering of local authority leaders that 'the party is over'; *The Times*' report was headlined 'Councils are told to curb rise in spending'.[1] His warning was strengthened by the balance of payments crisis of the following year.

The broad postwar consensus – encompassing an interventionist state and mixed economy as well as shared principles of foreign policy – that had shaped British politics since the war was eroding, as criticism of the efficiency and effectiveness of publicly owned institutions expanded and unemployment increased. Margaret Thatcher, elected party leader in 1975, personified a neoliberal turn in Conservative politics. This approach, favouring free-market capitalism, deregulation and cuts in government spending, believed private enterprise best adapted to meet consumer needs or, failing that and particularly in housing, thought third-sector organisations more responsive and flexible. In power, this was reflected in a particular antipathy towards the Labour-controlled councils, considered profligate and inefficient, that owned and managed much public housing. The latter was a view shared to a significant extent by New Labour governments after 1997. New Right ideologues also believed that council tenancies encouraged a 'dependency culture' inhibiting the personal and social mobility thought central to an enterprise culture.

Council housing emerged as a major site of neoliberal intervention, but the ground had been prepared earlier. The first use of the term 'sink estate' occurred in a *New Society* article in November 1976.[2] A government investigation of 30 'difficult-to-let' estates (those to which applicants were unwilling to move) was launched in the same year, and such estates were formally enumerated from 1978. By 1983, it was estimated that around 6.6% of council homes could be classified as difficult-to-let, typically those on Modernist, often system-built, estates in the larger urban authorities. While council housing had once represented aspirational housing for most (as it still was for the many on waiting lists, of course), owner-occupation increasingly came to be seen as the gold standard and council homes as something inferior.

After 1979, central government spending on public housing was drastically curtailed, both in terms of maintenance and newbuild, even as the housing benefit bill increased enormously. In essence, a supply-side system of bricks and mortar subsidies that built new council homes was replaced by a demand-side system of personal allowances, reflecting consumer spending on both private and social rental. The right of sitting council tenants to purchase their homes introduced in 1980 was, of course, the Conservatives' flagship housing policy and, such was its popularity that some 1.7 million former council homes were lost to Right to Buy by 1997.

This perfect storm of policy, combined with the decline of traditional manufacturing employment, led to a process of 'residualisation' by which council estates were increasingly occupied by a poorer and more vulnerable population while council housing itself was sometimes seen – by right-wing politicians but also by a broadening swathe of the general public – as 'housing of last resort'.

Regeneration was an attempt by governments of right and left to improve council estates and, by extension, their residents – but it must also be understood as a critique of the form and ethos of public housing that preceded it. The intellectual origins of these criticisms might be traced across the Atlantic, to Jane Jacobs' 1961 book *The Death and Life of Great American Cities* that celebrated the street life of dense mixed-used neighbourhoods, and, more directly, to Oscar Newman's 1972 book *Defensible Space*, that condemned the design of some of America's large urban public housing schemes. In the UK, such ideas gained more powerful traction and simplified form when taken up by Alice Coleman, author of *Utopia on Trial: Vision and Reality in Planned Housing*, published in 1985. The 16 elements of 'design disadvantage' Coleman identified were, in essence, a description of the principal features of Modernist public housing – multiple storeys, common entrances, shared walkways and decks. All were held to contribute to blurred boundaries between public and private space and the antisocial behaviour and crime allegedly prevalent. Coleman's theories provided a basis for much of the estate remodelling that followed, most obviously in the replacement of multi-storey housing with lower-rise alternatives and the revival of traditional streetscapes. Estates as such were increasingly questioned. As Southwark planned the redevelopment – essentially the demolition – of the Aylesbury Estate, it was 'determined to break down the estate concept … By the end of the development we no longer want the area to be conceived as a single perceptible entity but feel that it belongs to the city around it'.[3]

At the same time, regeneration sought to reform estates, criticised as mono-tenure and mono-class (their fault, of course, was to be working-class). They were to be 'mixed communities' containing a range of tenures; owner-occupied, privately rented as well as, though in declining numbers, social rent homes owned by local authorities and, increasingly, housing associations.

Regeneration

Regeneration addressed real problems. Many estates required renovation, the result of both expected obsolescence and cutbacks in maintenance since the 1970s. Some, often those system-built, were poorly constructed. But there was also a broader perception that many estates were failing socially and that some were subject to particular problems of crime and antisocial behaviour. Though their severity was exaggerated by stridently negative media coverage and elements of moral panic, broader social tensions may indeed have led to such problems. However, it was estates themselves – their form and composition – that were held to blame, understood as not the victim of wider dynamics but as the agent of their own misfortune.

Reflecting the belief that these problems had confined spatial causes rather than broader societal ones, area-based regeneration became the watchword. The programme began modestly in 1980 with the Priority Estates Project, initially covering just 20 estates, focusing on more responsive local management and enhanced tenant participation. Estate Action, covering 350 estates by 1991, added diversified tenure and stock transfer (from councils to housing associations or, in a few cases, tenants' organisations) to the mix alongside initiatives intended to increase residents' employability. Housing Action Trusts, from 1988, pursued similar goals by transferring the ownership and management of estates to independent boards. The Single Regeneration Budget established in 1994 was intended to enable a holistic approach combining the range of these initiatives.

New Labour's Decent Homes Standard, announced in 2000, differed from earlier policies in setting quality benchmarks for all public and private rental housing by requiring every home to be in a reasonable state of repair and enjoying up-to-date facilities and services. Around 1.6 million social rent homes were judged non-decent, 39% of the total. The legislation has played a major role in improving homes and estates across the country, but its implementation was funded in large part by the transfer of council housing stock to housing associations, or the new 'Arms-Length Management Organisations' permitted borrowing powers to finance the estimated £19 billion backlog of repairs and renovation denied local government.

The form and financing of regeneration contained other dynamics. The new model of public–private partnership and cross-subsidy (by which the construction of social rent and 'affordable' housing was financed by homes built for sale and private rental) impelled redevelopment – demolition and newbuild that would reward investors – rather than renovation. The high price of land and its lack of availability in the inner city made existing estates, treated as a form of brownfield land, attractive to local authorities looking to develop new schemes and increase housing density.

The social costs to existing tenants and inadequately compensated leaseholders who had bought their council homes were high, however – years of blight and disruption and often forced relocation to homes distant from existing

A History of Council Housing in 100 Estates

residences. Nor was there an increase in social rent homes, as many were replaced with housing built for owner-occupation or shared ownership, or let at so-called 'affordable' rents set at 80% of prevailing market rates. The frequent charge of 'state-led gentrification' – the criticism that working-class residents were being deliberately replaced by middle-class incomers – directed at many regeneration schemes, particularly in London, had genuine force. In the current climate crisis, a model of demolition and newbuild, so profligate of embodied energy used in original construction, is also coming under increasing fire.

North Hull Estate, Kingston upon Hull

The first housing on the North Hull Estate was built under the 1919 Housing Act; by 1939 it contained 4,371 homes. All apart from 32 cottage flats were self-contained two-storey houses built, cottage suburb-style, along the most 'most approved and advanced Town Planning lines' of the day.[4] Once nicknamed 'the Queen of the Estates', by the 1990s North Hull had fallen on hard times. It was a poorer and ageing community – one in five of the economically active population were unemployed, around a third of residents were over 60 – and its housing required modernisation. Around half the estate's homes had been improved under the Estate Action programme, but a further £50–60 million required to complete the job was refused.

Meanwhile, the Conservative government's Housing Action Trust (HAT) initiative launched in 1988 had hit a roadblock. Tenant activism had successfully resisted the attempt to impose a HAT in Hulme, Manchester, and had established the principle of tenants' ballots in future proposals; the first, in the North Peckham Estate, had decisively rejected the idea. North Hull was very far from being one of the 'worst estates' initially targeted in the government's programme, but the Conservatives needed a compliant local authority willing to transfer part of its stock to an independent body – most were not – and to help achieve

Bottom
Greenwood Avenue, the North Hull Estate's main thoroughfare, named after Arthur Greenwood, Labour's Minister of Housing between 1929 and 1931

Opposite left
Housing on Greenwood Avenue

Opposite right
Semi-detached corner homes on 22nd Avenue

tenant consent. Hull was an overwhelmingly Labour council but the interest of its Housing Committee chair, John Black, lay, in his own words, 'in seeking to achieve results, not some theory of government'.[5] A two-hour car journey with Deputy Housing Minister David Trippier helped secure a deal. The unmodernised homes of North Hull would become a HAT while the council, for its part, would receive (uniquely) a £5.75 million payment to fund housing renovations elsewhere in the city and the agreement that tenants could, if they wished, return to the council as a landlord once the HAT was wound up. Concerted campaigning and the promise of improved housing secured a 69% vote in favour of transfer from tenants in April 1991.

The new HAT comprised 2,436 homes, of which 2,109 were council-owned and 327 owner-occupied. On average, £31,000 was spent on each as, after mandatory structural repairs, residents were empowered to choose from a 'menu' of home upgrades including rear porches, French windows, wall lights and new kitchen units. Environmental and landscaping improvements were added, alongside other typical elements of the regeneration playbook including programmes to raise residents' health, 'self-esteem' and employability.

It might be seen as a sign of relative ingratitude (or satisfaction with local authority ownership) that 48% of tenants opted to return to the city council when the trust was wound up in 1999. Some 33% joined local housing associations, while the rate of owner occupation increased from 14% to just 18%. In that sense, the results of the North Hull HAT may have been disappointing to government, but the project prepared the way for the five further HATs that followed in Liverpool, Birmingham and London.

Raffles Estate, Carlisle

The novelist Margaret Forster was born in 1938 'in the front bedroom of a house in Orton Road, a house on the outer edge of Raffles, a council estate'. She considered herself 'a lucky girl'.[6] The estate, Carlisle's largest interwar scheme, contained 1,518 homes by 1939 – a garden suburb of two- and three-bedroom non-parlour homes, 12 to the acre. 'When they were nearing completion, young families would walk round Raffles on Sunday afternoon to admire the new houses and all the greenery and the new shops.'[7]

But in 1994 the estate made it into the *Independent*'s report on 'No-go Britain', apparently plagued by car theft and youth gangs. One resident allegedly commented 'If you've got a problem in Raffles, get a shotgun'.[8] A survey showed it the most stigmatised estate in Carlisle, rejected by fully three-quarters of local residents as a desirable place to live and with a void rate (proportion of empty properties) of around 30%. The obvious explanation of this decline lay in the circumstances of its tenants: around two-thirds of households were in receipt of state benefits, and some 28% of the estate's population were under 16, with many living in disadvantaged single-parent households.

Between 1987 and 1995, Raffles received £16 million of Estate Action funding, mostly spent on measures to physically improve the estate – traffic calming, landscaping, window replacements and so on. A later £3 million grant from the Single Regeneration Budget went on employment and training initiatives. All this apparently achieved 'no material change in the prosperity and stability of Raffles'.[9]

Bottom
Raffles in its early heyday: Dalton Avenue, 1937

Opposite left
Brookside Place, 1937

Opposite right
The new Raffles

A History of Council Housing in 100 Estates

In 1999, the city council determined on a more extensive scheme of regeneration – a four-year programme that would demolish almost half the estate's council houses and build new homes for private rental and ownership. The team eventually appointed in 2002 to carry out the project comprised the Riverside Group (a housing association), the Lovell Group (a private sector development company) and Ainsley Gommon Architects. The residents played their part by voting (albeit by a rather narrow 52% majority) to accept the transfer of their homes to the housing association.

By 2006, local media were proclaiming Raffles 'The trendy new place to live'.[10] Long-standing residents praised the changes; 'I've lived here 45 years and love it ... It's nice now. At one time you couldn't leave your house, but it hasn't half quietened down'.[11] Local crime statistics supported this impression. The drastic surgery had apparently achieved its aims, though in 2021 press reports still talked of the necessity of evictions 'sparked by adults and their teenagers whose anti-social behaviour is causing others to fear living in the area'.[12] At the same time, the demolition of over 500 council homes and their replacement by homes for sale or a few at so-called affordable rent has contributed to a shortage of genuinely affordable homes for those on local waiting lists. The costs and benefits of regeneration and its copybook solutions are perhaps more complex than sometimes allowed.

Hulme Crescents, Manchester

Hulme V – the Hulme Crescents – were officially opened in 1971. Described just seven years later by Allan Roberts, then chair of Manchester City Council's Housing Committee, as an 'absolute disaster – it shouldn't have been planned, it shouldn't have been built', the scheme was finally demolished in 1994, replaced by the very different Hulme we see today.[13]

Initial hopes had been high. The planning brief of its architects, Hugh Wilson and Lewis Womersley (responsible for Sheffield's Park Hill Estate), had seen in the estate's four large six-storey, crescent-shaped, deck-access blocks a deliberate echo of Georgian Bath. System building, they argued, promised a 'high quality of finish, both internally and externally'.[14] A local councillor proclaimed, 'highways in the sky, safe from cars ... the future of housing now'.[15]

What went wrong? Construction flaws from poorly executed prefabrication were disastrous from the outset. The closure of city streets and the enclosure of the estate by large two large dual carriageways isolated it. The decks apparently promoted antisocial behaviour rather than the neighbourliness foreseen. By 1975, a survey showed 96% of tenants wishing to relocate. As the estate became hard to let, these problems multiplied as it became increasingly occupied by a poorer and more troubled population. The city council struggled to maintain the estate, and by the 1990s it had 'become unmanageable'.[16] 'Planet Hulme' emerged, an anarchic land of misrule occupied by squatters – 'a

Bottom
Hulme Crescents layout, City of Manchester (October 1965), Hulme 5 Redevelopment. Report on Design by Hugh Wilson and Lewis Womersley.

Opposite left
Hulme Crescents visualisation, City of Manchester (October 1965), Hulme 5 Redevelopment. Report on Design by Hugh Wilson and Lewis Womersley.

Opposite right
Hulme Crescents, 1971

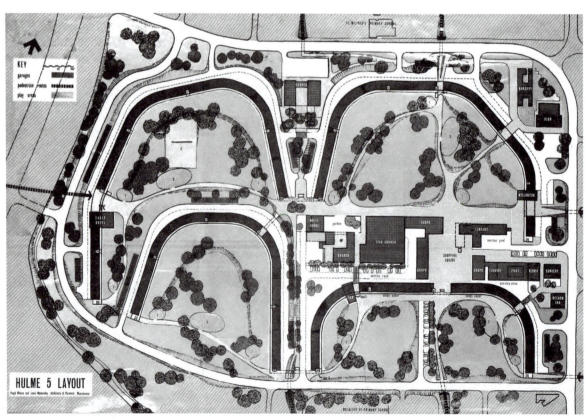

HULME 5 LAYOUT
Hugh Wilson and Lewis Womersley, Architects & Planners, Manchester

Modernist utopia decaying, gone crumbled and decadent' according to Owen Hatherley, but one deeply uncomfortable for more established residents.[17]

Plans to impose a Housing Action Trust in 1988 were blocked, but Manchester won City Challenge funding four years later. Hulme Regeneration Ltd, comprising the council's Hulme Subcommittee (representing the housing department, housing associations and tenants) and construction company AMEC was formed to oversee regeneration. This complex structure oversaw a process whose outcomes were essentially shaped by the 40-page *Guide to Development in Hulme*. It prescribed a mix of tenures, a 'built environment … of high quality', more family life, and permeability – a new streetscape that reintegrated the area into the city proper.[18] The aspirations of one tenant were expressed more simply: 'we wanted more houses than flats, gardens, lots of greenery and safe areas for children'.[19]

What evolved was a pretty conventional mix of redbrick semi-detached homes, terraces and functional low-rise flats along streets south of the reopened Stretford Road. The cooperative housing scheme Homes for Change – a small oasis of deck-access Brutalism – emerged as a solitary reminder of the 'alternative Hulme' of the 1980s. In all, £200 million was spent on the area's redevelopment. The outcome was a modest but telling 'back to the future' signifier of changed times and fashions, and a rebuke to the sometimes misplaced ambitions of the 1960s or, at the very least, their flawed execution.

Five Estates, Peckham, Southwark, London

The so-called Five Estates, wedged between Peckham High Street and Burgess Park, had little in common save a loose geographical proximity, but together they formed the subject of the largest successful Single Regeneration Budget (SRB) bid – a grant of £60 million in 1994. The Sumner Estate comprised interwar tenement blocks; the Willowbrook Estate, completed in 1963, low-rise maisonette blocks and one 12-storey tower. The later estates were also a mix. Gloucester Grove, built by the Greater London Council, brick-clad, of panel construction, contained over 1,200 homes in linked blocks ranging from three to eight storeys. Two Southwark schemes completed the ensemble: the Camden Estate, six- to eight-storey deck-access blocks of traditional brick construction and, most notoriously, another traditionally built, deck-access scheme, the North Peckham Estate described fully on page 185. 'It wasn't', as one local councillor commented, 'as if the area was all a sink estate' but the design flaws and social problems of the latter two in particular and the nature of the bidding process compelled a wholesale response that radically transformed the district as a whole.

There had been earlier renovation. The North Peckham Project had secured Estate Action funding in 1987, but tenant opposition to the formation of a Housing Action Trust the following year stymied further regeneration until the Peckham Partnership's successful SRB bid six years later. The partnership was a consortium of Southwark Council, tenant representatives, Countryside Properties plc, the Laing Group, housing associations and other interested local bodies. The

Bottom
Shurland Gardens, Willowbrook Estate – early 1960s maisonette blocks with later pitched roof 'improvements'

Opposite
The Five Estates, showing past and projected regeneration, 1994

creation of a more socially diverse and affluent, less working-class, community was central to its aims as described by Steve Chance, a director of Pollard Thomas Edwards, the firm of architects appointed to oversee the scheme:

The intention was to have a mixed tenure neighbourhood and make it possible for people to want to buy private property in an area that was not popular. We are not trying to build a new estate, we are trying to build a bit of ordinary London.

Estates were held to have failed as such and, in his eyes at least despite their ubiquity, did not represent the 'ordinary London' that new times demanded.

This entailed drastic surgery. The Willowbrook Estate, renovated previously – its harmless point block had been demolished and the maisonette blocks were given pitched roofs – survived; the Camden Estate was thoroughly refurbished

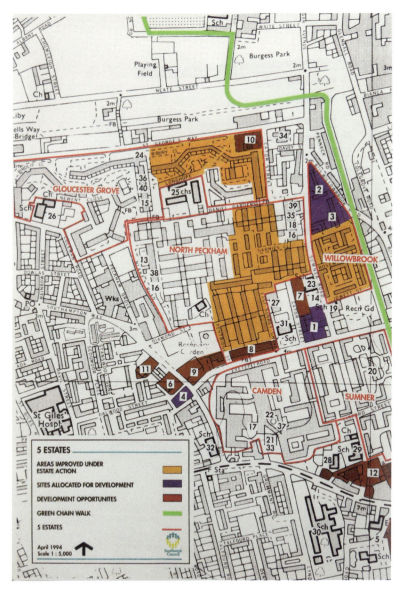

but left substantially intact. Most of the other estates were cleared. The number of homes across the Five Estates was reduced from 4,532 to 3,694. And the area shifted from 99% council-rented to 60%; housing associations let some 915 homes and 625 were built for owner-occupation. Streets were reinstated, and of 1,854 new homes built, 70% had gardens.

At the end of the process, according to one gushing journalistic account, the estates had 'been transformed from pits of urban blight into shining examples of regeneration'. A residents' survey conducted in 2002 showed 83% felt that their quality of life had improved. Visually, the result is a rather bland low-rise suburbia executed chiefly in the New London Vernacular architectural style currently favoured.

Top
Andoversford Court, part of the Gloucester Grove Estate, which has survived largely unscathed

Bottom
New housing, Tilbury Close

Broadwater Farm, Haringey, London

A troubled past and more recent ill-informed commentary have combined to make the Broadwater Farm Estate in Tottenham one of the most notorious in the county. The 1985 riots and the murder of PC Keith Blakelock as well as further disorder in 2011 etched the estate in public consciousness; unwanted publicity that increased when it featured as one of the 100 'sink estates' to be tackled by prime minister David Cameron's evanescent 'Blitz' on Britain's 'worst estates' in 2016. Its actual history and long-running regeneration provides a more complex and, in many ways, more positive story.

The estate, built by Haringey Council between 1967 and 1973, was typical of its time: a mixed development scheme comprising two 19-storey towers, nine six-storey blocks and a number of lower-rise maisonette blocks joined by deck-access walkways to separate pedestrians and traffic. Construction using the Larsen-Nielsen large-panel system was briefly halted after the Ronan Point collapse in May 1968 to allow existing and future blocks to be modified and strengthened. An unusual feature of the estate – a product of a site thought prone to flooding – was the use of piloti to raise all the principal buildings above ground level.

Bottom
Broadwater Farm Estate – a forbidding view of the underground parking areas, 1980

Construction flaws were apparent soon after completion. Flat roofs created severe problems of water penetration and damp in many flats; the district heating system was found noisy and inefficient. Antisocial behaviour became

a wider issue. Jim Sneddon, an architect and one of the fiercest critics of the estate's design, blamed the under-block parking areas for creating 'a concrete "underworld" for crime to thrive. Badly lit and overlooked by nothing, these "dark arches" became a muggers' paradise'.[20]

The estate became hard to let. Even in 1973, a council report – in language reinforcing the prejudices it documented – commented on '"problem" families – many of them single-parent families' and racial tensions apparently aggravated by 'the sight of unmarried West Indian mothers walking about the estate'.[21] Clasford Stirling, who moved to the estate in 1978, described it as a 'dumping ground ... just a mass of graffiti, shit everywhere'.[22]

In 1980, the Priority Estates Project set up a new neighbourhood housing office and spent £1 million on renovations, improved security and maintenance. The Broadwater Farm Youth Association, founded by Dolly Kiffin in 1981 (Clasford Stirling was an early member), was a vital community-led initiative. Intractable problems remained, however, not least the residents' anger at racist policing that underlay the tragic events of 1985.

Further regeneration under the Estate Action programme followed. A 'Ground-Level Reinstatement Plan' relocated deck-level shops to Willan Road and created new lobbies with concierge services at surface level for the larger blocks. Walkways were removed in 1993. The Council's Building Design Services, headed by John Murray, made a point of recruiting underrepresented minority community members to area-based design teams. A new community centre, children's nursery and health centre have been built since. By the time of Cameron's speech in 2016, Broadwater Farm was, in many respects and through this combination of top-down reform and bottom-up activism, a success story. Controversy remains, however. In 2018 a survey found Tangmere and Northholt blocks structurally unsound; both are now scheduled for demolition. Despite the council-owned replacement housing promised, some residents are sceptical and many fear the dislocation and disruption ahead.

Left
Tangmere, 2016

Right
Hawkinge and
Kenley Tower, 2016

Opposite
Croydon, 2016

CHAPTER 9

Social Housing Today –
Regeneration, Newbuild
and Sustainability

Prohibitive restrictions on council housing newbuild continued into the 2000s, though Scotland's devolved government has recently pursued more supportive policies towards council housebuilding. In 2011, Scottish local authorities were given access to the affordable housing grants previously restricted to housing associations, and in 2015 the Scottish government announced a flagship five-year, £3.5 billion programme to build 50,000 new affordable homes, 35,000 at social rent. In England, a small revival in council housing had been promised by legislation in 2012. This allowed the 169 local authorities still owning and managing council housing – many had transferred their stock to housing associations – to borrow on their housing assets. However, it had little immediate impact, offset by continuing Right to Buy sales and capped social rents.

Nevertheless, a variety of ingenious means have been found to support limited building programmes. Section 106 agreements and the Community Infrastructure Levy (by which councils secured contributions from developers via the planning system to pay for local amenities and affordable housing) were a favoured means, but were always constrained by the private developers' ability to limit social provision and game the system to their benefit. Increasingly, local authorities have turned to wholly council-owned housing companies and public–private joint ventures to build, a shift facilitated by the easing of borrowing restrictions in 2018. By 2021, it was reported that 80% of English councils were directly engaged in housebuilding, but of these new homes just 11% were let at social rent, given the financial necessity to cross-subsidise council housing by the construction and marketing of homes for sale and private rental. Furthermore, while 70,000 new social rent homes had been built since 2012, 210,000 existing homes had been lost to Right to Buy.

For all the recent small uptick in newbuild, social housing remains beleaguered. Coalition and Conservative governments since 2010 have viewed it as a residual sector serving only those who could afford or aspire to no better. Attempts to impose so-called flexible fixed-term tenancies (ending security of tenure) and 'Pay to Stay' policies to charge higher-income council tenants market rates were successfully resisted, but the 2013 Bedroom Tax, which increased rents for those tenants with a bedroom deemed surplus to their needs, was a harsh indication of tenants' second-class status. These policies do not apply to Scotland, which also abolished Right to Buy in 2016. Wales followed suit two years later.

The Grenfell fire, in which 72 residents died in June 2017, seemed – in the starkest form – to confirm the failure of social housing. The poor administration of the tenant management organisation that ran the North Kensington tower block and the cost-cutting agenda that governed its refurbishment will rightly be held accountable. However, the scandal of the flammable cladding that caused the fire lay in a government programme of deregulation that has weakened building control since 2010 and has afflicted private sector schemes to greater effect (and with, to date, far less remediation).

Conversely, local authorities continue for the most part to aspire to build well and, in many respects, to set a benchmark of quality and innovation that commercial developers might emulate. Regeneration of existing estates continues, on a large scale such as Glasgow's Sighthill, and on a smaller scale where, at best, sensitive architect-designed infill development can add to social housing provision. While local government has for the most part lost the in-house expertise that once planned and designed its council housing, private architectural practices with a real commitment to social housing's role and purpose have emerged to build some of the outstanding new homes of the 21st century. As the climate crisis heightens, councils are at the forefront of providing the more sustainable homes that might mitigate its impact.

Regeneration

Estate regeneration has continued on a significant scale into the present decade. There is now less talk than in the 1980s and 1990s of 'failing estates' and fewer (exaggerated) claims of crime and antisocial behaviour. More typically, regeneration is justified by the new mantras of 'mixed community' and 'mixed tenure'. The latter, of course, justifies the building of homes for sale and private rental that public–private partnership and the cross-subsidy model compel in the current financial regime of public housing. The growing population of London in particular adds another rationale – the need to house more people on less land. The argument has genuine force as we seek to create more sustainable modes of urban (as opposed to suburban) living, but 'densification' too has its more pragmatic drivers. Estates are publicly owned land and, as such, far more readily available to development and redevelopment than prohibitively expensive private land for purchase. 'New Urbanism' talks of 15-minute neighbourhoods of walkable streets and accessible amenities, a return to how cities and towns were held to have worked in the past. Again, planning ideals aligned readily with property interests as when, for example, the estate agents Savills talked of replacing 'old blocks of [council] flats' with 'new streets of terraced housing and mid-rise mansion blocks'.[1]

To those displaced by estate regeneration or communities suffering the years of blight it often entails, it is experienced very differently: as something imposed by external interests but not planned, in the words of one long-term resident of the Carpenters Estate in Newham, east London, 'for the likes of us'.[2] Since 1997, it is estimated that 54,263 council homes in London have either been demolished or scheduled for demolition and at least 135,658 households displaced. The Heygate Estate in Southwark is the most notorious example, where between 2011 and 2014 1,200 council flats were demolished and replaced by the luxury Elephant Park development on which just 82 of 3,000 new homes were for social rent. Southwark is one of a number of London boroughs with a significant newbuild social housing programme, but the statistics here and elsewhere demonstrate a clear net loss of public housing.

The peculiar forces of land and capital operating in London may not be replicated as strongly elsewhere but the broad dynamics and preferred outcomes of regeneration are similar. In Glasgow, where in 1981 63% of the population lived in a council home, reforms to the management, magnitude and form of public housing have been the most sweeping in the country.

Sighthill Transformational Regeneration Area, Glasgow

The Sighthill Transformational Regeneration Area (TRA) is the UK's largest regeneration project outside London. In the 1960s, it had been part of the Springburn Comprehensive Development Area, one of 20 such in Glasgow, in which slum tenements were cleared wholesale to make way for the mass public housing of the new era – 10 20-storey slab blocks designed and built by Crudens Ltd, interspersed among lower-rise maisonette blocks, housing together some 7,500 residents. An unpopular estate by the 1970s, in the following decade it became a 'byword for deprivation', unfairly stigmatised but also suffering real problems of unemployment, crime and drug use.[3] By the turn of the century, the scheme was being used to house those with least housing choice, including refugees and asylum seekers.

Housing allocations to Fountainwell, the northern half of the area, were halted in 2005 and two of Fountainwell's five slab blocks were demolished in 2008, the rest the following year. Glasgow's bid in 2012 to host a forthcoming Youth Olympics was rejected (there had been plans to use empty blocks to accommodate competitors) but the city council agreed a £250 million redevelopment programme to transform the area, accomplished firstly by the demolition of Pinkston's five slab blocks by 2016.

Sighthill became one of Glasgow's eight TRAs to be overseen by Transforming Communities: Glasgow, a partnership between Glasgow City Council, Glasgow Housing Association and the Scottish government, supported by 'Local Delivery Groups' for each of the project areas. Tellingly, in the overall programme, just 600 homes let at social rent are planned against some 6,500 'for affordable sale or mid-market rent'.[4] At peak in the late 1970s, Glasgow City Council owned and

Left
A surviving low-rise maisonette block and newbuild on Fountainwell Drive

Right
Newbuild and landscaping with low-rise maisonette blocks

Left
Children's play area
and newbuild

Right
Newbuild

managed some 180,000 homes and was by some way the largest public sector landlord in Europe.

In Sighthill, the first major elements completed, in 2020, have been a community campus comprising a new school and sports facilities and new parkland – 74 acres of 119 are designated 'green infrastructure'. (The latter includes the restoration of Sighthill's most famous landmark – an astronomically aligned stone circle, first created in 1979.) In contrast to many earlier municipal schemes, the intention here has been to ensure 'a useable neighbourhood was available to residents from the first'.[5] Of 1,000 new and energy-efficient homes planned by 2027, 140 were completed the following year.

Another major component of the overall scheme has been to better integrate Sighthill into the city as a whole and capitalise on its relatively central location, just a 15-minute walk from George Square but separated from it by the M8 motorway. A new pedestrian and cyclist bridge over the M8 and a road bridge over the Glasgow–Edinburgh railway line will improve its connections with the centre and neighbouring areas.

All this will add up to a change that can be properly called transformational. In most eyes, it will be seen as a sharp corrective to the planning and design missteps of the 1960s. If the scheme lives up to its publicity such a view will be justifiable, though we might remember at least the ambitions to provide genuinely affordable housing of that earlier era.

Newbuild

The 2020 report of the cross-party Housing, Communities and Local Government Select Committee, 'Building more social housing', provided a succinct summary of the recent evolution of housing policy and priorities:

> Between 1946 and 1980, an average of 126,000 council homes were built every year. Last year, just 6,827 were built. In the early 1990s, social rent made up over 75 per cent of all new affordable housing supply; last year it made up just 11 per cent … Social housing delivery has dropped to an average of around 35,000 a year in the last decade, with the majority of these let at more expensive affordable rent levels.[6]

The report went on to note that, according to official figures, around half a million households are homeless or living in unsatisfactory housing conditions. In England, around 1.2 million households are on social housing waiting lists. In overall terms, state spending on housing remains high, but whereas in the 1970s some 80% of housing expenditure went towards the construction of social housing, by 2000, 85% was spent on Housing Benefit. The UK currently spends around £20 billion annually on Housing Benefit, a figure predicted to rise to £30 billion as a result of the pandemic. Beyond legal and financial restrictions, the capacity of local authorities to build has been severely constrained by the loss of in-house expertise. In the mid-1970s, 49% of qualified architects worked in the public sector. That figure now stands at around 1%.

Nevertheless, as the research of Janice Morphet and Ben Clifford testifies, many local authorities are ambitious to build and, amid such difficulties, 'are increasing their levels of housing delivery in all ways including development, acquisition, regeneration and joint working … there was increased corporate priority around housing development, particularly around maximising affordable housing delivery, in many councils and a growing sense of momentum'.[7] Beyond simple numbers, there is a growing emphasis on the architectural and design quality of newbuild, particularly in relation to environmental standards. There is also increased interest in so-called 'modern methods of construction' using forms of prefabrication. As evidenced, there is in fact little that is modern in this approach, and it remains to be seen if this latest iteration of the long-held aspiration to build rapidly and more cheaply using mechanised methods will be more successful, practically and aesthetically, than some in the past.

Donnybrook Quarter, Old Ford Road, Tower Hamlets, London

The Donnybrook Quarter, designed by Peter Barber for the Circle 33 housing association and completed in 2006, has been described as 'one of the most innovative housing projects to be undertaken in the UK for decades'; one that 'might be remembered as a significant turning point in the culture of British housing provision'.[8] With a quarter of its 42 homes ranging from one-bedroom studios to a four-bedroom family house let at social rent and the rest for sale on the open market, it's a modest scheme in essence – four short terraces on a tight corner site in Bow, east London – but it stands out in both appearance and conception.

To a passer-by, it is the look of the small estate that is most striking: flat-roofed, white-washed housing, facades enlivened by balconies and oriel windows, deployed tightly around narrow pedestrian streets and a small central square, graced when I visited by cherry trees in full bloom. It's reminiscent of the Mediterranean. Barber describes discussing plans with residents: 'We were thinking, Le Corbusier, Adolf Loos, JJP Oud; the residents were thinking, "Spain! Holidays! Marbella!"'[9]

Barber was, he declared, 'happy with that' but he also had a more local reference, the Victorian 'back of pavement terrace' where front doors opened directly on to the street. Having removed the need for communal stairwells, lobbies and corridors, in Donnybrook it is the streets themselves that provide the estate's circulation space. The plan allows an unusually high-density design – the typical three-storey unit comprises a ground-floor flat and a two-bedroom maisonette above entered from the street through a courtyard garden. It is

Left
The scheme on completion, 2006

Right
The scheme on completion, 2006

Opposite left top
Axonometric drawing of layout

Opposite top right
Floor plan of flat

Opposite left
Photographed in spring 2021

also a celebration of public space, or 'a piece of the city' as Barber described it. A similar space-saving ethos is applied to the internal layout of the homes, in which the front door opens directly into an open-plan living room/kitchen and, so far as possible, unnecessary hallways are avoided. It's a compact design – the two-bedroom flats range from 55 to 65 m² in size – but each home is provided its own outside terrace.

As Barber acknowledges, the commission, selected as the winner of an Innovations in Housing competition organised by the Architecture Foundation and attracting 150 entries, also reflected the work of Richard Rogers' Urban Task Force convened by the Department of the Environment in 1998. Charged with arresting urban decline and outlining a new, greener, vision for cities based on affordable design excellence and social wellbeing, the group recommended denser urban living and mixed-use neighbourhoods. Barber, who established his architectural practice in far more restrictive times in 1989, recalled that he had 'projects like this in sketchbooks for years, and they just weren't possible before now'.

The scheme received a RIBA Regional Design Award in 2006 and was longlisted in the same year for the Stirling Prize, conferred by the Royal Institute of British Architects on the architect of the building that has made the greatest contribution to the evolution of architecture in the past year.

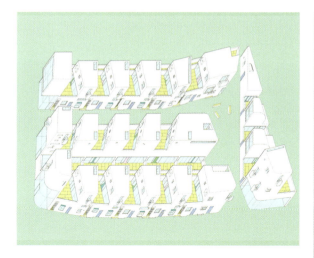

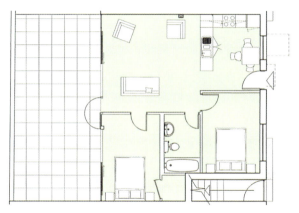

Dujardin Mews, Ponders End, Enfield, London

Dujardin Mews in Ponders End, completed in 2017, was the first housing built by the London Borough of Enfield for 40 years. Ostensibly, it represents a reaction to high-rise schemes such as the neighbouring Alma Estate: 'a full-blooded return to the idea of the traditional street of attached houses'. But, as Hugh Pearman continues, it is 'not traditionalist in style'.[10] A difficult location – the site of a former gasworks bounded by a new school, interwar housing and an industrial estate – demanded innovative solutions. The original brief envisaged a single terrace facing the school, but the school's objection to being overlooked alongside council regulations stipulating a 21-m distance between adjacent housing resulted in a scheme of varied forms but broadly unified style that achieved higher density, designed jointly by Karakusevic Carson Architects and Maccreanor Lavington.

The street is its dominant element, but it's a pedestrian-friendly thoroughfare softened by shared surfaces and thoughtful landscaping. Two- and three-storey redbrick terraces run either side. In the architects' description, 'all dwellings open onto the street with regular front doors and windows, ensuring a sociable and active space, but also natural surveillance and security'.[11]

That on the west, designed by Maccreanor Lavington, comprises 12 pitch-roofed two-storey family homes and a three-storeyed, flat-roofed row made up of a mix of family houses, maisonettes and flats. Green glazed brick surrounds emphasise entrances and add colour.

On the eastern side, where space was more confined, Karakusevic Carson Architects devised what they call 'slimline family houses' with 'a uniquely shallow layout making full use of a narrow and elongated site'.[12] The trick here was to rotate the typical housing footprint sideways, allowing the construction of eight wide-fronted, three-bedroom triple-aspect family houses. Rear gardens, precluded by lack of space, are replaced by a small backyard and a second-floor terrace over a garage to the side of each house. The ingenious design creates homes that, at some 100 m², are above those stipulated in the London Housing Design Guide.

Bottom left
Architect's model of the scheme

Bottom right
This sectional axonometric drawing illustrated the design and layout of 'slimline family houses'

Opposite top
Looking south; the school can be glimpsed immediately to the left

Opposite right
Looking south

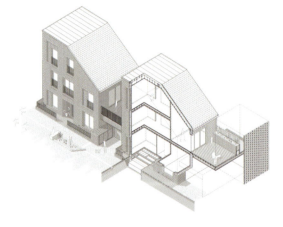

A History of Council Housing in 100 Estates

Of Dujardin Mews' 38 new homes, from one-bedroom flats to four-bedroom houses, half were provided for social rent and half for subsidised sale. Initially, all were occupied by former residents of the Alma Estate though future onward sales can be expected to shift this balance. The scheme remains slightly isolated in its very mixed locale but its self-contained character looks likely to fulfil its architects' intentions to design 'an intimate setting for a new sociable community'. Described as 'a totally convincing revisit of a very London human-scale domestic typology' that deserved 'to be studied and replicated widely', the quality of its design was recognised by awards from the Civic Trust and Royal Institute of British Architects in 2017 and 2018.[13]

Catmoor Road, Scone, Perth & Kinross, Scotland

The Catmoor Road scheme on the outskirts of the historic market town of Scone was one of the first undertaken directly by Perth & Kinross Council as Scotland's devolved government looked to boost the country's stock of council housing. It provides 65 new homes, all at social rent – a mix of 53 terraced two-, three- and four-bedroom houses and 12 cottage flats. The £10.9 million project, with a £5.1 million subsidy from the Scottish government, was agreed in September 2019.

Having previously delivered new affordable housing through local housing associations, the council faced the problem common to many contemporary local authorities of lacking the in-house resources and expertise to implement its own programme of housebuilding. To expedite procurement, it was agreed to contract the scheme to CCG Group who in turn, after consultation with the council, employed MAST Architects to design it. Council oversight was strengthened by its employment of a cost consultant and creation of a design guide stipulating quality, space and sustainability standards and addressing, after discussions with the local community, particular housing needs.

The completed scheme, opened in summer 2021, is notable for its attractive appearance, drawing upon 'elements of traditional detailing found within the existing buildings around the site' (a mix of owner-occupied and older council housing) and energy efficiency as all homes were built to conform to the Silver Standard (aspects 1 and 2) of the Scottish Building Standards.[14] Four of the homes are designed to be wheelchair accessible and all ground-floor flats have wet rooms for people with limited mobility. Local wildlife is catered for by bat and swift boxes and 'hedgehog highways' incorporated into back gardens.

As the council's experience in housebuilding grows, it may look in future to a more strongly design-led approach reflecting the Scottish government's emphases on quality and sustainability outlined in its 2021 policy statement, 'Housing to 2040'.

Left and right
Photographs of the recently completed scheme

Sustainable housing

The climate crisis perhaps confronts humanity with its greatest challenge to date. The British government is committed to reaching 'net zero' greenhouse gas emissions by 2050; over two-thirds of councils have declared a climate emergency. It is estimated that houses account for 30% of the UK's total energy use, 27% of its carbon dioxide emissions and around 24% of greenhouse gas emissions. A primary objective must be to retrofit the UK's ageing housing stock of 29 million homes to new energy-efficient standards, and local authorities have taken the lead in modernising existing homes with improved insulation and glazing. New thermal cladding added to existing high-rise has been one means, though implemented with disastrous consequences at Grenfell.

New social housing is uniformly constructed to higher environmental standards than in the past, and in many cases contemporary schemes offer examples of best practice that should be emulated by the private sector. Some specific instances follow. Passivhaus provides the gold standard, built to rigorous energy-efficient design standards to maintain an almost constant temperature with minimal fuel usage. Its five principles require high-quality insulation, airtight construction, heat recovery ventilation and thermal bridge-free design (thermal bridging occurs where heat is transferred across components from the inside to the outside of a building in cold weather). The EnerPHit standard is an equivalent of the Passivhaus hallmark applied to retrofit schemes.

An estimated 5.5 million households in the UK live in fuel poverty, spending over 10% of their income on energy bills. Fifteen per cent of these live in social housing. This is a little lower than the overall percentage that occupy social rent homes (proportionately the worst-off live in the private rental sector) but the problem, affecting the poorest and most vulnerable of social housing tenants, has been another significant factor driving councils to improve the energy efficiency of their homes.

Environmental arguments have also been deployed by housing campaigners to challenge a prevalent form of regeneration that demolishes existing housing that is structurally sound or could be renovated to be so. A full assessment of embodied carbon (essentially a calculation of the carbon footprint of the original construction plus that of projected newbuild) may often challenge environmental arguments advanced to support demolition.

BedZED, Hackbridge, Sutton, London

The Beddington Zero Energy Development (BedZED) project, opened in Hackbridge in the London Borough of Sutton in 2002, was claimed as the UK's largest low-carbon development at the time and the first in which a local authority had sold land at below market price for environmental reasons. It's a mixed-use scheme combining commercial space and some 82 flats, maisonettes and townhouses (each with a rooftop garden or terrace), originally planned to use only energy from renewable sources and to produce as much energy as it consumed. It was the brainchild of architect Bill Dunster, developed in partnership with engineers Ellis & Moore and Arup, and the environmentalist social enterprise BioRegional. The Peabody Trust agreed to fund the development in 2000.

The approach to sustainability was holistic, ranging from location and lifestyle to materials and construction. The site was selected for its good public transport links; residents also operate a car sharing scheme. Renewable and recycled building materials were sourced from within 50 miles of the site wherever possible. The scheme was designed in south-facing terraces to maximise heat gain from the sun and the buildings themselves as heavy-mass, highly insulated, triple-glazed structures that stored daytime warmth or harnessed night-time cool as appropriate to the season to achieve a comfortable natural ambient temperature. Solar panels and a biomass woodchip boiler were installed to supply the scheme's energy needs. Rainwater was collected, and a 'Living Machine' system of wastewater recycling minimised water usage.

The scheme, with a quarter of its homes let at social rent by the Peabody Trust, a quarter for shared ownership and the rest sold on the open market,

Left
General view

Right
A view showing walkways connecting homes and gardens

Opposite left
General view

Opposite right
Ventilation chimneys

A History of Council Housing in 100 Estates

proved extremely popular and has met many of its ecological goals. A 2003 survey found space heating requirements were 88% less than the UK average and overall energy usage 25% less; hot-water consumption was 57% less. Conversely, the original woodchip boiler proved inadequate but a gas boiler, in use from 2005, was replaced in 2017 by a new biomass pellet boiler that supplies the district heating system while electricity is supplied on a green tariff from the national grid. The wastewater recycling facility also proved ineffective. Some residents have reported problems with overheating of properties in warmer weather.

While some of BedZED's sustainability features were found technically unfeasible and some of its ambitions foundered on their relatively small-scale operation, the overall scheme received much acclaim and has provided a model for many similar schemes since. Architecturally, the scheme is unusual for making a structural feature of some of its energy-saving devices, notably the multi-coloured wind funnels (providing passive ventilation) prominently displayed on roofs. The bridges, spanning walkways and connecting some homes to their gardens, are another idiosyncratic feature of the scheme.

The indoor community space, communal green field and 'village square' conceived in the original plans as a means to foster neighbourliness appear to have been successful. The BedZED 'eco-village' remains a magnet for 'urban professionals looking for a more eco-conscious lifestyle', but not yet a model for social housing more widely.[15]

Chester Balmore, Chester Road and Raydon Street, Camden, London

The Chester Balmore development in Highgate New Town, completed in 2015, included the first council housing built by the Borough of Camden since 1999. It provided 53 new homes, of which 23 were for council rent, four for shared ownership (for those living or working in the borough and earning between £35,000 and £39,000) and 26 for market sale – part of the borough's Community Investment Programme aiming to build 50 new homes at social rent funded largely by the construction and sale of private homes.

It was at the time the largest residential Passivhaus scheme in the UK. Passivhaus buildings are defined by rigorous technical standards but are in essence characterised by their thermal comfort, good indoor air quality and very low energy consumption. Beyond pressing environmental concerns, when poorer families may spend up to 10% of their income on energy for heating, lighting, and cooking, Camden also wished to address the issue of fuel poverty. Additionally, 10% of the homes were adapted for wheelchair access.

Passivhaus achieves a 75% reduction in space heating requirements by super-insulating the buildings' fabric and making them exceptionally airtight. In the Chester Balmore scheme designed by Rick Mather Architects in partnership with contractors Willmott Dixon that involved brick-clad, reinforced concrete structures containing 250 mm of insulation within walls almost half a metre thick, and triple glazing. The buildings' hermetic seal required mechanical ventilation in the form of two low-energy fans to circulate fresh air within the homes; one to supply, the other to extract. The single form of conventional heating comprised

Left
Raydon Street frontage

Right
Chester Road frontage

Opposite
Gated courtyard

a heated towel rail in the bathrooms. All this provided a constant ambient temperature of 16°C that was calculated to reach a comfortable 20–21°C with human occupation and usage.

New residents were given guidance to accustom them to adaptations required. As Ivan Christmas, Camden's Senior Development Manager, explained, this was sometimes counterintuitive: 'We knew it would stay warm in winter but keeping cool in summer was more of an issue. It's best not to open your window and let hot air in during the day, for example; you open the windows at night.'[16] Fuel bills at then-current rates were estimated to amount to less than £100 a year.

The scheme, on a sensitive corner location amid Victorian terraces and facing the Modernist Whittington Estate, was designed to blend in with its surroundings while maximising use of its restricted site. Three articulated three-storey blocks, comprising terraces, stacked maisonettes, flats, and retail and community space, were oriented around a central communal garden while each dual-aspect home benefited from its own private outside space and front doors with direct street access.

Chester Balmore set a benchmark for new, high-quality sustainable housing, receiving a Civic Trust special award for sustainability in 2015. While the hope expressed by Ivan Christmas that the development would demonstrate 'Passivhaus has crossed over into the mainstream' has not been fully fulfilled, it remains a model that many local authorities are seeking to emulate.[17]

Wilmcote House, Tyseley Road, Portsmouth

Wilmcote House in central Portsmouth, opened in 1968, was a building typical of its time – a system-built scheme comprising three connected 11-storey slab blocks characterised by poor insulation and serious heat loss caused by thermal bridging. Resultant issues of condensation and mould were exacerbated for residents when – after the Ronan Point disaster – gas heating was replaced by more expensive electric storage heaters that many could not afford to run. By 2010, it was clear that the scheme needed either thorough renovation or demolition, but most residents wanted to stay in their homes.

Conventional refurbishment and an upgrade of the existing heating system were found impractical, and the city council's decision to renovate the estate to EnerPHit standards was confirmed two years later following a feasibility report and survey finding the buildings structurally sound. The proposal enabled the retention of existing homes, relieved fuel poverty and avoided the wasteful loss of embodied carbon caused by demolition. The scheme, overseen by ECD Architects and completed in 2018, was the largest ever residential EnerPHit project delivered with residents in situ. In practice, around two-thirds of the original residents remained as existing residents in unsuitable accommodation were transferred and other flats falling vacant were not re-let.

The basic solution applied to achieve the thermal efficiency and airtightness required by Passivhaus was to overclad the buildings within new thermal envelopes. That entailed enclosing previously external decks, constructing external steel frames to support new insulated facades and replacing roofs. (The changes had the additional benefit of allowing a small extension to existing living areas.) Triple-glazed windows were installed alongside the mechanical ventilation and heat recovery systems required by Passivhaus. New, more efficient heating and hot water systems were installed, though residents kept their storage heaters.

Left
Before refurbishment, 2014

Right
Courtyard view before refurbishment, 2014

Opposite top left
The blocks after refurbishment, 2018

Opposite top right
Corridor before refurbishment, 2014

Opposite bottom
Corridor after refurbishment, 2018

A History of Council Housing in 100 Estates

Despite the technical challenges of the scheme and inevitable disruption to residents while works were being carried out, the results have been overwhelmingly positive. The building's life has been extended in sustainable fashion for a minimum of 30 years, and residents are estimated to save up to 90% on their fuel bills. A study of an unused and unheated flat after the works were complete found it maintained an average temperature of 18°C even in deep midwinter.

At a cost of £12.9 million (around £117,000 for each of the 107 homes), Wilmcote's deep retrofit was not a cheap solution – but it may, in the longer run, provide a more cost-effective and certainly more sustainable one. Its residents are the direct beneficiaries, but Portsmouth City Council, which funded the scheme in its entirety, may offset some of that expense by a more reliable rental income in future years.

A similar recent scheme, involving the retrofitting of three 22-storey blocks in Woodside, Glasgow, carried out for the Queens Cross Housing Association by Collective Architecture, is further evidence of the potential of this approach.

Goldsmith Street, Norwich

Goldsmith Street in Norwich provides a fitting finale to this survey, as the 2019 winner of the Royal Institute of British Architects' Stirling Prize and the inaugural Neave Brown Award for the best new example of affordable housing in the UK. And it is a local authority scheme providing 100% social housing.

The development originated in an international design competition in 2008, but Norwich City Council's plans to sell the land and have the scheme completed by a local housing association were stymied by the financial crash. Eventually, the council took the brave decision to build itself, employing Mikhail Riches as both architects and contract administrators on a project that it now determined should be built to Passivhaus standards. Respected local firm R.G. Carter, which had built much of the city's council housing in its earlier heyday, carried out the works.

Goldsmith Street comprises 45 two-storey terraced houses and 48 flats located in 'bookend' three-storey blocks, each with their own garden and front door on to the street. (It's a small touch but a significant break with past local authority practice that each front door is painted a different colour.) Around a quarter of its three-acre site is communal space, most innovatively in the form of a landscaped alleyway running to the rear of the homes: 'a reinterpretation of a traditional [Norfolk] "ginnel"', according to David Mikhail, intended 'to encourage a sense of community and provide a safe, overlooked place for small children's play'.[18] There are other local references too in the use of traditional light Gault brick and glossy black pantiles for roofing.

In outward appearance, the scheme's Passivhaus credentials are lightly worn but are essential to its overall design and detail. In layout, streets running east–west and the homes' internal design align three-quarters of rooms due south to

Left
Bookend flats and terrace

Opposite clockwise from top left
Bookend flats and terrace

Greyhound Opening street section

Greyhound Opening open space

The enclosed 'ginnel' running to the rear of the terraces

maximise solar gain. Roofs are angled to optimise the impact of warming winter sun while providing shading in summer. South-facing windows are provided with a metal shade to reduce the risk of overheating. Projecting walls house external letterboxes that help secure the rigorously tested airtight seal that is essential to the homes' energy efficiency.

This finely calibrated design and engineering adds 5–10% to the scheme's overall construction costs, but results in household energy bills 70% below the average. In practical terms, one resident estimates he saves around £220 a month in utility bills: 'it just does not feel like a council property at all – it is brilliant. People we know own properties and are jealous of ours'.[19]

Julia Barfield, chair of the Stirling Prize judging panel, described Goldsmith Street as 'a modern masterpiece ... high-quality architecture in its purest, most environmentally and socially conscious form'.[20] To Gail Harris, the city council's cabinet member for social housing, the scheme has set 'a benchmark for social homes – not just for us as a council but across the country'.[21] Its co-architect Annalie Riches thought it 'not a showy project [but] a very pragmatic solution ... what housing should be'.[22] We might hope that what one architectural commentator described as Goldsmith Street's 'radical normalcy' does indeed provide a model that others will follow.

Afterword

In a speech to the National Housing Federation in 2018, then UK prime minister Theresa May stated that the 'rise of social housing in this country provided what has been called the "biggest collective leap in living standards in British history"'. Her pledge to build on that 'more than a century of history, and [carry] forward the torch of high-quality, affordable housing for generations to come' was, however, only very modestly fulfilled, not least because those 'affordable' homes so often proved to be unaffordable to those who needed them most. In 2020/21, just 6,566 new social rent homes were completed in England; in the same year, 9,319 were lost to Right to Buy. There are now approximately 1.4 million fewer social rent homes than at peak in 1980. Of those former council homes acquired over the years under Right to Buy, around 40% are now in the private rental sector; some are rented back from private landlords by local authorities desperate to house at least a few of the 1.2 million households on social housing waiting lists.

We are in the midst of a housing crisis. The historic contribution of public housing to meeting this country's housing needs is obvious; the need to build more social rent homes now and into the future equally so. In the words of Michael Gove, then Secretary of State for Levelling Up, Housing and Communities, 'we've reached a situation for a variety of reasons where the number of people living in social housing, the availability of social housing, is simply inadequate for any notion of social justice or economic efficiency'.

If that, in the most summary form imaginable, is the politics of council housing, it is important to remember that for the many millions who have lived – and live today – in a council house, maisonette or flat it is above all else their home. And, overwhelmingly, it's been a decent home – more secure, affordable, spacious and better equipped than any otherwise available to them; a refuge, a springboard – a foundation for the best life they might live. This was obviously and dramatically true for the many moving from slum housing in the 20th century; as one new resident of the Lansbury Estate in east London stated, 'I'd never thought I'd see such luxury'. But it's equally true now for those moving from insecure or unaffordable or overcrowded accommodation and provided a decent home of their own.

Many continue to ask what *form* of council housing provided the best type of home. Readers may form their own conclusions; a sometimes friendly, often hostile, commentariat has frequently been quick to express its opinions. I will disappoint some by withholding easy judgment. Firstly, every form of council housing – from the derided, apparently monotonous and soulless cottage suburb to the anathematised high-rise block – has been lauded by those who matter most, the people who lived in them (while others of their neighbours, of course, found reasons to complain). Secondly, many estates subsequently labelled as 'failed estates' were successful in their earlier years. Excepting some with particular construction flaws, very few were born bad, as it were – but many, from the 1970s, did fall on hard times. Often, working communities stopped working, literally and figuratively as unemployment rose and previously stable communities fragmented when estates came to house a disproportionately poorer and more vulnerable cross-section of our community. In none of this was architectural form the deciding influence on lived experience. 'Problem estates' came in all shapes and sizes; the common factor was hostile circumstance. We can celebrate the ideals and best intentions of architects and planners, but should always acknowledge the broader politics and social and economic forces that have been more powerfully determinant of the reality of estate lives.

Secondly, and in relation to just those ideals and best intentions, what this book makes clear is how our ideas shift and how readily the unquestioned common sense of one era is challenged by that which follows. The broad notion that people and traffic should be separated, for example – whether by Radburn layouts, 'streets in the sky' or the enclosed estate more generally – doesn't seem inherently eccentric despite the more recent embracing of 'the street' and its virtues that followed from an uncritical acceptance of methodologically flawed 'defensible space' theories in the 1980s. In the long-running contest between low-rise and multi-storey solutions, high-rise housing is fashionable once more as we look to a higher-density, more sustainable urbanism – though ironically this is now an approach confined principally to a private sector catering for middle-class residents. We should therefore, as a matter of historical integrity, be humble in our judgments.

At its best, over the years and in varied forms, council housing has been at the vanguard of housing progress – an example to the private sector and an essential substitute for it, as the latter so often proved uninterested in or incapable of meeting the housing needs of working-class people. That, despite the constraints imposed on public housing under the contemporary regime of politics and finance, remains as true today as ever. While the amount of new genuinely social rent housing remains for the moment woefully inadequate, we are fortunate in having local authorities anxious to build and a new generation of architects committed to public sector ideals and best practice. The politics may change; the wellbeing of our community and environment demands that it should. When that happens, this book, I hope, will not be merely a history but an inspiration.

A note on the selection of estates

My choice of case studies is deliberately eclectic. It is not a selection of the 'best' or 'most successful' estates; sometimes, manifestly, the opposite is true. What I have attempted is to portray a representative range of schemes; some deemed significant in their time, others unheralded but for that reason more illustrative of the broader history of council housing. Within this, I have identified the forms and trends of planning and design that were most characteristic of their era. The arrangement is obviously chronological, though real life isn't quite as neat as the periodisation I have applied. Finally, to the best of my ability, I have tried to tell a UK-wide story that gives proper weight to the nations and regions of our country.

Southmere Lake
and Southmere
Towers, 1970

Index

Endnotes

Chapter 1

1. Nigel Goose, 'The English almshouses and the mixed economy of welfare: medieval to modern', *The Local Historian*, vol. 40, no. 1, February 2010, pp3–39.
2. John Broad, 'Housing the rural poor in southern England, 1650–1850', *Agricultural History Review*, vol. 48, no. II, 2000, p157.
3. Quoted in John Broad, '10. The parish poor house in the long eighteenth century' in Joanne McEwan and Pamela Sharpe (eds), *Accommodating Poverty: The Housing and Living Arrangements of the English Poor, c. 1600–1850*, Basingstoke, Palgrave Macmillan UK, 2011, p246.
4. W.M. Mavor, *A New Description of Blenheim, The Seat of His Grace the Duke of Marlborough*, Oxford, Slatter, 1820, p116.
5. A Charity Commissioners' report of 1823 quoted in Historic England, 'Kenton School', https://historicengland.org.uk/listing/the-list/list-entry/1097676?section=official-listing, n.d. (accessed 28 January 2022).
6. Marcia Rice, *Abbots Bromley*, Shrewsbury, Wilding and Son, 1939, p187.
7. Eric Midwinter, *Social Administration in Lancashire, 1830–1860*, Manchester, Manchester University Press, 1969, p84.
8. Quoted in Rose Pipes, 'Edinburgh's colonies', *Vernacular Building 24*, 2000, p6.
9. Quoted in 'Peabody Square', *Illustrated London News*, 10 March 1866, p233.
10. Irina Davidovici, 'The depth of the street', *AA Files*, no. 70, 2015, p104.
11. *The Builder*, 30 June 1883, quoted in *Noel Park Conservation Area Appraisal and Management Plan Consultation Draft*, Haringey Council, n.d., p9.
12. *Pall Mall Gazette*, 23 January 1884, quoted in Haringey Council, *Noel Park Conservation Area*, p20.

Chapter 2

1. London County Council, *Housing of the Working Classes, 1855–1912*, London, Odhams Ltd, 1913, p70.
2. William Thompson, *Housing Up-to-Date*, London, National Housing Reform Council, 1907, p105.
3. C.G. Pooley, 'Housing for the poorest poor: slum-clearance and rehousing in Liverpool, 1890–1918', *Journal of Historical Geography*, vol. 11, no. 1, January 1985, p78.
4. W.W. Knox, *A History of The Scottish People: Urban Housing in Scotland 1840–1940*, https://www.scran.ac.uk/scotland/pdf/SP2_4Housing.pdf, n.d. (accessed 22 September 2021).
5. See Steven Robb, 'Conservative surgery in Edinburgh', *Context*, Institute of Historic Building Conservation, no. 150, July 2017, pp19–22.
6. Steven Robb, 'Health is greater than history: an introduction to Edinburgh's social housing, 1890–1945', https://municipaldreams.wordpress.com/2019/02/19/edinburgh_social_housing_1890-1945/, 19 February 2019 (accessed 22 September 2021).
7. 'Housing in Hackney', *Shoreditch Observer*, 22 August 1903, p2.
8. Quoted in Duncan Bowie, *The Radical and Socialist Tradition in British Planning*, Routledge, London, 2017, p126.

9. Patrick Abercrombie, 'A comparative review of examples of modern town planning and "Garden City" schemes in england (concluded)', *Town Planning Review*, vol. 1, no. 2, July 1910, p119.
10. Quoted in Michael Harrison, 'Burnage Garden Village: an ideal for life in Manchester', *The Town Planning Review*, vol. 47, no. 3, July 1976, p257.
11. Ibid., p259.
12. *Building News*, 17 September 1909, p418.
13. Abercrombie, 'Modern town planning in England', p18.
14. Quoted in Peter Shapeley, *The Politics of Housing: Power, Consumers and Urban Culture*, Manchester, Manchester University Press, 2017, p95.
15. Quoted in Rupert Hebblethwaite, 'The municipal housing programme in Sheffield before 1914', *Architectural History*, vol. 30, 1987, pp148–9.
16. S. Beattie, *A Revolution in London Housing: LCC Housing Architects and their Work 1893–1914*, London, Greater London Council, 1980, p106.
17. London County Council, *Housing of the Working Classes, 1855–1912*, London, Odhams Ltd for the London County Council, 1912, p83.
18. Mark Swenarton, *Homes Fit for Heroes: The Policy and Architecture of Early State Housing in Britain*, Routledge Revivals, Abingdon, 2018, p35.

Chapter 3

1. Mark Swenarton, *Homes Fit for Heroes. The Politics and Architecture of Early State Housing in Britain*, Routledge, Abingdon, 2018, p191.
2. Quoted in David Englander, *Landlord and Tenant in Urban Britain: The Politics of Housing Reform, 1838–1924*, University of Warwick PhD, 1979, p384.
3. Swenarton, *Homes Fit for Heroes*, p60.
4. Susan Gleave, *The Influence of the Garden City Movement in Fife, 1914–23 with Particular Reference to Rosyth*, MPhil thesis, Department of Art History, University of St Andrews, 1987, p105.
5. Ibid., p110. The succeeding quotation is drawn from the same source, p129.
6. Swenarton, *Homes Fit for Heroes*, p53. Other quotations are drawn from the same source.
7. 'The site planning of housing schemes', *The Town Planning Review*, December 1920, vol. 8, no. 3/4, p142.
8. E.G. Culpin, *The Garden City Movement, Up-To-Date*, Garden Cities and Town Planning Association, London, 1913, p70.
9. Ernest Morgan, 'The development of the Town Hill Estate, Swansea', *Perspectives in Public Health*, vol. 51, no. 10, 1930, p580. Subsequent quotations are drawn from the same source.
10. Seán Damer, *Scheming: A Social History of Glasgow Council Housing, 1919–1956*, Edinburgh, Edinburgh University Press, 2018, p28.
11. Terence Young, *Becontree and Dagenham: A Report Made for the Pilgrim Trust*, Becontree Social Survey Committee, 1934.
12. Quoted in Christopher Middleton, 'A cultural feast in Corned Beef City', *Daily Telegraph*, 14 September 2002.

13. Elisabeth Blanchet and Sonia Zhuravlyova, *Prefabs: A Social and Architectural History*, Swindon, Historic England, 2018, p2.
14. Nissen-Petren Concrete Houses advertisement, *The Times*, 7 April 1925, p50.
15. 'The Nissen-Petren House', *Western Chronicle*, 13 March 1925, p1.
16. 'Housing in Tiverton Area', *Exeter and Plymouth Gazette*, 1 May 1925, p7.
17. Roland Jeffery, 'Housing Happenings in Somers Town', *Twentieth Century Architecture, Housing the Twentieth Century Nation*, no. 9, 2008, p29.

Chapter 4

1. Seán Damer, *Scheming: A Social History of Glasgow Council Housing, 1919–1956*, Edinburgh, Edinburgh University Press, 2020, p7.
2. R.J. Allerton, 'Housing in Norwich', Annual Conference of the Institute of Housing, September 1938, p21.
3. Rosamond Jevons and John Madge, *Housing Estates. A Study of Bristol Corporation Policy and Practice Between the Wars*, Bristol, 1946, p25.
4. Ibid., p76.
5. Quoted in 'Manchester housing estate', *The Times*, 2 February 1932, p7.
6. Quoted in Andrew Davies and Steven Fielding, *Workers' Worlds: Cultures and Communities in Manchester and Salford, 1880–1939*, Manchester, Manchester University Press, 1992, p80.
7. '2,166 White City Flats', *The Times*, 21 July 1939, p11; 'A town is born', *Architects' Journal*, 27 July 1939, p128.
8. LCC, *Working-Class Housing on the Continent and the Application of Continental Ideas to the Housing Problem in the County of London*, report by the Chairman of the Housing and Public Health Committee of the Council, Mr Lewis Silkin MP, as the result of a visit to Continental Housing Estates in September and October 1935 (October 1936).
9. Quoted in Matthew Whitfield, *Multi-Storey Public Housing in Liverpool During the Inter-War Years*, Department of History and Economic History, Manchester Metropolitan University, PhD, 2010, p371.
10. Lancelot Keay, 'Housing and the redevelopment of central areas', *Journal of the Royal Institute of British Architects*, vol. 43, no. 2, 23 November 1935, p60.
11. 'Flats in Hackney', letter to *The Times*, 25 March 1937, p10.
12. Quoted in E. Robinson, *Twentieth Century Buildings in Hackney*, London, Hackney Society, 1999, p57.
13. Le Corbusier, 'The Mars Group exhibition of the elements of Modern architecture: a pictorial record', *Architectural Review*, vol. 83, no. 496, 1 March 1938, p110. The succeeding quotation is on p111.
14. Le Corbusier, 'The Mars Group exhibition of the elements of Modern architecture: a pictorial record', *Architectural Review*, vol. 83, no. 496, 1 March 1938, p110.
15. Quoted in Elizabeth Darling, 'Kensal House: the housing consultant and the housed', *Twentieth Century Architecture, 2007*, no. 8, 2007, p108.

16 Mark Llewellyn, '"Urban village" or "white house": envisioned spaces, experienced places, and everyday life at Kensal House, London in the 1930s', *Environment and Planning D*, vol. 22, no. 2, 2004, p233.

17 Alison Ravetz, *Model Estate: Planned Housing at Quarry Hill, Leeds,* London, Routledge, 2013, p73.

18 Ibid., p63.

Chapter 5

1 Aneurin Bevan, Housing Bill, Second Reading: Hansard, HC Deb, 16 March 1949, vol. 462, c.2127.

2 Patrick Abercrombie and J.H. Forshaw, *The County of London Plan*, Macmillan, London, 1943, p78.

3 Quoted in E. Blanchet and S. Zhuravlyova, *Prefabs: A Social and Architectural History*, Swindon, Historic England, 2018, p48.

4 *Post-War Building Studies No. 1, House Construction*, by an Interdepartmental Committee Appointed by the Minister of Health, Secretary of State for Scotland and the Minister of Works (The Burt Committee), London, 1944, p1.

5 Blanchet and Zhuravlyova, *Prefabs*, p34.

6 'Here's a real house-builder', *Daily Mirror*, 25 January 1943, p4.

7 'June Kapitan's prefab memories', The Prefab Post, https://www.prefabmuseum.uk/wp-content/uploads/2018/04/PRM0013774_Prefab_Post5_04.pdf, June 2017 (accessed 24 February 2022).

8 These and succeeding quotations are drawn from R.D. Smith, 'Flats going up', BBC Home Service, 6 June 1947 (Transcript: Pamphlet 331.3 Box 1, Tower Hamlets Archives).

9 J.M. Richards, 'London housing', *Architects' Journal*, vol. 109, 10 March 1949, p228.

10 Seán Damer, *Scheming: A Social History of Glasgow Council Housing, 1919–1956*, Edinburgh, Edinburgh University Press, 2018, p126.

11 Damer, *Scheming*, p127.

12 '250 Houses for Derry', *Londonderry Sentinel*, 2 December 1944, p4.

13 Quoted in Michael McGuinness and Gharbán Downey, *More than a History: Creggan*, Guildhall Press, Derry, 2000, p61.

14 'Boasts that Warn', *Londonderry Sentinel*, 26 June 1954, p4.

15 Councillor Cathal Crumley in McGuinness and Gharbán Downey, *More than a History*, p4.

16 'High costs having "disastrous effect" on living standards', *Derry Journal*, 2 June 1950, p1.

17 Hansard: Housing Shortage, House of Commons Debate, 17 October 1945, vol. 414, c.1222.

18 Hansard: Housing Bill Second Reading, House of Commons Debate, 16 March 1949, vol. 462, c.2126.

19 'Bath's new housing estate', *Bath Weekly Chronicle*, 18 May 1946, p3.

20 '"Follow Bath's example", Bevan will tell other council house planners', *Bath Weekly Chronicle*, 26 February 1947, p7.

21 Owen Hatherley, *A New Kind of Bleak. Journeys through Urban Britain*, Verso, London, 2013, p226.

22 Quoted in Karolina Szynalska, 'Yesterday's church of tomorrow: St John the Baptist, Ermine Estate' presented at the symposium 'The history and heritage of post-war council estates', June 2011, Bishop Grosseteste University College, Lincoln, p4.

23 Jones the Planner (Adrian Jones and Chris Matthews), *Towns in Britain*, Five Leave Publications, Nottingham, 2014, p309.

24 John Newman, *Gwent/Monmouthshire*, Penguin Books, London, 2000, p458.

25 Quoted in Judith Alfrey, 'Themes and sources for public housing in Wales', *Twentieth Century Architecture*, no. 9, 2008, p80.

26 This quotation and the later one are drawn from David Hunt, *A History of Preston*, Carnegie Publishing and Preston Borough Council, Preston, 1992, pp292–3.

27 Ruth Durant, *Watling, A Survey of Life on a New Housing Estate*, P.S. King, London, 1939, p119.

28 Forshaw and Abercrombie, *The County of London Plan*, p101.

29 County Borough of Derby, *The Mackworth Estate*, Derby, 1959.

30 Wilson writing in *Observer*, 20 July 1952, quoted in Nicholas Bullock, *Building the Post-War World: Modern Architecture and Reconstruction in Britain*, Routledge, London, 2002, p105.

31 J.M. Richards, 'Old and new at Lansbury', *Architectural Review*, 1 December 1951, p363.

32 John Westergaard and Ruth Glass, 'A profile of Lansbury', *Town Planning Review*, vol. 25, no. 1, April 1954, p37.

33 Quoted in Westergaard and Glass, 'A profile of Lansbury', p39.

34 Quoted in Stuart Jeffries, 'Bilston's revival: the pursuit of happiness in a Black Country town', *Guardian*, https://www.theguardian.com/cities/2016/aug/02/pursuit-happiness-black-country-town-bilston, 2 August 2016 (accessed 24 February 2022).

35 *Birkenhead News*, 12 April 1944.

36 See Lawrence Woolf, *The Reilly Plan: A New Way of Life*, Nicholson and Watson, London, 1945.

37 P.J. Larkham, 'New suburbs and post-war reconstruction: the fate of Charles Reilly's Greens', University of Central England School of Planning and Housing Working Paper, no. 89, 2004, p9.

38 M.A. Neill, 'Rathcoole: a study in social relationships'; Hons Arts Thesis, Dept of Geography, Queen's University, 1971, quoted in John Darby, *Intimidation in Housing*, https://cain.ulster.ac.uk/issues/housing/docs/nicrc6.htm (accessed 24 February 2022).

39 Stanley Gale, *Modern Housing Estates*, B.T. Batsford Ltd, London, 1949, p254. Other quotations are drawn from the same source.

40 Personal communication, 20 April 2022.

41 Quoted in A.W. Cleeve Barr, *Public Authority Housing*, B.T. Batsford, London, 1958, p35.

42 Cleeve Barr, *Public Authority Housing*, p36.

43 Nicholas Bullock, *Building the Post-War World*, Routledge, London, 2002, p84.

44 George L.A. Downing, 'Some aspects of housing in a metropolitan borough', *Journal of the Royal Society for the Promotion of Health*, September 1949, vol. 69, no. 5, p598.

45 Frederick Gibberd, 'Housing at Hackney', *Architectural Review*, vol. 106, no. 633, September 1949, p146.

46 'Mixed housing at Hackney', *The Times*, September 6 1949, p2.

47 These quotations are drawn from 'A £403,000 development "showpiece pointer" to future housing', *Walsall Observer*, 20 October 1961, p5.

48 M.E. Habershon, A.T. Parrott and G.F. Elliott, 'New housing at Walsall', *Official Architecture and Planning*, vol. 24, no. 11, December 1961, pp.487–9.

49 Ibid.

50 'A £403,000 development', *Walsall Observer*.

51 Quoted in K. Powell, 'Powell, Sir (Arnold Joseph) Philip (1921–2003), architect', *Oxford Dictionary of National Biography*, https://www-oxforddnb-com.liverpool.idm.oclc.org/view/10.1093/ref:odnb/9780198614128.001.0001/odnb-9780198614128-e-89996 (accessed 6 August 2021).

52 Elaine Harwood, 'Post-war landscape and public housing', *Garden History*, vol. 28, no. 1, summer 2000, p113.

53 Giles Worsley, 'Estate of grace: the Churchill Gardens Estate has been voted Britain's most outstanding building', *Daily Telegraph*, 25 March 2000; 'Rent shock for tenants', *The Times*, April 30, 1962, p8.

54 Cleeve Barr, *Public Authority Housing*, p42.

55 Alison Ravetz, *Council Housing and Culture: The History of a Social Experiment*, Routledge, Abingdon, 2001, p103.

56 Gordon Stephenson, 'The Wrexham experiment: the Queen's Park South Estate', *Town Planning Review*, vol. 24, no. 4, January 1954, p291.

57 Stephenson, 'The Wrexham experiment', p283.

58 Cleeve Barr, *Public Authority Housing*, p278.

59 Stephenson, 'The Wrexham experiment', p286.

60 Ibid., p290.

61 Quoted in Ian Waites, 'Middlefield: the development of a provincial post-World War Two council estate in Lincolnshire, 1960–1965', *Midland History*, vol. 40, no. 2, 2015, p271. Succeeding quotations and references are drawn from the same source. For a more personal and photographic record, see also Ian Waites, *Middlefield: A Postwar Council Estate in Time*, Uniformbooks, Axminster, 2017.

62 'Housing at Beaumaris, Anglesey', *Architects' Journal*, 13 April 1950, p466.

63 Judith Alfrey, 'Themes and sources for public housing in Wales, twentieth century architecture, no. 9', *Housing the Twentieth Century Nation*, 2008, p. 80.

64 Alfrey, 'Themes and sources for public housing in Wales', p80.

65 New Towns Bill, Second Reading, House of Commons Debate, 8 May 1946, vol. 422, c.1088.

66 Gordon Cullen, 'Prairie planning in the new town', *Architectural Review*, vol. 114, no. 679, 1953, p34.

67 J.M. Richards, 'Failure of the new towns', *Architectural Review*, vol. 114, no. 679, 1953, p31.

68 Anthony Minoprio, 'Crawley New Town', *Perspectives in Public Health*, vol. 69, no. 5, September 1949, p606.

69 Frederic J. Osborn and Arnold Whittick, *The New Towns: The Answer to Megalopolis*, McGraw-Hill Book Company, New York, 1963, p178.

70 1952 Development Corporation report quoted in Osborn and Whittick, *The New Towns: The Answer to Megalopolis*, p174.

71 Quoted in 'Cwmbran New Town', *The Times*, 15 November 1950, p3.

72 Anthony Minoprio, Hugh G.C. Spencely and Peter W. Macfarlane, *Cwmbran New Town: A Plan Prepared for the Cwmbran Development Corporation*, March 1951, p5.

73 Marcus Hughes, 'New town – with inside toilets; residents recall their first glimpse of 'garden city'', *Wales on Sunday*, 19 August 2018.

74 Susan Fielding, *Cwmbrân New Town: An Urban Characterisation Study*, Royal Commission on the Ancient and Historical Monuments of Wales, 2021, provides a detailed account of the town's history and form.

75 David Cowling, one of the Development Corporation's design team, *An Essay for Today: Scottish New Towns 1947–97* quoted in Katy Lock and Hugh Ellis, *New Towns: The Rise, Fall and Rebirth*, RIBA Publishing, London, 2020, p106.

76 Miles Glendinning, 'Cluster homes: planning and housing in Cumbernauld New Town', *Twentieth Century Architecture*, no. 9, 2008, p141.

77 Quoted in Alan Middleton, 'Cumbernauld: concept, compromise and organizational conflict', *Built Environment*, vol. 9, no. 3/4, 1983, p221.

78 Quoted in John Gretton, 'Out of London', *New Society*, 15 April 1971.

79 Thetford Borough Council and Greater London Council, 'Abbey Farm Housing Estate'; DG/TD/2/93, London Metropolitan Archives.

80 Rotary Club of Thetford Norfolk, 'Thetford town expansion: report on social survey', March 1964, DG/TD/2/95, London Metropolitan Archives.

81 Quoted in Keystone Development Trust, *A Profile of Thetford*, August 2004, p4.

82 Ian Nairn, 'Rural housing: post-war work by Tayler and Green', *Architectural Review*, no. 741, vol. 24, 1 October 1958, p236.

83 Quoted in Elain Harwood, 'Tayler & Green and Loddon Rural District Council' in Harwood and Powers (eds), *Tayler and Green, Architects 1938–1973: The Spirit of Place in Modern Housing*, Prince of Wales's Institute of Architecture, London, 1998, p49.

84 'Rural housing for Loddon RDC, Norfolk; Architects: Tayler & Green', *RIBA Journal*, vol. 54, October 1947, p607.

85 'Rural housing at Gillingham for Loddon Rural District Council; Architects: Tayler & Green', *RIBA Journal*, vol. 66, no. 3, January 1959, p99.

86 'High flats: report of a symposium held on 15 February 1955 by the Royal Institute of British Architects', RIBA, London, 1955.

87 'Redcliff Hill Flats plan to house port key workers goes forward', *Western Daily Press*, 20 December 1949, p1.

88 'Canynge House, Bristol', *Architect and Building News*, 28 April 1955, p498.

89 Ibid., p498.

Chapter 6

1 'More than half of British homes don't have a bathroom – archive, 1950', *Guardian*, https://www.theguardian.com/society/2018/mar/21/british-homes-without-bathroom-archive-1950, 21 March 2018 (accessed 27 September 2021).

2 Patrick Dunleavy, *The Politics of High-Rise Housing in Britain: Local Communities Tackle Mass Housing*, University of Oxford PhD thesis, 1978, pp48–50.

3 Ruth Harman, John Minnis, Roger H. Harper, *Sheffield*, Yale University Press, London, 2004, p35.

4 Stefan Muthesius and Miles Glendinning, *Towers for the Welfare State: An Architectural History of British Multi-storey Housing, 1945–1970*, Scottish Centre for Conservation Studies, Edinburgh, p163.

5 Housing Development Committee, *Ten Years of Housing in Sheffield*, Sheffield Corporation, 1962, p3. This celebratory account was published in English, French and Russian.

6 Lionel Esher, *A Broken Wave: The Rebuilding of England, 1940–1980*, Pelican Books, Harmondsworth, 1983, p203.

7 Gordon Aspland, 'Achievements in bulk housing', *The Times*, 10 November 1969, Sheffield supplement, pVI.

8 Keith Marriott, 'Gleadless Valley remembered', https://municipaldreams.wordpress.com/2021/02/09/gleadless-valley-remembered/, 9 February 2021, (accessed 24 September 2021).

9 G.E. Kidder Smith, *The New Architecture of Europe: An Illustrated Guidebook and Appraisal*, Pelican Books, Harmondsworth, 1961, p40.

10 Nikolaus Pevsner, 'Criticism: Roehampton: LCC housing and the picturesque tradition', *Architectural Review*, vol. 126, no. 750, July 1 1959, pp21–35.

11 Elain Harwood, 'Post-war landscape and public housing', *Garden History*, vol. 28, no. 1, summer 2000, p113.

12 John Allan, *Berthold Lubetkin. Architecture and the Tradition of Progress*, RIBA Publications, London, 1992, p553.

13 Civic Trust, Chinbrook Estate, Lewisham/Bromley, https://www.civictrustawards.org.uk/benet/schemes/chinbrook-estate-lewisham-bromley, n.d., (accessed 4 October 2021).

14 Anne Power, *Hovels to High Rise: State Housing in Europe since 1850*, Routledge, London, 1993, p225.

15 Peter Claxton, personal communication, 21 September 2021.

16 Peter Hall, 'Regeneration policies for peripheral housing estates: inward- and outward-looking approaches', *Urban Studies*, vol. 34, no. 5/6, 1997, pp873–90.

17 George Legg, 'Contradictory capitalism, geographical inertia and the new city of Craigavon', *The Irish Review (Cork)*, no. 52, summer 2016, p7.

18 Craigavon Development Commission, *Brownlow, Craigavon: the New Community*, n.d.

19 BBC Northern Ireland, 'The lost city of Craigavon', https://www.youtube.com/watch?v=VKw-T-47oqo, 28 August 2008 (accessed 5 October 2021).

20 BBC News 'Craigavon "most desirable place to live" – Royal Mail', https://www.bbc.co.uk/news/uk-northern-ireland-39139264, 3 March 2017 (accessed 5 October 2021).

21 Lynsey Hanley, *Estates: An Intimate History*, Granta, London, 2007, p38.

22 Quoted in Solihull Metropolitan Borough Council, 'Chelmsley Wood history', https://www.solihull.gov.uk/About-Solihull/Chelmsley-Wood-history, 29 August 2019 (accessed 7 October 2021).

23 Quoted in Phil Jones, *The Rise and Fall of The Multi-Storey Ideal: Public Sector High-Rise Housing in Britain 1945–2002, With Special Reference to Birmingham*, University of Birmingham, PhD, 2003, p157.

24 Lynsey Hanley, 'My children are teaching me to love the housing estate I fled', *Guardian*, https://www.theguardian.com/commentisfree/2019/aug/29/children-housing-estate-chelmsley-wood-birmingham, 29 August 2019 (accessed 7 October 2021).

25 Margaret Willis, 'My job' transcript for a BBC broadcast, 23 January 1955, quoted in Thaddeus Zupančič, 'London's modernist maisonettes: "going upstairs to bed"', https://municipaldreams.wordpress.com/2021/03/23/londons-modernist-maisonettes/, 23 March 2021 (accessed 11 October 2021).

26 'Proposed LCC estate at Loughborough Road', *Architects' Journal*, vol. 116, no. 2997, 7 August 1952, p157.

27 Reyner Banham, 'The new Brutalism', *Architectural Review*, vol. 118, no. 708, 1 December 1955, p361.

28 Ian Nairn, *Modern Buildings in London*, London Transport, London, 1964, pp64–5.

29 Historic Environment Scotland, Designation Report of Handling, https://www.historicenvironment.scot/media/7149/aberdeen-multi-storey-flats-report-of-handling.pdf, January 2021 (accessed 11 October 2021).

30 BBC News, 'Eight Aberdeen high-rise blocks awarded category A listed status', https://www.bbc.co.uk/news/uk-scotland-north-east-orkney-shetland-55711650.amp, 19 January 2021 (accessed 11 October 2021).

31 This and subsequent quotations are drawn from Greater London Council, *The Pepys Estate – a GLC Housing Project*, 1969.

32 Quoted in Les Back, *New Ethnicities and Urban Culture. Racisms and Multi-culture in Young Lives*, UCL Press, London, 1996, p83.

33 Quoted in Sarah Lonsdale, 'Tears of a clown as his tower gets a fancy facelift', *Daily Telegraph*, 12 November 2004.

34 Owen Hatherley, 'Brave new Southampton: Wyndham Court, modern architecture and the municipal socialist city', https://www.in-common.co.uk/2020/08/12/3030/, 12 August 2020 (accessed 14 October 2021).

35 Elain Harwood, *Space, Hope and Brutalism: English Architecture 1945–1975*, Yale University Press for the Paul Mellon Centre for Studies in British Art, New Haven and London, 2015, p81.

36 Owen Hatherley, *A Guide to the New Ruins of Great Britain*, Verso, London, 2011, p11.

37 Alison and Peter Smithson, *Ordinariness and Light*, Faber and Faber, London, 1972, quoted in Christopher Bacon, '"Streets in the sky": the rise and fall of modern architectural utopia', University of Sheffield, PhD, 1982, pp83 and 86.

38 Alison Ravetz, *Council Housing and Culture: The History of a Social Experiment*, Routledge, Abingdon, 2001, p109.

39 Quoted in Open University, 'Park Hill, Sheffield: continuity and change', https://www.open.edu/openlearn/society/park-hill-sheffield-continuity-and-change, 4 May 2012 (accessed 2 November 2021).

40 Quoted in Rachel Cooke, 'How I learnt to love the streets in the sky', *Observer*, https://www.theguardian.com/artanddesign/2008/nov/23/sheffield-park-hill-estate-architecture, 23 November 2008 (accessed 2 November 2021).

41 Quoted in Ravetz, *Council Housing and Culture*, p186.

42 Quoted in Glendinning and Muthesius, *Tower Block: Modern Public Housing in England, Scotland, Wales and Northern Ireland*, Yale University Press, New Haven and London, 1994, p300.

43 'Yorkshire Development Group: Industrialised housing: large-scale production scheme proposed', *Architects' Journal*, 16 December 1964, vol. 140, no. 2516, p1425.

44 Douglas Frank, 'YDG 1 R.I.P.?', *Architects' Journal*, 9 September 1970, vol. 152, no. 36, p566.

45 The quotation from a former tenant is drawn from Jason Flack, 'Leek Street flats – a social history shared on Facebook', South Leeds Life, https://southleedslife.com/leek-street-flats-social-history-shared-facebook/, 13 March 2014 (accessed 4 November 2021); the latter from Richard Hoggart, *A Local Habitation: Life and Times Volume One 1918–40*, Random House, London, 2015, p139.

46 Elain Harwood, 'White light/white heat: rebuilding England's provincial towns in the sixties', *Twentieth Century Architecture*, 2002, no. 6, p69.

47 Jesse Meredith, 'Decolonizing the New Town: Roy Gazzard and the making of Killingworth Township', *Journal of British Studies*, April 2018, no. 57, p355.

48 John Grundy, et al., *Northumberland*, Yale University Press, New Haven and London, 2002, pp361–2.

49 P.J. Taylor, '"Difficult-to-let", "difficult-to-live-in", and sometimes "difficult-to-get-out-of": an essay on the provision of council housing, with special reference to Killingworth', *Environment and Planning A*, vol. 11, 1979, p1314.

50 Geoffrey Rippon, MP, Minister of Public Building and Works, quoted in Association of Metropolitan Authorities, 'Defects in housing part 2: industrialised and system built dwellings of the 1960s and 1970s', 1984, para 2.4.

51 Quoted in Muthesius and Glendinning, *Towers for the Welfare State*, p90. The following direct quotation is found on the same page.

52 Salford City Reporter, April 1965, quoted in Tony Flynn, '50 years ago: "Space-age" Salford high-rise dream comes true', Salford-Online.com http://salfordonline.com/1330-50-years-ago-space-age-salford-high-rise-dream-comes-true.html, 21 March 2018 (accessed 10 November 2021).

53 Councillor Albert Jones, Foreword, in Robert Matthew and Percy Johnson-Marshall, *Report on the Plan*, Bella Vista, Edinburgh, 1963, p1.

54 Quoted in David Kynaston, *Modernity Britain, 1957–62*, Bloomsbury Publishing, London, 2015, p650.

55 Matthew and Johnson-Marshall, *Report on the Plan*, p6.

56 Nigel Pivaro, 'Salford street loss', *Salford Star*, http://www.salfordstar.com/article.asp?id=575, 14 May 2010 (accessed 10 November 2021). Pivaro, now a journalist, played Terry Duckworth in Coronation Street (set in Salford), that archetypal evocation of traditional community.

57 Quoted in Gerry Mooney, 'The rise and fall of Glasgow's Red Road Flats, part 1: Glasgow housing in historical context', https://municipaldreams.wordpress.com/2015/10/20/the-rise-and-fall-of-glasgows-red-road-flats-part-1-glasgow-housing-in-historical-context/, 20 October 2015 (accessed 11 November 2021).

58 Quoted in Muthesius and Glendinning, *Towers for the Welfare State*, p236.

59 Quoted in Jane M. Jacobs, Stephen Cairns and Ignaz Strebel, '"A tall storey ... but, a fact just the same": the Red Road high-rise as a black box', *Urban Studies*, vol. 44, no. 3, March 2007, p616.

60 Mooney, 'The rise and fall of Glasgow's Red Road Flats, part 1'.

Chapter 7

1 Quoted in Michael Romyn, *London's Aylesbury Estate: An Oral History of the 'Concrete Jungle'*, Palgrave Macmillan, London, 2020, p137.

2 Quoted in Stefan Muthesius and Miles Glendinning, *Towers for the Welfare State: An Architectural History of British Multi-Storey Housing, 1945–1970*, Scottish Centre for Conservation Studies, Edinburgh, 2017, p6.

3 H.F. Wallis, 'A living showpiece at North Peckham?', *Municipal Review*, November 1972, (North Peckham Cuttings File, PC 711.5, Southwark Archives).

4 'Life at deck level', *Southwark Civic News*, July 1968.

5 Quoted in Luna Glücksberg, *Wasting the Inner-City: Waste, Value and Anthropology on the Estates*, PhD in Social Anthropology, Goldsmiths College, University of London, January 2013.

6 *Southwark Sparrow*, February 1987.

7 Alice Coleman is referenced in Joanna Coles, 'Is there life in Peckham?', *The Spectator*, 4 July 1987, p16; the space syntax study in Matt Weaver, 'Dangerous structures?', *Building Design*, 15 December 2000.

8 Quoted in Robert Chesshyre, *The Return of the Native Reporter*, Penguin, London, 1987, p101.

9 Quoted in Lisa Hutchinson, 'What life was REALLY like in the Dunston Rocket – the "Heartbreak Hotel" where people "urinated in lifts"', *ChronicleLive*, https://www.chroniclelive.co.uk/news/north-east-news/dunston-rocket-derwent-tower-gateshead-16684382, 4 August 2019 (accessed 18 November 2021). The following quotation is drawn from the same source.

10 Quoted in Jake Tharp, 'Gateshead's Derwent Tower to be demolished', *Architects' Journal*, https://www.architectsjournal.co.uk/archive/gatesheads-derwent-tower-to-be-demolished, 30 October 2009 (accessed 18 November 2021).

11 Macintosh, interviewed in Tom Cordell's film *Utopia London* (2010).

12 This and succeeding quotations are drawn from Henrietta Billings, 'Dawson's Heights: the "Italian" hill town in Dulwich', *Twentieth Century Society*, https://c20society.org.uk/casework/dawsons-heights-the-italian-hill-town-in-dulwich, 22 May 2012 (accessed 18 November 2021).

13 Macintosh, *Utopia London*.

14 Shumi Bose and Justine Sambrook, 'Dawson's Heights: hilltop community', *The Journal of Architecture*, 8 April 2019, vol. 24, no. 2, p287.

15 The book authored by Hook's would-be planners Oliver Cox and Graham Shankland in 1961, *The Planning of a New Town*, became a widely read guide to the innovative thinking of the day.

16 Ariana Markowitz, *The making, unmaking, and remaking of Thamesmead. A story of urban design, decline, and renewal in postwar London*, Bartlett Development Planning Unit Working Paper No. 13, November 2017, p15.

17 John Grindrod, introduction to Peter Chadwick and Ben Weaver (eds), *The Town of Tomorrow: 50 Years of Thamesmead*, Here Press, London, 2019, p14.

18 Mark Swenarton, *Cook's Camden: The Making of Modern Housing*, Lund Humphries, London, 2017, p17.

19 This and the following quotation are drawn from Swenarton, *Cook's Camden*, p41.

20 Ibid., p42.

21 Quoted in Historic England, 'Dunboyne Road Estate', https://historicengland.org.uk/listing/the-list/list-entry/1393894?section=official-listing, n.d. (accessed 22 November 2021).

22 David Percival, 'Redevelopment work in Norwich', *Housing Review*, July–August 1960, p112.

23 Quoted in Miles Horsey and Stefan Muthesius, *Provincial Mixed Development, Norwich Council Housing 1955–1973*, Norwich, 1986, p61 and p24 respectively.

24 Peter Davey, 'Perimeter: Duffryn', *Architectural Review*, 1 April 1980, vol. 167, p214.

25 'Special report: Duffryn social survey', *Architects' Journal*, 6 May 1981, vol. 173, no. 18, p855 and p854 respectively.

26 Ibid., p856.

27 Ibid., p849.

28 Jill Craigie, 'People versus planners', *The Times*, 14 September 1968, p17.

29 Hollamby speaking on 'The architect's approach to architecture' at the RIBA, 24 January 1974, quoted in *Architects' Journal*, vol. 159, no. 6, 1974, p251.

30 Quoted in 'Smallness inside the bigness', *Concrete Quarterly*, vol. 92, January–March 1972, p1.

31 Quoted in Social Life, 'Living on Cressingham Gardens, Social Life's conversations with residents', http://www.social-life.co/media/files/SMALL_FINAL_Exbtn_boards_updated.pdf, 20 October 2013 (accessed 23 November 2021).

32 This and the following quotation are drawn from Roger Stonehouse, 'Building study: housing of Highgate New Town, London N19', *Architects' Journal*, 12 August 1981, p295.

33 Quoted in Camden Council, 'HNT Stage 2 – 107 new homes – got Civic Trust award', 29 November 1983.

34 Lionel Esher, *A Broken Wave: The Rebuilding of England 1940–1980*, Pelican Books, Harmondsworth, 1981.

35 Quoted in Susanne Palsig Christiansen, *Housing and Improvement: A Comparative Study Britain–Denmark, Volume II*, University of York, DPhil, 1985, p165, from which much of the information in this section is drawn.

36 Quoted in Phil Child, 'Landlordism, rent regulation and the Labour Party in mid-twentieth century Britain, 1950–64', *Twentieth Century British History*, vol. 29, no. 1, 2018, p94.

37 Harley Sherlock, *An Architect in Islington*, The Islington Society, London, 2006, p86. The succeeding quotation is drawn from p82.

38 Ibid., p90.

39 Rob Rowlands, *Forging Mutual Futures – Co-operative and Mutual Housing in Practice: History and Potential*, Centre for Urban and Regional Studies, Birmingham Business School, University of Birmingham, 2009, p8.

40 David Clapham and Keith Kintrea, 'Importing housing policy: housing co-operatives in Britain and Scandinavia', *Housing Studies*, vol. 2, no. 3, April 2007, p166.

41 Speech by John Hands at the Sanford Open Day, https://vimeo.com/75850257#, 7 September 2013 (accessed 9 December 2021).

42 Quoted in Tjerk Ruimschotel, *Architectural Guide London*, DOM Publishers, Berlin, 2021, p210.

43 Borough of Lewisham, 'Lewisham self build: Segal Close and Walters Way, prepared by Scrutiny Manager & Jon Broome', https://

councilmeetings.lewisham.gov.uk/documents/
s20760/Segal%20Close%20-%20case%20
study.pdf, n.d. (accessed 13 January 2022).

44 Rowan Moore, *Slow Burn City*, Picador, London, 2016, p241.

45 Quoted in Rowan Moore, 'The story of Lewisham's radical self-builders', *Observer*, https://www.theguardian.com/artanddesign/2017/jul/16/story-of-lewishams-radical-self-builders, 16 July 2017 (accessed 13 January 2022).

Chapter 8

1 Anthony Crosland quoted in *The Times*, 10 May 1975, p1.

2 See Tom Slater. 'The invention of the "sink estate": consequential categorization and the UK housing crisis', *The Sociological Review*, vol. 66, no. 4, 12 June 2018, p5.

3 Catherine Bates, Southwark planning officer, quoted in Ike Ijeh, 'Aylesbury Estate: "taking back the streets"', *Building*, https://www.building.co.uk/focus/aylesbury-estate-taking-back-the-streets/5040143.article, 3 August 2012 (accessed 5 January 2022).

4 W.H. Whitby, 'Some aspects of the housing problem: a public lecture delivered at the Guildhall, Hull on 7th May, 1930', Hull Education Committee, Hull, 1930.

5 Quoted in Brian Lewis, *New for Old: The Story of the First Housing Action Trust*, Pontefract Press, Pontefract, 1988, p18.

6 Margaret Forster, *My Life in Houses*, Chatto and Windus, London, 2014, p3.

7 Hunter Davies, *The Biscuit Girls*, Ebury Press, London, 2014, p21.

8 'No-go Britain: where, what and why', *Independent*, 16 April 1994, https://www.independent.co.uk/news/uk/nogo-britain-where-what-why-1370749.html, 16 April 1994 (accessed 7 January 2022).

9 'Raffles: from riots to show homes in 10 years', *The Cumberland News*, 6 September 2013.

10 Deborah Kuiper, 'Raffles: the trendy new place to live', *News and Star*, 14 September 2006.

11 Quoted in 'Raffles: from riots to show homes'.

12 Gareth Cavanagh, 'Problem residents on Carlisle's Raffles Estate face eviction', *News and Star*, https://www.newsandstar.co.uk/news/19173616.carlisle-estate-residents-last-chance-evicted/, 20 March 2021 (accessed 7 January 2022).

13 Councillor Allan Roberts, interviewed in 'There's no place like Hulme', *World in Action*, https://www.youtube.com/watch?v=S1qpf9hogl0, 10 April 1978 (accessed 11 January 2022).

14 City of Manchester, *Hulme 5 Redevelopment. Report on Design by Hugh Wilson and Lewis Womersley*, October 1965, p8.

15 Quoted in Peter Shapely, *The Politics of Housing. Power, Consumers and Urban Culture*, Manchester University Press, Manchester, 2007, p162.

16 *Manchester Evening News*, 19 June 1989 cited in Julia Kay Horne, *Managing Hulme: Survival, Adaptation and Reputation*, University of Manchester PhD thesis, 1995, p110.

17 Owen Hatherley, *A Guide to the New Ruins of Great Britain*, Verso Books, London, 2010, p126.

18 Hulme Regeneration Ltd, *Private Sector Development Brief: The Crescents*, n.d., p3.

19 Quoted in Laurette Ziemer, 'Social Climbing: Estates are Transformed', *Daily Mirror*, 23 June 2001.

20 Jim Sneddon, 'My years of misery on Broadwater Farm', *Building Design*, 25 October 1985, p13.

21 Quoted in Dominic Severs, 'Rookeries and no-go estates: St Giles and Broadwater Farm, or middle-class fear of "non-street" housing', *Journal of Architecture*, vol. 15, no. 4, August 2010, p477.

22 Quoted in Ben Willis, 'Out of the darkness', *Inside Housing*, 30 September 2005, p20.

Chapter 9

1 Savills Research Report to the Cabinet Office, 7 January 2016. 'Completing London's streets', p5.

2 Quoted in Paul Watt, *Estate Regeneration and its Discontents*, Policy Press, Bristol, 2021, p1.

3 Chris Leslie, 'Not built to last?', https://www.disappearing-glasgow.com/portfolio/sighthill-3/, n.d. (accessed 19 January 2022).

4 Glasgow City Council, Transforming Communities Partnership, https://www.glasgow.gov.uk/index.aspx?articleid=19842, n.d. (accessed 19 January 2022).

5 The Pineapples, Sighthill Transformational Regeneration Masterplan, Glasgow, https://www.festivalofplace.co.uk/project-showcase/gallery-shortlisted-entries-for-the-pineapples-awards-2021/sighthill-transformational-regeneration-masterplan-glasgow---glasgow-city-council-keepmoat-homes-scotland-with-lda-design, n.d. (accessed 19 January 2022).

6 Housing, Communities and Local Government Committee, 'Building more social housing', 2020, p11.

7 Janice Morphet and Ben Clifford, *Local Authority Direct Provision of Housing: Third Research Report*, Bartlett School of Planning, University College London, p6.

8 Ellis Woodman, 'Streets ahead', *Building Design*, 24 February 2006, p13.

9 This and the following quotations are drawn from Steve Rose, 'Marbella on the Thames', *Guardian*, https://www.theguardian.com/artanddesign/2006/feb/06/architecture.communities, 6 February 2006 (accessed 20 January 2022).

10 Hugh Pearman, 'Dateline: London. Architect: Karakusevic Carson & Maccreanor Lavington. Model: Row Houses', *Architectural Record*, vol. 206, no. 10, p114.

11 This and following quotations drawn from Karacusevic Carson Architects, *Public Housing Works*, Lund Humphries, London, 2021, p122.

12 Karacusevic Carson Architects, *Public Housing Works*, p122.

13 Pearman, 'Dateline: London', p117.

14 MAST Architects, Residential Brochure, https://mastarchitects.co.uk/wp-content/uploads/2019/12/MAST-Architects-Residential-Brochure-2019-min.pdf, n.d. (accessed 1 March 2022).

15 Tjerk Ruimschotel, *Architectural Guide London*, Dom Publishers, Berlin 2021, p219.

16 Quoted in 'Passive position', *Building Construction Design*, https://www.buildingconstructiondesign.co.uk/news/passive-position/, 18 November 2014 (accessed 25 January 2022).

17 Quoted in Rick Mather Architects, 'Passivhaus principles lead the way on housing scheme', http://www.cnplus.co.uk/on-site/project-report/major-willmott-dixon-passivhaus-assessment-takes-shape-in-camden/8642713.

article, 21 February 2013 (accessed 25 January 2022).

18 Quoted in 'Passivhaus for the mass market: Mikhail Riches' Goldsmith Street development for Norwich City Council', *Architects' Journal*, vol. 246, no. 4, 28 February 2019, p26.

19 David Hannant, '"Home-owners are jealous of us" – how award-winning council home changed life for this couple', *Eastern Daily Press*, https://www.edp24.co.uk/news/local-council/goldsmith-street-area-stirling-award-couple-1459114, 9 October 2019 (accessed 27 January 2022).

20 RIBA, 'Goldsmith Street wins RIBA Stirling Prize 2019', https://www.architecture.com/awards-and-competitions-landing-page/awards/riba-stirling-prize/riba-stirling-prize-2019, n.d. (accessed 27 January 2022).

21 Quoted in Hannant, '"Home-owners are jealous of us"'.

22 Quoted in George Kafka, 'Goldsmith Street: Mikhail Riches with Cathy Hawley – RIBA Stirling Prize shortlist 2019', *Architects' Journal*, vol. 246, no. 18, p44.

Image Credits

IX Thaddeus Zupančič, X Architectural Press Archive / RIBA Collections, 3 Graham Horn, 4l Owl Prints, 4r Out of copyright, 6l Architectural Press Archive / RIBA Collections, 6r Bill Harrison (CC BY-SA 2.0), 8t, 8br Out of copyright, 8bl Colin Lourie, 9l Out of copyright, 9r John Boughton, 10l Bruce Castle Museum (Haringey Archive and Museum Service), 10r-11 John Boughton, 12 Paul Wood, 15 President and Fellows of Harvard College, 16t Paul Wood, 16b Martin Charles / RIBA Collections, 17 President and Fellows of Harvard College, 18t Out of copyright, 18b President and Fellows of Harvard College, 20 Steven Robb, 21 Dale Harvey, 22 John Boughton, 24-25t Manchester Tenants Ltd, 25b Peter Warrington, 27t PictureSheffield.com, 27b President and Fellows of Harvard College, 28t PictureSheffield.com, 28bl President and Fellows of Harvard College, 28br PictureSheffield.com, 29 Out of copyright, 30-31 John Boughton, 32 Swansea Council: Swansea Museum collection, 35 Royal Incorporation of Architects in Scotland. Courtesy of HES, 36 Out of copyright, 37 Architectural Press Archive / RIBA Collections, 38 John Boughton, 40t Out of copyright, 40b Royal Pavilion & Museums Trust, Brighton & Hove, 41t The Regency Society. The whole of the James Gray archive may be viewed at regencysociety-jamesgray.com, 41b © Mat Sunderland for Sunipa Picture Ltd 2020, 42-3 Swansea Council: Swansea Museum collection, 44 Out of copyright, 45 Keith Moore, 46 David Martyn, 47l Bristol Archives, 43207/4/17, 47r David Martyn, 48l RIBA collections, 48r LBBD Archives, Valence House, 49 John Boughton, 51t Out of copyright, 51b-52 Chris Matthews, 53-54 John Boughton, 55 Liverpool Central Library and Archives, 56t Russ Oakes, 56b-59 John Boughton, 60 RIBA Collections, 63 Bristol Archives, 17563/1/848, 64 Hedley Bashforth, 65 John Boughton, 66l © Garden City Collection, Letchworth Garden City Heritage Foundation (www. gardencitycollection.com), 66r-67 John Boughton, 69l London Metropolitan Archives (City of London), 69r-70l Out of copyright, 70r John Boughton, 71 Liverpool Central Library and Archives, 72 John Boughton, 73l Ninos Merza, 73r John Boughton, 74l Ninos Merza, 74r John Boughton, 76 RIBA Collections, 77-78l RIBA Collections, 78r-79 By kind permission of Leeds Libraries. www. leodis.net, 80 RIBA Collections, 83 Craig McCracken, 84 picturenottingham. co.uk, 85 John Boughton, 87 Out of copyright, 88 John Boughton, 89-90 Keith Moore, 91-92l Northern Ireland Housing Executive, 92r John Boughton, 94l Image courtesy of Bath Preservation Trust, 94r Elliot Guise/Curo, 95 Tim Beale, 96l Ian Waites, 96r-97 Chis Matthews, 98 Crown copyright: RCAHMW, 99 Chris Matthews, 101 RIBA Collections, 102t Architectural Press Archive / RIBA Collections, 102b Thaddeus Zupančič, 103 By Courtesy of the University of Liverpool Library, 104 Jay Mason-Burns, 105-106 Northern Ireland Housing Executive, 107-108 Tim Morton, 110 RIBA Collections, 111-113 John Boughton, 114-115t RIBA Collections, 115bl John Boughton, 115br Thaddeus Zupančič, 117-118 John Boughton, 119-120 Ian Waites, 121-122 John Boughton, 124-125 Architectural Press Archive / RIBA Collections, 125br Tony Ray-Jones / RIBA Collections, 127l Gwent Archives: C/MISCR/184, 126 Architectural Press Archive / RIBA Collections, 128 Crown copyright: RCAHMW, 127r Tiia Monto (CC BY-SA 3.0), 129l Architectural Press Archive / RIBA Collections, 129r-130 RIBA Collections, 131-135 John Boughton, 137-138l David Martyn, 138r John Boughton, 139 David Martyn, 140 John Maltby / RIBA Collections, 143l Architectural Press Archive / RIBA Collections, 143r-144t RIBA Collections, 144b John Boughton, 145 Architectural Press Archive / RIBA Collections, 146tl RIBA Collections, 146tr Architectural Press Archive / RIBA Collections, 146bl John Donat / RIBA Collections, 146br Thaddeus Zupančič, 147 John Maltby / RIBA Collections, 148 John Boughton, 149 London Metropolitan Archives (City of London), 150 Rob Clayton, 151 John Boughton, 152 Miles Glendinning, 153-154t Craigavon Museum Services, 154b Owen Griffiths, 155 Miles Glendinning, 156 John Boughton, 158 Architectural Press Archive / RIBA Collections, 159t John Maltby / RIBA Collections, 159b Thaddeus Zupančič, 160-161 Andrew Stevenson, 162-163t Tony Ray-Jones / RIBA Collections, 163bl Architectural Press Archive / RIBA Collections, 163br John Boughton, 164 Marco Catellan, 165t John Boughton, 165b Marco Catellan, 167l RIBA Collections, 167r-168t Architectural Press Archive / RIBA Collections, 168bl John Donat / RIBA Collections, 168br John Boughton, 169 Northern Ireland Housing Executive, 170t Judah Passow, 170b Northern Ireland Housing Executive, 171 Architectural Press Archive / RIBA Collections, 172 Miles Glendinning, 173 Architectural Press Archive / RIBA Collections, 173b John Boughton, 176 Miles Glendinning, 177 John Boughton, 178 Architectural Press Archive / RIBA Collections, 179 Richard Chivers / RIBA Collections, 180r Architectural Press Archive / RIBA Collections, 181l RIBA Collections, 180l Jon May / RIBA Collections, 181r John Boughton, 182 Colin Westwood / RIBA Collections, 185-186 Southwark Archives, 187 Peter McDermott, 188-189l Architectural Press Archive / RIBA Collections, 189r John Boughton, 190 Tony Ray-Jones / RIBA Collections, 191l Christopher Hope-Fitch / RIBA Collections, 191r Thaddeus Zupančič, 193-194t Martin Charles / RIBA Collections, 194b-196 John Boughton, 197 Mark Scott, 198 Chris Matthews, 199-200tl Colin Westwood / RIBA Collections, 200tr-200b John Boughton, 201-202 Martin Charles / RIBA Collections, 203 John Boughton, 205l Public domain, 205r-206 Mike Quinn (CC BY-SA 2.0), 208-213 John Boughton, 214 Architectural Press Archive / RIBA Collections, 218-219 John Boughton, 220-221l Carlisle Library, Cumbria Image Bank, 221r Alf Plant, 222-223l Out of copyright, 223r RIBA Collections, 224-226 John Boughton, 227 Architectural Press Archive / RIBA Collections, 228-229 John Boughton, 230 Christopher Hope-Fitch / RIBA Collections, 233-234 Hilary Mooney, 236 Morley von Sternberg, 236l Peter Barber Architects, 236r John Boughton, 238 Karakusevic Carson Architects, 239t Tim Crocker, 239b Jim Stephenson, 240 Scott Watson, Perth & Kinross Council, 242-243 Christopher Hope-Fitch / RIBA Collections, 244-245 John Boughton, 246-247 Portsmouth City Council, 248-249 John Boughton, 252-3 Tony Ray-Jones / RIBA Collections, Endpapers Tony Ray-Jones / RIBA Collections